The Risen Adam

Virginia Hyde

The
Risen Adam

D. H. LAWRENCE'S
REVISIONIST TYPOLOGY

The Pennsylvania State University Press
University Park, Pennsylvania

Library of Congress Cataloging-in-Publication Data

Hyde, Virginia Crosswhite.
    The risen Adam : D.H. Lawrence's revisionist typology / Virginia
Hyde.

        p.   cm.
    Includes bibliographical references and index.
    ISBN 0-271-00776-1 (alk. paper)
    1. Lawrence, D. H. (David Herbert), 1885–1930—Religion.
2. Christian art and symbolism in literature. 3. Typology
(Theology) in literature. 4. Medievalism in literature. 5. Bible
in literature. I. Title.
PR6023.A93Z631933 1992
823'.912—dc20   91–8043
                                                               CIP

It is the policy of The Pennsylvania State University Press to use acid-free
paper for the first printing of all clothbound books. Publications on
uncoated stock satisfy the minimum requirements of American National
Standard for Information Sciences—Permanence of Paper for Printed
Library Materials, ANSI Z39.48-1984.

To my parents, Frank and Hazel Crosswhite,
and
To my husband, David Barnes

Contents

List of Illustrations

Fig. 1.   One of the Cherubim with Six Wings, from a fourteenth-century English psalter, in the British Library (included in Jenner's *Christian Symbolism*). By permission of the Trustees of the British Library.

Fig. 2.   Tree of the Two Advents, by Joachim of Fiore, from his *Liber Figurarum,* in the library of Corpus Christi College, Oxford University. The First and Second Comings of Christ are represented in the sketch. By permission of Corpus Christi College (and with the assistance of the Bodleian Library), Oxford.

Fig. 3.   Typology of Adam, on the central western tympanum of Strassburg Cathedral (detail): Crucifixion of Christ over the grave of Adam (bottom); Christ, holding the staff of Resurrection, with Adam and Eve at the harrowing of hell (middle); the Ascension (above these two levels). The foliage of the tree-cross appears on several levels. By permission of Foto Marburg, Marburg/Lahr, and Art Resource, New York.

Fig. 4.   *Throwing Back the Apple,* watercolor painting by D. H. Lawrence (1927-28), whereabouts unknown. By permission of the Harry Ransom Humanities Research Center, the University of Texas at Austin; and Laurence Pollinger, Ltd., and the Estate of the late Mrs. Frieda Lawrence Ravagli.

Abbreviations

(For complete references, see Bibliography.)

Works by D. H. Lawrence:

A	*Apocalypse and the Writings on Revelation*
AR	*Aaron's Rod*
BB	*The Boy in the Bush* (with M. L. Skinner)
CP	*Complete Poems of D. H. Lawrence*
CSN	*Complete Short Novels of D. H. Lawrence*
CSS	*Complete Short Stories of D. H. Lawrence*
E	*England, My England and Other Stories*
EC	*The Escaped Cock*
EP	*Etruscan Places*
F	*Fantasia of the Unconscious*
K	*Kangaroo*
LCL	*Lady Chatterley's Lover*
Letters	*Letters of D. H. Lawrence* (Cambridge)
MEH	*Movements in European History*
MEM	*Memoir of Maurice Magnus*
MM	*Mornings in Mexico*
MWD	*The Man Who Died*
P	*Phoenix*
PII	*Phoenix II*

Plays	*Complete Plays of D. H. Lawrence*
PO	*The Prussian Officer and Other Stories*
PS	*The Plumed Serpent*
Psy	*Psychoanalysis and the Unconscious*
Q	*Quetzalcoatl*
R	*The Rainbow*
RDP	*Reflections on the Death of a Porcupine*
SCAL	*Studies in Classic American Literature*
SL	*Sons and Lovers*
SM	*The Symbolic Meaning*
STH	*Study of Thomas Hardy and Other Essays*
TI	*Twilight in Italy*
WL	*Women in Love*

Works by other authors:

Isis	Madame Helena Blavatsky, *Isis Unveiled,* 2 vols. in one.
SD	——, *The Secret Doctrine,* 2 vols. in one.
Schiller	Gertrud Schiller, *Iconography of Christian Art,* 5 vols.

Preface

Edward Garnett, in 1924, described D. H. Lawrence as a combination of a knight errant and a prophet wielding a blossoming staff. "I've watched him," Garnett said, "since he came riding into the arena of literature ... , flourishing a thorned stick blossoming with odd flowers. With this he hit his opponents and floored 'em. He watered the flowers with pain and grief, pruned them with bleeding fingers, tended them with obstinate care and avoided grafting from other writers."[1] The editor had evidently become caught up in the novelist's own imagery from *Aaron's Rod* (1922) and thereby happened to associate him appropriately with a flowering shepherd's staff that, in one form, is a primitive "wild man" motif and, in another, is Aaron's rod itself. Lawrence not only alludes to this biblical image but also appropriates and revises an entire system in which Old Testament figures, like Aaron with the rod, were held to prefigure Christ and his church. Although I show the significance of this plan to Lawrence's work, this book is not a "source study," depending as it does on the credibility of its new readings of particular texts. Nonetheless, if Lawrence's art displays little predictable "grafting," it is nurtured in part by biblical and still more exotic sources.

1. Skinner, *The Fifth Sparrow*, 149, recounts Garnett's remark to her.

A question inevitably arises: How likely is a modern writer to know—never mind to employ—such materials?[2] But Lawrence's canon argues anew the necessity of our learning unfamiliar systems in order to understand some modern literature most fully; his works require such treatment as Blake's have received, unlocking the "code" of typological meaning.[3] Lawrence's texts, in fact, prove saturated with biblical typology as, by his own account, he had himself been steeped in the Bible in his youth. His uses must be categorized as "extensions" of such typology; by no means orthodox, they are often as ironic and revisionist as Blake's.

Despite the great number of books already written about Lawrence, the times are especially auspicious for further studies. Volumes of the Cambridge Edition of his letters and works are still appearing, including previously unpublished material, and new critical approaches illuminate his techniques and ideas. It is not surprising that, just now, as several critics explore his anticipation of deconstructionist tenets, he is also the subject of this study, looking back to medieval iconography and biblical typology, in which he sought metaphorical equivalents for things he believed in. His work has been known, from early criticism through the present, for what George Ford calls "double measure,"[4] for the complexity acknowledged in Christopher Pollnitz's remark that there are "more Lawrences than we have discovered in the first hundred years."[5] With his multiple interests, both traditional and modernist, Lawrence produced a body of literary paradox so rich that it can scarcely be categorized.

When I began this study of his biblical typology a few years ago, I could not foresee the diverse channels into which it would lead. Lawrence's intensely modernist texts seem at first to make only passing use of this form of biblical exegesis, which we associate rarely with the twentieth century. True, his preoccupation with Adam and Eve is well known. So, too, is his use of "Christ figures." But the connection between the two has never properly been placed within the full-scale typological pattern casting Christ as the "new Adam" and the savior of the "old Adam." Ford's initial

2. See, for example, Ziolkowski, "Some Features of Religious Figuralism," 345–69, designating biblical elements in some modern literature while holding their discontinuity with biblical typology; and see his *Fictional Transfigurations of Jesus.*

3. Tannenbaum, *Biblical Tradition,* 8–24, 86–123.

4. Ford, *Double Measure.*

5. Pollnitz, " 'Raptus Virginis,' " 129.

identification of some Lawrentian typology and Frank Kermode's readings centered on Apocalypse do not account for all that goes on in Lawrence.[6] The longtime emphasis upon his apocalyptic vision has, in fact, obscured his use of the other aspects of biblical typology.

One need not look far to discover likely sources of his knowledge of such typology. Beyond pointing to his reading and religious background, I focus on the graphic arts that were important to him throughout his lifetime. His own home area near Nottingham was rich in cathedral art, as were some of his later locations in Italy and southern Germany. Lincoln Cathedral alone is so important in *The Rainbow* (1915) that it has sparked debate for a quarter of a century, one that continues to yield new claims about whether Lawrence preferred Gothic or Romanesque arches.[7] This cathedral, like some of his other settings, displays carvings of typological motifs. In addition, his practice of copying Giotto and Fra Angelico prints would have familiarized him with typological themes, and Lawrence, surprisingly, seems to have continued this practice well into his "middle" period. His well-known interest in Joachim of Fiore—whose elaborate uses of typology ranged from orthodox to esoteric—must also be considered in ways that have been previously neglected. Finally, Lawrence also imbibed theosophical variants of typology from a variety of sources, including Madame Helena Blavatsky, and these color his work significantly.

The comprehensive system of typology offered him a cast of characters, or "types" (Old Testament forerunners of Christ), which he invokes somewhat like archetypes (though the two are distinct); it also provided a historic scheme, a cosmology, a set of rituals, and a pattern of fall and resurrection fitting to his central preoccupations. While he combined the biblical types eclectically with classical and more exotic primitive materials, and while he produced many ironic and parodic permutations on typology, he never dispensed with its underlying vision—although sometimes he tried. When studying the early and final versions of works like *The Plumed Serpent* (1926) and "The Border Line" (1924), for example, I find that he often dropped the most blatant references to types from his later drafts. But they left indelible imprints.

The question of whether an author or an artist is entirely in

6. Ford, *Double Measure,* 130-31, 136-37; Kermode, "Lawrence and the Apocalyptic Types," 14-38, and *D. H. Lawrence.*
7. See note 65 to my introduction and note 24 to chapter 2.

control of his or her results arises today in criticism of both literature and graphic arts.[8] E. H. Gombrich refers to the "open question" of how "the arousal potential of symbols" may tap unconscious human reserves.[9] Lawrence himself claims that the symbols of myth (unlike emblems or images in allegory) may bypass the author's conscious mind (*A* 49).[10] Thus the artist "knows that his work was never in his mind"; rather, "out of the struggle with his material, in the spell of the urge, / his work took place, it came to pass, it stood up and saluted his mind" (*CP* 690). This is why Lawrence asserts, as a literary critic, "Never trust the artist. Trust the tale" (*SCAL* 2). Still, we have learned to be cautious at times of his insistence that his "pollyanalytics" always derive from the "pure passionate experience" of his fiction rather than the other way around (*F* 57). While I acknowledge, then, that symbols, types, and iconographic patterns, like words themselves, may have a life of their own beyond artistic intention, I do assume Lawrence's awareness and shaping of many of these features in his writing. Despite current critical tendencies to dispense with intentionality altogether, Lawrence's works remain notoriously difficult to separate from both his life and his didacticism, and my study reveals this fact anew.

Related to this issue of intent is the fact that, since traditional forms may carry their own content, they may function as ideograms—either in accord with or in spite of the author's wishes. Classical-subject painting of the nineteenth century, for example, is said to carry patriarchal assumptions engaging it not only in aesthetic roles but also in "social discourse."[11] How much more likely it is, then, that biblical typology, dealing directly with a

8. On this issue in iconography, see, for example, Rothenberg, "Provisional Vision of Blake's *Jerusalem,*" 305–11, and essays in *Unnam'd Forms,* ed. Hilton and Vogler, especially Carr, "Illuminated Printing," 177–96, and Essick, "How Blake's Body Means," 197–217.

9. Gombrich, *The Image and the Eye,* 152.

10. Lawrence argues this point in the introduction he wrote for Frederick Carter's *Dragon of the Apocalypse* (1931), which was not published with that volume but in the *London Mercury* of July 1930. Lawrence was, on occasion, disingenuous about conscious meaning, as in "Introduction to These Paintings," for the 1929 exhibition of his paintings, stating: "That the cross by itself was supposed to *mean* something always mystified me" (*P* 567). The claim is surprising from the author who explained (and even drew) forms of the cross in nonfiction (*SM* 177, 184) and whose works have such titles as "The Cross" (poem) and "The Crucifix Across the Mountains" (in *Twilight in Italy*).

11. Kestner, *Mythology and Misogyny.*

series of patriarchs—like Adam and Moses—should carry similar
assumptions, partly accounting for the patriarchal leadership ideal
often traced in Lawrence's works. Because this study shows that
his use of biblical typology affects some of his most controversial
themes, it is necessary to reassess how early his patriarchal strains
appear; I conclude that they are present, along with the typology
itself, from an early date. Although he was undoubtedly deeply
concerned with women's issues in several periods of his life,
especially before the First World War, his mode of thought (or his
"myth"), reflecting a major strain in his culture itself, was charged
with figures and themes of dominant kings and heroes, biblical
and otherwise.

Lawrence depicts the Old Testament types as tribal patriarchs
and lords whose dispensation is due for a return in the place of
depleted modern civilization. His interest in them, especially Adam,
is far wider than any political formulations can allow. His central
mystique is regeneration through sexuality; his central metaphor
is marriage, which he commonly casts, like the typologists, in
terms of the mystic union of Bride and Bridegroom in the Song of
Solomon and the Book of Revelation.12 Therefore, Adam and Eve
together are meaningful to him for their archetypal marriage. Combining two sacraments, Lawrence often associates marriage with
the Eucharist, which he adapts to his own metaphysic of "blood
knowledge," the deep, sensual consciousness he believed to be
submerged by the cerebral modern age.

In the course of my study, I have often considered whether
typology contributed more to Lawrence's utopian hopes or his
dystopian fears.13 The issue is a difficult one, partly because
scholars do not invariably understand the main thrust of typology
in the same way. Frank Kermode has pointed to the "rigid, life-
denying schema" inherent in a system of foreordination.14 Northrop Frye, however, in the first volume of his recent study of the
Bible, refers to the "forward-moving" orientation of biblical typology,
always looking ahead to fulfillment in Christ:

12. Sometimes Lawrence is also referring to the alchemical "marriage" of
opposites, as traced in *The Plumed Serpent* by Cowan, *D. H. Lawrence and
the Trembling Balance*, 201-3. Jung, in *Mysterium Coniunctionis*, cites a
connection between the biblical and the alchemical marriage imagery (*Collected
Works* 14:410-34), a link of which Lawrence often seems aware, probably
from theosophical sources.
13. See Goodheart, *Utopian Vision of D. H. Lawrence.*
14. Kermode, "Lawrence and the Apocalyptic Types," 25.

What typology really is as a mode of thought, what it both
assumes and leads to, is a theory of history, or more accurately of historical process: an assumption that there is
some meaning and point to history, and that sooner or later
some event or events will occur which will indicate what
that meaning or point is, and so become an antitype
[typological fulfillment] of what has previously happened.
Our modern confidence in historical process, our belief
that despite apparent confusion, even chaos, in human
events, nevertheless those events are going somewhere and
indicating something, is probably a legacy of Biblical typology:
at least I can think of no other source for its tradition.[15]

Examples of both effects, the rigid and the fluid, appear in
Lawrence's work, but it is the latter that seems to me to explain
why he found typological patterns congenial enough to use them
frequently.

The biblical type and antitype appealed to him partly because
they place, in George P. Landow's words, "simultaneous emphasis"
on "two levels of existence," realistic and symbolic or physical and
spiritual.[16] The more physical "type," like Adam, prefigures the
spiritual "antitype," Christ; that is, the former signifies the latter.
Yet both signifier and signified are held to be historical and both
are necessary to the typological scheme. This system is in accord
with Lawrence's interest in uniting opposites, as he often sees
type and antitype to be. "The old Adam of power," he wrote, must
be kept in "a balance" with "the new Adam of love" (A 163). His
usual valorization of the physical type is based upon a dislike of
abstract personification, of the antitype's perfection in "meaning"
as opposed to the human predecessor's erring but active quest for
meaning.[17] But Lawrence is quick to acknowledge in other contexts that even seeming opposites do not negate each other, that
neither term of a twin reality can preclude the other.

Even at a time when his logocentricity is being challenged (as,
indeed, he challenged it himself), it is not anomalous to explore
his search for meaning in biblical and other models. While

15. Frye, *The Great Code,* 80–81.
16. Landow, *Victorian Types, Victorian Shadows,* 4.
17. Lawrence's intuition of the relationship between type and antitype
accords in some ways with a modern interpretation. Whitman, *Allegory,* 86,
holds that, in the antitype, the personification or the "meaning" of the type
emerges to "take over the narrative foreground."

Lawrence deconstructed both words and the Word, his search was not only genuine but insistent and pervasive, informing much of his output. Gerald Doherty finds the novelist's work full of the "unchecked sublimations" of supernaturalism in his "leadership" period.[18] Daniel J. Schneider asserts that, despite Lawrence's own sense of the limitations of words as the means of expressing or knowing truth, he was far from denying an absolute, but, on the contrary, sought more essential truth than he believed words could convey.[19] Diane S. Bonds also concludes her look at Lawrence's deconstructive practices by emphasizing his will to faith in "some transcendental signified."[20]

My study has necessarily included some consideration of Lawrence's religious beliefs. One of the recently published *Apocalypse* fragments, in which he interprets the Book of Revelation, reveals a Lawrence who both affirms and questions: "From the last far corner of the soul comes the confession: There is Almighty God. . . . If there is Almighty God, I care about nothing else. There is Almighty God, and . . . the whole burden of my fear shifts over" (175). However tenuous the message, the tone is that of the religious zealot. It is also the urgent tone of the modernist as defined by Lawrence B. Gamache.[21] Lawrence might have agreed with one of his recent critics, who finds his beliefs "worse than pantheism . . . pure theriolotry."[22]

One of the most challenging aspects of this study lies in the attempt to sort out Lawrence's biblical typology from his use of theosophy or comparative mythology. His syncretic art combines both strains. In fact, typology itself had accommodated heterodoxy, especially during the Renaissance, when parallels between biblical and classical figures afforded, as Frye puts it, "a cultural citizenship for the Classics within Christendom."[23] In keeping with this movement, not only in the Renaissance but before and after, Christian iconography also absorbed pagan variations, another reason for Lawrence's interest in it: the eclectic writer was attracted to the eclectic art. The church itself, Lawrence points out, had assimilated pagan features with an ease he admired (*PII* 509).

A large body of scholarship concerns the important subject of

18. Doherty, "White Mythologies," 485.
19. Schneider, "Alternatives to Logocentrism," 35–47.
20. Bonds, *Language and the Self,* 112.
21. Gamache, "Toward a Definition of 'Modernism,' " 32–45.
22. Pollnitz, " 'I Didn't Know His God,' " 18.
23. Frye, *The Great Code,* 92.

the relation between the literary and visual arts, and I have added little to it beyond pursuing Lawrence's own interests and practice. I refer to graphic-arts motifs that influenced or paralleled his work in various ways, as I also refer to his own paintings and drawings when they illustrate the subjects at hand. I acknowledge the pioneering work of such scholars as Keith Alldritt and Jeffrey Meyers, whose studies of Lawrence and the graphic arts persuaded me that I was not far afield in seeking his affinities in nonmodernist art, and the efforts of Jack F. Stewart, Marianna Torgovnick, Deborah Schnitzer, and others, whose explorations of Lawrence and "modern art" show that he was also very much of his own age. Investigations by my colleague Diane Gillespie into Virginia Woolf's relation to the graphic arts have also enriched my thinking.

I have been guided by the works of many other scholars before me. For texts, I have used the *Cambridge Edition of the Letters and Works of D. H. Lawrence* (James T. Boulton and Warren Roberts, general editors), whenever the volumes had been issued. I have also used manuscripts and typescripts when their content was pertinent to my argument.

Acknowledgments

For the use of manuscript and typescript materials, I am indebted to the Harry Ransom Humanities Research Center at the University of Texas at Austin, especially Cathy Henderson; the Houghton Library at Harvard University, especially Rodney G. Dennis; Laurence Pollinger, Ltd., and the Frieda Lawrence Ravagli Estate; and George Lazarus, the generous collector who is a special friend to Lawrence scholarship.

For information about Lawrence paintings, I wish to thank Keith Sagar, Alvin Sullivan, Beatrice (Mrs. Harry T.) Moore, Christopher Miles, and Keith Cushman. I owe special thanks to Enid Hilton for sharing with me her unpublished recollections of Lawrence and his interests in art. For the artworks in this volume, I am indebted to the Harry Ransom Humanities Research Center at the University of Texas at Austin, especially Kathleen Gee and Sally Leach; Laurence Pollinger, Ltd., and the Frieda Lawrence Ravagli Estate; Christopher Miles; the trustees of the British Museum and the British Library; the Österreichische Nationalbibliothek, Vienna; Foto Marburg, Marburg/Lahr; Art Resource, New York; Corpus Christi College and the Bodleian Library, Oxford University; and the Museo Civico, Padua.

I gratefully acknowledge permission to reprint brief passages or sections of these articles that I have previously published:

"*Aaron's Rod:* D. H. Lawrence's Revisionist Typology," originally published in *Mosaic: A Journal of Interdisciplinary Studies* 20.2 (1987), 111-26;
"Architectural Monuments: Centers of Worship in *Women in Love,*" originally published in *Mosaic* 17.4 (1984), 73-92; and
"Will Brangwen and Paradisal Vision in *The Rainbow and Women in Love,*" originally published in *D. H. Lawrence Review* 8 (1975), 346-57.
Thanks are due as well to the Washington State University Foundation for a grant-in-aid that allowed me to begin this book and to the Humanities Division of the College of Arts and Sciences for a completion grant that allowed me to finish it. I am appreciative of the help of Philip Winsor and Cherene Holland of Penn State Press, Frank Austin, and the scholars who read and commented on my manuscript in whole or in part: L. D. Clark, James C. Cowan, Keith Cushman, Daniel J. Schneider, Evelyn J. Hinz, Diane Gillespie, and others. I am grateful to Stanley Weintraub for helpful advice and to Louis Martz for information on his edition of *Quetzalcoatl.* To Karl Kroeber, Virginia Randall, and the late Paul Wiley, I am indebted for encouragement of my initial interest in iconography in literature, including Lawrence. And I thank my husband, David Barnes, and my parents, Frank and Hazel Crosswhite, for assisting me in countless ways past, present, and future.

Introduction:
Wanting the Scene

Lawrence's Ecclesiastical Imagery

When D. H. Lawrence sought communication beyond words, he often turned to religious symbols and graphic arts to try to express himself with particular fullness.[1] The words of the Bible have long been associated with a graphic mode of perception and a "sensual" language.[2] Furthermore, the Bible's images carry metaphysical meanings and could not fail to be attractive to a writer who was always seeking vehicles for such meanings. I begin exploring Lawrence's religious symbology by considering a specific passage in which an iconographic scheme's inherent content is subtly revalued, but not without leaving its original imprint on the reader's mind.

In *The Rainbow* (1915), Lawrence states that one of his characters, Will Brangwen, "wanted the scene" of a biblical story, the Marriage at Cana. This line is one over which Lawrence labored in composition, evidently wishing to stress it: "In his blood and bones, he wanted the scene" (*R* 159).[3] The passage illustrates a

1. Lydia Blanchard's "Lawrence, Foucault, and the Language of Sexuality," 17–35, also finds Lawrence interested in "a different system of signs," one of touch and sexuality, often related to "Adam and Eve, before the fall, in a time before consciousness and language" (31).
2. Tannenbaum, *Biblical Tradition*, 77, records literary attempts to regain a "sensual language" like that lost at Babel.
3. In both the manuscript and the final typescript of 1915, Lawrence

common feature of Lawrence's works, the evocation of biblical
scenes, and also offers a preview of his techniques in religious
iconography and revisionary biblical typology. It further serves
to exemplify his metaphysic of the blood. The passage is an
extended one, including the details of narrative and image that
the young ecclesiastical artist wanted: "the wedding, the water
brought forward from the firkins as red wine: and Christ saying
to His mother: 'Woman, what have I to do with thee?—mine hour
is not yet come.'" The account ends in the novel with the
judgment of the wedding guests on the water transformed by
Christ into wine: "But thou hast kept the good wine until now"
(R 159-60).

This is, of course, a Bible story (John 2:1-10), but it is also a
scene in graphic art, one having a standard iconographic identity
in painting, the *Marriage at Cana* (Schiller 1:162-64), as Lawrence
must have known from his interest in art by such painters as
Giotto and Fra Angelico.[4] Lawrence's passage, though, is less
remarkable for its pictographic quality (though this is present)
than for its symbolic content, which is integrated in the novel into
an expanding marriage theme. Besides providing a narrative picture,
it introduces the biblical typology that is common in his use of
selections from the Bible and from medieval and early Renaissance art.

The Marriage at Cana is sometimes correlated in iconography
with the divine marriage between Christ and the church, the
Bridegroom and the Bride—a connection linking it with the
Old Testament's Song of Solomon, often interpreted to signify
the love between Christ and the church, a love already uniting

---

continued to alter the passages on the Marriage at Cana. I refer to E331a and
E331b, respectively, in Roberts, *A Bibliography of D. H. Lawrence*.

4. Famous examples of the *Marriage at Cana* include one from the school
of Fra Angelico, in the Museo di San Marco, Florence, and one by Giotto in
the Arena Chapel, Padua. This Giotto painting is just across the room from
Joachim and the Shepherds, which Lawrence had once copied from a print
(*PII* 606) and *Meeting at the Golden Gate*, which may have influenced the
treatment of arches in *The Rainbow*; the *Marriage* is almost directly below
the *Miracle of the Rods* and *Marriage of the Virgin*, containing rods associated
with Aaron's rod. (See my article "*Aaron's Rod*," 111-26.) Christopher Miles,
the present owner of a Lawrence copy of *Joachim*, believes it possible that it
was copied from the original Giotto rather than from a print, and Enid
(Hopkin) Hilton, Lawrence's lifelong friend, has told me that she learned of
Giotto from a postcard Lawrence sent from Italy, a recollection suggesting
that he may have been at Padua itself.

them mystically though destined for utmost fulfillment at the end of time.[5] The combination of the human marriage at Cana with the divine union is well known, for the two are mentioned together in the traditional wedding ceremony, referring to matrimony as a holy estate figuring forth the union between Christ and the church and blessed by Christ's first miracle at Cana.[6] The Marriage at Cana is also seen as a forecast of Christ's Last Supper, which institutes the Mass, or ritual ingestion of bread and wine as the body and blood of Christ. The "good wine" at the marriage, then, can suggest the properties of divinity within the Eucharist (Schiller 1:162–64), and some paintings of the *Marriage at Cana* even show the wine vessel as a chalice centered ceremoniously on a white, altar-like table. All of these associations charge Lawrence's usage with special significance.

In *The Rainbow,* this scene, coming early in the marriage of the second-generation Brangwens, reflects on that marriage by contributing to a complex matrimonial motif in combination with eucharistic images. Lawrence merges the two, seeing in marriage the ultimate communion of blood between two people, and the imagery from the *Marriage* scene and from other icons in the same section of the novel—the *Pietà,* the *Agnus Dei,* and the *Creation of Eve* —radiate into the actions, thoughts, and feelings of the characters. Will's wife, Anna, is likened to Eve and even, for Will, to the serpent of Eden (*R* 189), but the less-noticed imagery of the Eucharist is at least as important in this novel as that of the loss of Eden.

5. See Abrams, *Natural Supernaturalism,* 37–46, on the centrality of the mystic marriage in Romanticism; Tannenbaum, *Biblical Tradition,* 124–84, shows Blake's use of Christ and the Bride, as well as of the antithetical figures the Beast and the Whore of Babylon, from the Book of Revelation. Behind the biblical tradition of Christ as the Bridegroom, some writers see primitive patterns of the "Sacred Marriage" of god surrogates, rituals intended to secure the earth's fruition, and Lawrence may borrow some of this meaning from James G. Frazer, whose *Golden Bough* he read in 1914 (*Letters* 2:470). See *The Magic Art* (1911), in *The Golden Bough,* 2:120–70. (I cite the edition available in Lawrence's time.) Lawrence himself, in a fragmentary draft for *Apocalypse,* written in 1929, finds the wine at the Marriage at Cana "very suggestive of Orphic rituals" (*A* 186).

6. The form for solemnizing matrimony in the Book of Common Prayer of Lawrence's time refers to marriage as "an honorable estate . . . signifying unto us the mystical union that is betwixt Christ and his Church: which holy estate Christ adorned and beautified with his presence and first miracle that he wrought in Cana of Galilee."

It should not be surprising that Lawrence often uses an elaborate metaphor of the Mass to convey what to him was the mystical significance of the blood; one critic, Marguerite Beede Howe, considering an anagogic layer in his works, finds that this ultimate mystical level refers to "the Blood" as Dante's refers to God.[7] I demonstrate in chapter 2 that, in *The Rainbow,* the wine that the young Will recalls from the Bible is related to the blood that he longs to give to Anna. After an estrangement, for example, he desires "to give everything . . . , all his blood, his life, to the last dregs," to "restore" her (*R* 144, 145). This imagery resembles that in a poem originally called "Eve's Mass" but retitled ("Birth Night") when the publisher protested the combination of "amorous" and religious elements before the publication of the 1917 poetry volume *Look! We Have Come Through! (Letters* 3:145-46). The poem suggests that the birth of Eve is from the man's blood (rather than his rib) and that sexual communion brings rebirth.[8] Of course, Lawrence uses such metaphors to reveal profound human realities: "The great religious images," he states, "are only images of our own experiences, or of our own state of mind and soul" (*PII* 571).[9]

It is dangerous to relate an author's view to that of a character, especially one like Will, who is less than sympathetic. Quite independent of this figure, however, "wanting the scene" seems to me an appropriate way of describing one side of Lawrence's creative work. Elsewhere in his writings, he repeatedly relates the scene, the image, to the blood even more clearly than in the example of Will's feeling for the Marriage at Cana. To Lawrence, "blood knowledge" is an instinctive, sensuous faculty that modern man has lost as his mental consciousness has overbalanced it. The blood's knowledge lies to a great extent beyond words; it is both a sensuous and a religious faculty. Lawrence came to believe that its mysteries had been taught by a priesthood in a grand universal theocracy—which included Atlantis—and that its symbols had later been known to such ancient civilizations as the Etruscan,

7. Howe, *The Art of the Self,* 35.

8. See also chapter 2.

9. Lawrence sounds somewhat like Annie Besant, "many" of whose works he had read, according to what his wife, Frieda, told William York Tindall, as recorded in *D. H. Lawrence and Susan His Cow,* 134. In her book *Mysticism,* 30-58, Besant explains "the God-Idea," a term Lawrence sometimes uses, and further observes that each person's life reflects the events in the life of Christ (80-82).

Druidic, Chaldean, Amerindian, and Chinese.[10] The "old wisdom" was "remembered as ritual, gesture, and myth-story" so that "the intense potency of symbols is part at least memory," shared to some degree by "every country and every people" (*F* 55). This idea of symbolism is much like that of Jung in his theory of universal archetypes, but it draws as well from ancient assumptions in the exegetical tradition: biblical symbolism of the Old and New Testaments had often been linked with Egyptian, Chaldean, and other sources — as Lawrence would have known from such eclectic savants as Madame Blavatsky and James M. Pryse, who incorporated earlier scholarship.[11] Lacking a communicable imagery from Atlantis — and having only a limited one directly from Etruria, Chaldea, and the like — Lawrence often resorts, like Blake before him, to biblical imagery and medieval or early Renaissance graphic art for symbols by which to restore the lost mode of perception. As Keith Sagar puts it, "When Lawrence spoke with the tongues of his own blood, or at least of his own inheritance, he spoke in the symbolism of the Judaeo-Christian tradition."[12]

The *Rainbow* passage on the Marriage at Cana, discussed at greater length in chapter 2, is no isolated example of Lawrence's technique of introducing scenes into his fiction. Keith Alldritt, Jeffrey Meyers, Marianna Torgovnick, and Deborah Schnitzer, among others, have discussed his use of visual art and its methods

10. Lawrence postulates further that "the great pagan world of which Egypt and Greece were the last living terms . . . once had a vast and perhaps perfect science . . . in terms of life" (*F* 54), a "science" communicated through a priesthood; and Asia, Polynesia, America, Atlantis, and Europe were all in touch with each other until the melting of the glaciers brought changes in the landmasses and in their peoples. See also Schneider, " 'Strange Wisdom,' " 183–93, and *The Consciousness of D. H. Lawrence*, especially 152–75 ("Blood Consciousness"); and Tracy, *Lawrence and the Literature of Travel*, 91–127, detailing Lawrence's "Myth of Archaic Consciousness."

11. Views from William Warburton, *The Divine Legation of Moses* (1738), and Charles Daubuz, *A Perpetual Commentary on the Revelation of St. John* (1720), for example, filtered down through Blavatsky and Pryse, as did much earlier syncretic exegesis. Lawrence had read Blavatsky's *Secret Doctrine* (1888) by 1917 and *Isis Unveiled* (1887) by 1919; he had read Pryse's *Apocalypse Unsealed* (1910), with its combination of the Bible, the Upanishads, and other sources, by 1917 (*Letters* 3:150). Unless otherwise stated, my source on Lawrence's reading is Burwell, "A Checklist of Lawrence's Reading," 59–125.

12. Sagar, *D. H. Lawrence: Life into Art*, 300. Sagar's study of Lawrence's letters from the *Rainbow* period shows "just how much of himself Lawrence put into Will Brangwen" (128).

in his writing.[13] Torgovnick, rightly finding that Lawrence usually mentions modern art only to embody in it the failings of the
modern world, is wrong in adding that he "frequently denounced"
art of the past as well—and that he "tends to use linguistic,
unpictorial language . . . to express ideal moments."[14] I see him,
on the contrary, frequently utilizing past art to help make the
"ideal" intelligible—to give it concreteness and a kind of sensuous
realism, to help communicate difficult and esoteric meanings by
reference to traditional forms. Alldritt, Meyers, and Torgovnick
herself show how Fra Angelico's *Last Judgment* offers imagery for
a number of passages in *The Rainbow.*[15] It serves to reveal Will
Brangwen's religious longing, to express Anna's state of mind in
her first pregnancy, and to help Ursula chart her affair with her
lover Skrebensky in her own imagination. The art imagery allows
the abstract to be more concrete than it could otherwise be.
Schnitzer, while tracing Lawrence's interest in "the primitive
sense in Post-Impressionist art" and in Etruscan art, emphasizes
his preference for scenes "in which human forms participate in
cosmic events,"[16] and certainly this description fits much medieval religious art as well.

Somewhat closer to my purposes than the points of these critics
is L. D. Clark's demonstration of Lawrence's lifelong interest in
"visual" biblical images—his creation and re-creation of Holy
Land scenes;[17] the *Marriage,* with its wine vessels brought from
the firkins, is, in fact, an example of such a creation. In the essay
"Hymns in a Man's Life," Lawrence refers to "Galilee and Canaan,
Moab and Kedron" (*PII* 600) as compelling places in his imagination,

13. See Alldritt, *The Visual Imagination;* Meyers, *Painting and the Novel;*
Clark, "Immediacy and Recollection," 121–35; Torgovnick, *The Visual Arts,*
37–69, 124–56; Schnitzer, *The Pictorial in Modernist Fiction,* 138–58; Millett,
The Vultures and the Phoenix; Stewart, "Lawrence and Gauguin," 385–401;
Stewart, "Lawrence on Van Gogh," 1–24; Stewart, "Vital Art of Lawrence,"
123–48; Schvey, "D. H. Lawrence and Expressionism," 124–36; Remsbury,
"'Real Thinking,'" 117–47; Delavenay, "Lawrence and the Futurists," 140–62;
and the following essays in *The Paintings of D. H. Lawrence,* ed. Levy: Harry
T. Moore, "D. H. Lawrence and His Paintings," 17–34; Jack Lindsay, "The
Impact of Modernism on Lawrence," 35–53; and Herbert Read, "Lawrence as
a Painter," 55–64.
14. Torgovnick, *The Visual Arts,* 124.
15. See Alldritt, *The Visual Imagination,* 83–85, 105, 127; Meyers, *Painting
and the Novel,* 53–64 (chapter 5: "Fra Angelico and *The Rainbow*"); and
Torgovnick, *The Visual Arts,* 10–11, 143.
16. Schnitzer, *The Pictorial in Modernist Fiction,* 139, 147.
17. Clark, "Immediacy and Recollection," 126–29.

lingering over "the wonder of 'Canaan,'" which could never be localized" (*PII* 599). It was not simply the old Protestant hymns of his boyhood, either, that affected his view of biblical places and events; he was influenced at least as much by paintings such as those he copied in youth and manhood—from prints of Fra Angelico and Giotto, for instance (*PII* 606). Lawrence's own rendering of Giotto's *Joachim and the Shepherds*, apparently copied from a print, is extant. He continued this practice much longer than is generally recognized, for a 1919 letter to Mark Gertler shows him still planning such copies.[18] Even in *Etruscan Places* (1932), written to celebrate ancient Etruria and its sensuous consciousness, Lawrence still singles out Giotto for praise, finding an Etruscan quality in his work and that of "the early sculptors" (*EP* 75).

In Lawrence's fiction, however, descriptions that seem indebted to such graphic sources are not always related to specific locations or artists but often are, instead, generic scenes—revealing traditional iconographic patterns from which Lawrence worked his creative revisions. Features of such patterns often proliferate in a given text even before the introduction of the specific artifact to which they belong. For example, in *The Rainbow,* images of angels precede the description of them in Fra Angelico's *Last Judgment* and continue occasionally later in the book. Some of the novel's iconographic patterns have no identified sources within the texts. Will's soul, for instance, seems to have "six wings of bliss," and to Anna (now associated with the Virgin Mary) her husband seems like "an Annunciation" (*R* 158). One inspiration for this imagery is probably a medieval drawing of one of the cherubim with six wings, all the pinions elaborately designated with mystical attributes (Fig. 1); Lawrence would have encountered it in Katherine L. Jenner's *Christian Symbolism* (1910), which occupied him deeply while he was writing *The Rainbow* (*Letters* 2:249). But the *Rainbow* passage alludes also to the angel of the Annunciation in the New Testament, recalling countless other artworks, such as Giotto's, Fra Angelico's, and many anonymous examples. Will Brangwen's interest in the *Agnus Dei* and the *Pietà* has far-reaching impact in *The Rainbow,* as I demonstrate in

18. See *Letters* 3:341: writing from Derbyshire on 20 March 1919, Lawrence asked Gertler, his artist acquaintance, for reproductions of paintings by Fra Angelico, Giotto, Mantegna, Paolo Uccello (a fifteenth-century Italian artist), and Van Gogh. He intended to copy them—from black and white, if necessary, adding his own color—and asked Gertler to indicate what the colors should be.

chapter 2, but only the latter is explicitly named, while the former is represented by a lengthy description of the lamb in a stained-glass window at Cossethay Church. Lawrence uses such images for their ability to embody complex religious meanings. He wants not only "the scene" but also its religious content.

Even as I refer to his informed use of such models, I am far from denying that icons, like types, may carry content beyond the artist's specific knowledge and that they may vary in meaning beyond his or her conscious attempt at adaptation. Indeed, Lawrence counted on this process, and sometimes his results must have surprised even him. Because he is "pre-eminently and constantly" creative, his ontology, as shown by John B. Vickery, is more dynamic, Romantic, and transformational than static, classical, and fixed.[19] Lawrence states his disdain for what he calls the forced "didactic" character of "allegorical" images, which he contrasts with dynamic symbols that "don't 'mean something'" but can affect people "beyond comprehension" because they are latent beneath human consciousness and are capable of taking new directions there (A 49). "No man can invent symbols," he adds, although they are "embedded in the soul and ready to start alive when touched" (A 49). This account has much in common with Jung's description of symbolic images that are not prescriptive, not imposed by an external system.[20] Nonetheless, I see Lawrence's art mediating between well-established, even conventional, images and his vision of unrealized possibilities. According to Vickery, his view of the cosmos, for example, draws upon "aspects of antecedent structures" even while following a Romantic "fantasia form," allowing "free play" to his imagination. Thus one side of his work may represent a "ritual . . . derivative and firmly anchored in a largely forgotten and no longer viable past" while the other seeks to revise and revitalize that past imaginatively, often producing ironic effects when past and present meet in conflict.[21]

Despite the importance Lawrence himself gives to the "forever-

19. Vickery, "D. H. Lawrence and the Fantasias," 163, 166–67. Cowan, too, in *D. H. Lawrence and the Trembling Balance,* emphasizes the continual fluidity of Lawrence's work, which reflects in this style a dynamic "conception of life" (16).

20. Jung, *Archetypes and the Collective Unconscious,* in *Collected Works,* 9, 1:3–41, especially 6. Lawrence was familiar with some Jung, perhaps *Psychoanalysis of the Unconscious,* by 1918 and refers to him as "the *ex cathedra* Jung" in his own *Psychoanalysis and the Unconscious* (1921), 3.

21. Vickery, "D. H. Lawrence and the Fantasias," 166, 175, 179.

Fig. 1. One of the Cherubim with Six Wings, from a fourteenth-century English psalter, in the British Library (included in Jenner's *Christian Symbolism*).

unfolding creative spark," the "come-and-go" of "momentaneity"
(*CP* 182–83), the known forms are indispensable to his practice,
and he proves a remarkably conscious craftsman in choosing
forms with inherited implications and repeating them in con-
sistent ways. His iconography is best understood through the
strict etymology of the word: his *icons* have sacred associations,
thus involving his work in entire worldviews, cosmologies, and
typologies.[22] If *The Rainbow* presents fairly early examples, *The
Man Who Died* (1929), with its repetitive focus on the *Noli me
Tangere,* provides a late one. Numerous other instances, of small
and broad scale, appear throughout his canon. In this study, then,
I look at some lines of medieval iconography pertinent to his
work, but I am even more concerned with the aspects of biblical
typology and worldview that are interrelated with them — and with
Lawrence's reinterpretations of them.

His knowledge of biblical typology has been little explored despite
his interest in one of its most spectacular practitioners, Joachim
of Fiore. This twelfth-century abbot, whose ideas were partly
influenced by St. Augustine's typology,[23] not only knew traditional types but also employed new ones that focused uniquely
on an eschatological vision more intense than that of most fellow
churchmen. After his death, some of his thought was condemned
by the church, revalued in various hands, and channeled into
heresies, secret societies, and, eventually, secular philosophies.
Thus Joachimism came to influence both alchemy and Rosicrucianism, entering indirectly into the theosophy and other occult
lore that interested Lawrence.[24] Yet much of Joachim's work was
entirely orthodox, including most of his tripartite division of time
into the standard typological epochs of Law (Old Testament or Old
Law) and of Love (Christian or New Law) — and a third age, which
he named for the Holy Spirit and envisioned as a historic period
preceding the ultimate end of time.

22. Alldritt, *The Visual Imagination,* 128–35, identifies five scenes in *The
Rainbow* as "icons": a mother-and-child scene formed by Lydia and Anna as
seen by Tom early in the novel; the moonlight ritual between Will and Anna
in the sheaves; Anna's dance during pregnancy; Ursula's moonlight dance
with Skrebensky; and Ursula's encounter with the horses near the novel's
end. Except for the first of these, however, they are not based on traditional
Christian iconography. I refer to icons in a stricter sense as religious images.

23. West and Zimders-Swartz, *Joachim of Fiore,* 31–32, 78.

24. On a tie with alchemy, see Jung, *Mysterium Coniunctionis,* in *Collected
Works,* 14:30; on a contact with seventeenth-century Rosicrucianism, see
Reeves and Hirsch-Reich, *Figurae of Joachim of Fiore,* 299.

The first two ages are clearly mentioned in Lawrence's works as early as the preface to *Sons and Lovers* (1913) and the "Study of Thomas Hardy" (1914-15), but these are epochs of standard, not specifically Joachimite, typology; and Lawrence's early references to the "third age" are rather vague, though he deals with it unambiguously in his *Movements in European History* (1921) and seems to embody it silently in later fiction. Marjorie Reeves and Warwick Gould, including Lawrence in their book on the Joachimite tradition, find him influenced by the "Eternal Evangel," a radical heresy not promulgated by Joachim but by one of his followers.[25] In this view, the church is to be superseded in the third epoch—and certainly Lawrence obsessively proclaims the end of Christendom. From Joachim, too, Lawrence may derive his focus on the "trinitarian" third element in his schemes of history and relationship.[26] In addition, I suggest in later chapters that some of his curious images of trees argue for the long-term influence of Joachim or his followers, preoccupied as they sometimes were with graphic "tree" diagrams, like expanded family trees, representing the future era of the Holy Spirit in their topmost branches (Fig. 2). Lawrence's trees are diverse, but several curious passages associate the workings (if not the age) of the Holy Spirit with the growth of trees.

His typology is, however, far broader than to focus continually on that third epoch and the Apocalypse. Frank Kermode's approach, finding all of Lawrence's major novels "in a sense allusions to Revelation," has employed an entirely apocalyptic typology of the "third age" while neglecting the more standard messianic exegesis

25. It was a fanatical Franciscan, Gerard of Borgo, who in 1254 proclaimed the Old and New Testaments "utterly abrogated" and the church superseded by a third age; he first identified Joachim's works with the "Eternal Evangel" (from the Book of Revelation), and it was in this form that Joachimism was popularly transmitted (Reeves and Gould, *Joachim of Fiore,* 8-9).

26. See Reeves and Gould, *Joachim of Fiore,* 279-91. It is unclear how early Lawrence knew of the "third age" that most typifies the Joachimite model. In 1916, he read a book that included translated passages from the thirteenth-century Franciscan Salimbene, a disciple of Joachim (*Letters* 2:633), and this volume, Coulton's *From St. Francis to Dante,* may have been Lawrence's only source, according to Clark, *The Minoan Distance,* 209. Since the "trinitarian" pattern shows itself earlier in Lawrence, however, Reeves and Gould "suggest that he came across an account of Joachimism as expressed in the Eternal Evangel episode as early as c. 1914" (291). Coulton would not account for Lawrence's failure to differentiate, in *Movements in European History,* between Joachim and his radical disciples. Neither would Coulton account for Lawrence's possible echoes of Joachim's tree imagery.

Fig. 2. Tree of the Two Advents, by Joachim of Fiore, from his *Liber Figurarum,* in the library of Corpus Christi College, Oxford University. The First and Second Comings of Christ are represented in the sketch.

in which specific Old Testament characters, along with specific events and rituals, prefigure the New Testament Christ and the rituals of the church.[27] The general disregard for such typology in Lawrence's works is hard to understand, for they are imbued with it in essential ways. Perhaps his most direct study of it came in 1914, when he pored over Jenner's *Christian Symbolism,* with its important section on orthodox types, for *The Rainbow.* But the very titles of his works in diverse stages of his development—"The Old Adam" (1911), "New Eve and Old Adam" (1913), *The Rainbow* (1915), "Samson and Delilah" (1917), *Aaron's Rod* (1922), *Noah's Flood* (1924), *David* (1925)—insistently announce not just biblical but typological figures and motifs that do not cluster in a single period.

Biblical typology is a specialized form of scriptural exegesis that deeply influenced both literary and graphic arts in the Western world. Present in the Bible itself, it underwent major development under St. Augustine and throughout the Middle Ages, becoming increasingly eclectic in the Renaissance (though it had eclecticism, too, in the patristic period).[28] Perhaps it is best known in America for its popularity among the colonial settlers, who often saw their trek to New England in terms of the journey to the Promised Land, but it has also had its role in many other millennial and messianic movements.[29] Standard typology has three main branches—the Levitical, or ritual, the prophetic, and the "historical."[30] Lawrence's

27. Kermode, *D. H. Lawrence,* 57. See also his "Lawrence and the Apocalyptic Types," 14-33, and Doherty's "Salvator Mundi Touch," 70. The latter, while posing a Yogic system of "typology" in Lawrence, acknowledges that it has "no basis in orthodox Christian messianic typology." See also my preface, acknowledging George Ford's *Double Measure* for its initial identification of several orthodox types in Lawrence.

28. On Renaissance and seventeenth-century eclecticism, see, for example, Allen, *Mysteriously Meant,* and Korshin, *Typologies in England, 1650-1820.*

29. Brumm, *American Thought and Religious Typology,* 33, 44-47 passim; Bercovitch, *The American Jeremiad,* 95-131; and Lowance, "Typology and Millennial Eschatology," 228-73. On the influence of the Apocalypse in Western thought and art more generally, see also Cohn, *The Pursuit of the Millennium,* and Kermode, *The Sense of an Ending.*

30. See, for example, Landow, *Victorian Types, Victorian Shadows,* 23-34. On orthodox biblical typology, see also Schiller, *Iconography of Christian Art,* 5 vols.; Hoefer, *Typologie im Mittelalter;* Galdon, *Typology in Seventeenth-Century Literature;* and Taylor, *Christ Revealed.* Landow has identified both orthodox uses of biblical typology and secularized extensions of it in the Victorian and modern periods: see (besides *Victorian Types, Victorian Shadows*) *Images of Crisis,* 159-79, and other works cited below.

references to the Eucharist extend and reinterpret the Levitical rituals of Mosaic law, in which offerings of animal sacrifice forerun Christ's own offering (and its commemoration in the Mass). Prophetic types include objects, like Moses' or Aaron's staff, supposed to signify future attributes of Christ. The "historical" types provide a kind of genealogy of Christ's forebears (not always physical forebears but personages who forerun him in particular ways). In this line of typology, certain Old Testament *figurae,* "types," seen as both historic and prefigurative, precede Christ, the "antitype." They include Adam, Noah, Abraham, Moses, Samson, David, and others— but chief among them is Adam, for the "new Adam" is Christ, redeeming the old.

Because of the importance of knowing this scheme when reading Lawrence, it is particularly fortunate that his *Quetzalcoatl,* written in 1923 as the first version of *The Plumed Serpent* (1926), is now available to general readers.[31] It is a rich repository of specific typological motifs, including the following: the redemptive relationship between the first and the last Adam (Christ); the Brazen Serpent that Moses reared in the wilderness to save his people, as the uplifted (crucified) Christ would save his; the "smitten rock" from which Moses' rod released water prefiguring the redemptive blood of Christ, the Eucharist, and baptism; and the bruising of the serpent's head, signifying the defeat of evil.

All of these were known to Lawrence early from Jenner and probably from such Victorian predecessors as Carlyle, Ruskin, and the Pre-Raphaelites;[32] probably, too, from Nonconformist sermons; and certainly from paintings and cathedral art that he saw in copies and in person, in his home area and during his travels in Germany, Italy, and elsewhere. His interest in biblical types was whetted anew in mid-career, partly by the Roman Catholic art and culture that frequently surrounded him after his rupture from his homeland,[33] and also by theosophists and students

31. *Quetzalcoatl* is being edited with an introduction by Louis Martz. I quote from Lawrence's typescript (E313b in Roberts, *A Bibliography of D. H. Lawrence*), located in the Houghton Library, Harvard University; for convenience, I refer to *Quetzalcoatl* and *The Plumed Serpent* as separate works, although Martz believes the former is an unfinished version. I have also examined the manuscript of *Quetzalcoatl* (E313a in Roberts).

32. On Lawrence's early interest in these Victorians, see Chambers (E.T.), *D. H. Lawrence,* 101–2, 107, 119, 146.

33. See Delany, *D. H. Lawrence's Nightmare,* on Lawrence's disillusionment

of the occult like Blavatsky, Pryse, and Frederick Carter, who all adapted elements of typology on occasion. Blavatsky alone extended antique and medieval time to the turn of the century in that exotic form in which it flowers along with modernism in figures like W. B. Yeats, James Joyce, and even T. S. Eliot. Part of that florescence shows up in Lawrence's radically revised biblical typology.

Quetzalcoatl affords the fullest showcase of such combined orthodox and revisionary usage, and it deserves early discussion for its ability to illuminate much about Lawrence's symbolism in other works both earlier and later. The religious motifs in the penultimate chapter of this novel are said to be "old symbols" and images that make "the mysterious ... real" (Q 332). These "symbols" clearly resemble those attributed in *Fantasia of the Unconscious* (1922) to the "old wisdom" descending from the Atlantean world (55) and ascribed in *Apocalypse* (1931) to "ancient sense-consciousness," with its "knowledge based not on words but on images" or "symbols" (91). In fact, however, they frequently belong to biblical typology, as I will demonstrate. One catalogue of such "old symbols," for example, even includes "New Jerusalems and Rosy Crosses and Ankhs and Heavenly Brides" (Q 332). While two of these refer to shapes of the cross existing in heterodox forms (as well as orthodox), the New Jerusalem (the Heavenly Bride) is specific to Christian typology. Yet the novel's authority, Ramón, refers to all of these symbols as examples of "the semi-barbaric method of thinking in images: image-thinking" (Q 332). They and other types are further related to "the magic of the ancient blood, before men had learned to think in words, and thought in images and in acts" (Q 341).

The subject of this 1923 chapter is very much the same one that engaged Lawrence nearly ten years earlier in his handling of the Marriage at Cana. It presents something of a Last Supper tableau comprised of the three major characters: Ramón, the Mexican prophet who calls himself "the living Quetzalcoatl" after the ancient Aztec god; an Irish woman, Kate Burns (later Kate Leslie in *The Plumed Serpent*); and Cipriano, "the living Huitzilopochtli," who wants to marry Kate. At one point, Cipriano offers Kate a cup of

---

with his country during the First World War, when he was under surveil-lance because of his German wife; after he was allowed to leave in 1919, he was seldom to return. See also Moore, *The Priest of Love*, 261–305, and Meyers, *D. H. Lawrence*, 177–81, 222–30.

wine obviously intended to suggest the Eucharist, the marriage
union, and the combining of their two bloods. "It's my blood,"
Cipriano intones, asserting that his blood and Kate's meet in the
wine's "vortex" (Q 342).

This version of the Christian ritual seems totally ironic and
blasphemous since Cipriano is supposedly the modern avatar of
an Aztec god associated with bloodshed and violence (in one
account, a victim himself, commemorated in a crudely eucharistic
ceremonial).[34] Yet the entire chapter surprisingly attempts a
certain reconciliation, in the Mexican setting, between a neo-
Aztec movement and the Catholic church. Quetzalcoatl/Ramón
understandably amazes Kate by stating that he will accept Easter
Mass: "I will still kneel, at Easter, to the great mass of the Sacrifice.
I will take from the priest the sacrament of the Crucified Redeemer.
I will do it at Easter, in remembrance" (Q 331). At this point,
Lawrence demonstrates his knowledge of a legend, often found in
Italian panel paintings, that Christ's cross was reared at the world's
center (in this case, Golgotha) directly over the body of Adam so
that the blood of the Crucifixion bathed him in redemption: according to Gertrud Schiller, who describes this typological pattern,
"The new Adam [typologically, Christ] dies above the grave of the
old Adam, that the old may live" (2:131). Ramón himself expounds
the "Old Mysteries" largely in keeping with such typology: "In all
religions . . . the unredeemed Adam was buried at the foot of the
cross, and the blood of the Redeemer showered down on him. So
he rose again, as before the Fall" (Q 331). This is part of the
pattern in which not only Adam but also other Old Testament
personages prefigure Christ—a pattern that I explore in greater
detail in chapter 1. This *Adamtypologie* was particularly prevalent
in the thirteenth and fourteenth centuries, partly because of the
popular *Golden Legend* of Jacopo de Voragine, which was frequently
illustrated, as in Agnolo Gaddi's *Legend of the True Cross* in the
choir at Santa Croce, Florence; Piero della Francesca's in Arezzo;
and Cenni di Francesco's in Volterra.[35] These show that a branch

34. Jung cites a sixteenth-century account by Bernardino de Sahagún, in
Psychology and Religion, in *Collected Works,* 11:223-24. Whether or not
Lawrence knew of this source, he creates a similar context for Huitzilopochtli's
offer.

35. On Adam and the legend of the cross, see, for example, Clark, *Piero
della Francesca,* 38-50, and Eliade, *Patterns in Comparative Religion,* 292-93.
See also Jung, *Mysterium Coniunctionis,* in *Collected Works,* 14:382-456
("Adam and Eve").

or a seed of the tree of knowledge was rooted in Adam's body and that its wood eventually became the cross. In some legends of the cross and in standard typology, Christ's triumph over death revives the first Adam and turns the cross into the tree of life.

Lawrence would have known from Blavatsky a cabbalistic counterpart to the Adam of Eden, Adam Kadmon, an "Emanation" of God who originally "contained" all the universe (*SD* 1:443; 2:128-29, 234; *Isis* 1:302, 2:264-65).[36] This figure has been termed "an 'Idea' in the Platonic sense";[37] yet the two Adams have occasionally been identified together over the centuries, and Lawrence may blend them at times. While he does, like Blake, utilize the concept of a cosmic man,[38] I believe that this figure was too anthropomorphic and too nearly Platonic for Lawrence to be primarily interested in it — and that, rather, he preferred the earthy and erring Adam set in his typological drama with Christ.

Ramón's version of this drama is, in some ways, hardly distinguishable from some orthodox views as he explains that "the passion of the Lamb is consummated, the blood of Sacrifice had done its work and ceased to flow" because of the redemption (*Q* 331). But the cross of sacrifice is to be replaced by the "rosy cross." This reversal is doubtless influenced by theosophy — Lawrence had read Blavatsky at least a year before he himself wrote about the "rosy cross" in 1918 in "The Two Principles" (published in 1919). Despite his knowledge of the esoteric traditions about the "rosy cross," however, he was also demonstrably aware that the cross of Christ was often depicted as the barren tree of death for crucifixion but as the flowering tree of life for resurrection (Schiller 2:134-36 3:16, 555); such usage is common enough in Florentine and southern German church art of the thirteenth and fourteenth centuries.[39] As early as his poem "Almond Blossom," written in

36. Scholem, *Kabbalah,* 137, remarks on the "strong anthropomorphic coloring" of this concept and "the purely spiritual sense" in which it is to be understood. See also Bloom, *Kabbalah and Criticism,* 40-41.

37. Jung, *Mysterium Coniunctionis,* in *Collected Works,* 14:416.

38. Lawrence is connected with hermeticism by Woodman, "D. H. Lawrence and the Hermetic Tradition," 1-6, and Ballin, "Lewis Spence and the Myth," 74.

39. St. Bonaventura, in the thirteenth century, influenced a school of mysticism and art when he represented the cross as a flowering, fruit-bearing tree; it appears as both a rose-tree and a rose-bush (Schiller 2:135). Examples of the tree-cross are especially well known in work by Nicola and Giovanni Pisano, Florence, and throughout southern Germany. While affinities exist between Joachim of Fiore's elaborate tree imagery and St. Bonaventura's, the

1920, he uses this tradition of the flowering cross, as I show in chapter 5.

Cipriano, in *Quetzalcoatl,* mentions yet another standard Christian type: the Brazen Serpent that Moses lifted up in the wilderness trek toward the Promised Land. Christ in the attitude of the Brazen Serpent is the subject of artworks, including a well-known painting by the Pre-Raphaelite Holman Hunt, one that Lawrence may have known.[40] The Brazen Serpent, which appears a number of times in Lawrence's work, has a long history as a prophetic type. In the Old Testament, when the Israelites were assailed by poisonous snakes, Moses lifted up an image of a serpent on a pole so that all who looked upon it might escape death (Numbers 21:6-9). In the New Testament, Christ explicitly connects himself with this image: "And as Moses lifted up the serpent in the wilderness, even so must the Son of Man be lifted up" (John 3:14). Thus Moses' cruciform stave with its brass serpent is a typological prefiguration of Christ on the cross and a symbol of salvation (Schiller 2:125-26). Lawrence would have known of this usage at least as early as 1914 from Jenner.[41] He alludes to the Brazen Serpent in his poem "St. Matthew," written in 1920, and, in 1924, makes the device a symbol of renewal for a civilization: "When the worst comes to the worst, there is sure to be a Moses to set up a serpent of brass. And then we can start off again" (*RDP* 197). Later, in *Apocalypse,* as in "St. Matthew," he confirms his exact understanding of its relation to Christ: "The millions of little vipers [in the modern world] sting us as they stung the murmuring Israelites, and we want some Moses to set the brazen serpent aloft: the serpent which was 'lifted up' even as Jesus later was 'lifted up' for the redemption of men" (*A* 125).

---

saint's trees are distinguishable as trees of redemption (the tree of life and the cross) and Joachim's as illustrations of historic epochs (Reeves and Hirsch-Reich, *Figurae of Joachim of Fiore,* 299-307).

40. Lawrence refers to another Hunt painting, *The Light of the World,* in *Kangaroo* (290), describing it in detail. The chapter "The Light of the World" in "Study of Thomas Hardy" may refer to this painting as well as to John 8:12, according to Bruce Steele (*STH* 264). See Landow, *William Holman Hunt,* xvi, 116-25, on *The Shadow of Death* (in the Manchester City Art Galleries); Hunt mentions the Brazen Serpent in his statement about this painting and includes a heraldic Brazen Serpent in his design for stained glass, *Melchizedek* (12, 114-16) and a stylized one in the frame of his *Finding of the Saviour in the Temple* (122). See also Landow, "William Holman Hunt's 'Shadow,'" 212-15.

41. Jenner, *Christian Symbolism,* 49.

In *Quetzalcoatl,* however, Cipriano gives a radically revisionist meaning to the symbol, stating that "good desire is the Serpent in the Wilderness, all gold" (Q 342). The motif of Moses in the wilderness is an extended one in this discourse as Cipriano discerns in the "vortex" of the winecup "the Lord Almighty . . . dividing the waters of the Red Sea" to allow the soul to pass from Egypt to Canaan (Q 342). The meaning is not unlike earlier and later Lawrence messages about the power of vital, instinctive "blood knowledge" to transform the overly cerebral and spiritual modern consciousness. Lawrence wrote his friend Catherine Carswell in 1916 that "God in me is my desire" (*Letters* 2:635), an idea he may combine with Blavatsky's declaration that the Brazen Serpent was a sexual image (*SD* 2:473). Specifically, of course, Cipriano wants Kate to desire him as a major part of her salvation from the modern stalemate (Egypt). This is the personal and cultural renewal that is possible for this middle-aged, disillusioned woman who sees the shallowness and sterility of her European civilization. The "vortex of my blood with your blood," says Cipriano, creates "a Canaan of tomorrow" (Q 342). Thus the Promised Land serves Cipriano, like the biblical exegete, as an image of a desired future. While he means to share this Canaan with Kate, she cannot commit herself to the union.

The sacramental wine she drinks only leaves her repelled, and her lack of response is rendered in curious terms: "She was set into a hard rock, like the rock before Moses smote it and released the flow" (Q 344). Here is one of the most famous of all images in biblical typology—that of the Rock of Horeb which, smitten by Moses' staff, gave forth life-giving water as the smitten side of Christ would issue redemptive blood (Schiller 1:130, 2:23).[42] To some extent, Kate is seen as a potential savior, for Ramón and Cipriano think Mexico needs her as a goddess. The smitten rock is a major eucharistic symbol (and a baptismal one), fitting to the situation in this chapter. Even more fitting in this case is the typological reading that makes the smitten rock an image of the obdurate heart that needs to be softened, a common usage among Victorians—one occurring in works by Alfred Tennyson, Robert Browning, G. M. Hopkins, Christina Rossetti, and Emily Dickinson—and in famous graphic illustrations by Nicolas Poussin,

42. See Landow, "Moses Striking the Rock," 315–44, showing the survival of this type among Victorians.

Lucas van Leyden, and others.[43] While Ramón, and presumably Cipriano, have become "Redeemed Adam," Kate, far from being Mexico's goddess, does not even become the redeemed Eve but makes plans to return to Europe despite her attraction to the Mexican attempt to restore a kind of Eden.

Ramón even announces the new order with the words of Psalms 24:7—"Lift up your heads, O ye gates!" (Q 339), a passage that heralds the coming of "the King of Glory" (designating Christ, to the biblical typologist). According to one critic, the passage had phallic significance in some medieval church contexts, as it does in Lawrence's *Lady Chatterley's Lover* (1928).[44] Here, however, Ramón uses the quotation to suggest the coming of a new era, for "the wheel of the ÆEon has turned" (Q 339), doing away with the Christian era and bringing the next. This new period is in some ways similar to the "third age" as projected by radical thirteenth-century Joachimites. In *Quetzalcoatl,* as in the final *Plumed Serpent,* this new day has the guise of an ancient one: it is an age of renewed paganism, seen as an almost prelapsarian state.

Kate's position in such a scheme is elaborated in typological terms based on the passage from Genesis in which God tells Adam and Eve the consequences of their disobedience and tells the serpent, "And I will put enmity between thee and the woman, and between thy seed and her seed; it [the seed] shall bruise thy head, and thou shall bruise his heel" (Genesis 3:15).[45] Often interpreted as a prophecy of Mary and her "seed," Christ, the passage is commonly read to say, as in Lawrence's version, that the serpent will bruise the woman's heel while she bruises its head. As Ramón puts it, "The heel of Eve was as a bruise, the heel of her flesh which must forever kiss the earth" (Q 336). This serpent, to the biblical exegete, is not the Brazen Serpent but Satan, the tempter in the Garden of Eden. It will be "bruised" when evil is conquered by Christ (Schiller 3:31-37). Many artworks, from manuscript

43. Landow, *Victorian Types, Victorian Shadows,* 84-93.

44. Sheerin, "John Thomas," 297-300, shows that the bishop's staff, in certain medieval church dedications, had a masculine (phallic) character when allegorizing the marriage of Christ to the church: the staff's rapping on the church door signified the divine entry.

45. See Landow, "Bruising the Serpent's Head," 11-14. Lawrence refers to this type in *Fantasia of the Unconscious* (written in early 1920): "We bruise the serpent's head. . . . But his revenge of bruising our heel is a good one" (216).

miniatures to monumental paintings and sculptures, represent either Mary or Christ with foot upon the serpent or dragon, treading down evil; one example, the *Christus Triumphans,* from a medieval manuscript, appeared in Jenner.[46] While the first Eve lost paradise because of this serpent, the "second Eve" (Mary) would triumph over it by bringing forth Christ. Lawrence's reversal of this theme casts the serpent (combined with the bird in *The Plumed Serpent*) as the life principle itself, associated with and not contrasted with the Brazen Serpent. It is, says Cipriano, the "dragon" in the wine.

In *The Plumed Serpent,* a well-known scene depicts Kate's sense of "reconciliation" with a snake she happens to see on a walk. In *Quetzalcoatl,* however, the serpent looks directly from "a loop-hole in hell" (Q 354), and Kate feels that the creature is "poisonous" in its disappointment at not having risen higher in creation (Q 354). In the later version, she acknowledges that it may have its "own peace" (*PS* 425). In a passage that Lawrence canceled before its publication, Ramón makes the typological significance of the snake more explicit, telling Kate that "the snake coils in peace round the ankle of Eve, and she no longer tries to bruise his head" (*PS* 547); such is the reversal of the fall of man and woman. In *Quetzalcoatl,* Kate's more wary encounter with the serpent follows her refusal of a marriage proposal by Cipriano—a refusal based partly on her sense that the Mexicans despair and may even grow "wicked" (like the snake). The finished *Plumed Serpent,* on the other hand, places the reconciliation with the snake after Kate's marriage to Cipriano as she sees increasing signs of paradise in the Mexican setting. Both versions mention the "paradisal" aspect, but only the second Kate becomes the redeemed Eve. She does so not by "bruising the serpent's head" but by accepting the creature.

The example of *Quetzalcoatl* shows with particular clarity the preoccupations that consistently structure Lawrence's thinking— the fall from Eden and its reversal, such prefigurations of redemption and renewal as Moses' wilderness trek toward the Promised Land and the rearing of the Brazen Serpent, and the rituals of Eucharist and marriage. In all of these, he revises orthodox pat-

---

46. In the *Christus Triumphans,* it is Christ who treads down the serpent (Schiller 1:29, 3:31-37). Lawrence would have known, too, from Jenner's *Christian Symbolism,* 126, that "the crowned and sceptered personification of the church is sometimes shown with her feet upon the dragon, the symbol of sin."

terns of biblical typology, sometimes as startlingly as Blake.[47] Despite Lawrence's alterations, however, he retains from his typo-logical system its central interest in resurrection, its heightening of the mundane by the sacred frame of reference, and even some-thing of its worldview. Most of these types appear in well-known artistic representations, and their pictographic features, too, enter importantly into his texts.

Besides providing an elaborate example of the workings of a revised biblical typology in a "middle" Lawrence piece (one bear-ing importantly upon his earlier and later usage), *Quetzalcoatl* also explicitly illustrates "image-thinking," depending less upon the word than the image—a mode of perception belonging to an essentially religious vision that Lawrence seeks always to restore from a primeval past. Although these examples are in a novel that he later rewrote, they are not out of keeping with his more fin-ished works, as later chapters will demonstrate; *The Plumed Serpent*, for example, drops the obvious, formulaic types but retains some of their associations and combines them with aspects of Aztec mythology.

Since Lawrence eventually wishes to evoke the modes of Atlantis— from Etruria, for example, or from ancient Mexico—his interest in the Judeo-Christian types is a surprise to the modern reader. Are they not too traditional, too medieval for his purposes (even if often ironically employed)? Earl Miner explains, however, that the comprehensive system of typology "has continued to matter in various forms" because it "could only seem inviting to writers in search of meaning, even if their versions lacked religious purpose or if they worked to parodic ends."[48] Clearly, Lawrence was often drawn to material from medieval Europe, the heyday of legends of the cross and popular typology, and he undoubtedly did associate "blood knowledge" with the Middle Ages. In *Twilight in Italy* (1916), he refers to the "strong, primitive, animal nature" of medieval man (*TI* 34); even in an essay on Herman Melville (1919), one of the *English Review* essays later revised for *Studies*

---

47. Although Lawrence's proven reading of Blake is limited to *Songs of Innocence* and *Songs of Experience* (Chambers, *D. H. Lawrence*, 101), many commentators have noted similarities between the two writers: see, for example, Storch, *Sons and Adversaries*; Ballin, "D. H. Lawrence's Eso-tericism," 70–87; de Sola Pinto, "William Blake and D. H. Lawrence," 84–106; Colmer, "Lawrence and Blake," 9–20; and Glazer, "Why the Sons of God," 164–85.

48. Miner, "Afterword," 393.

in Classic American Literature (1923), Lawrence associates the medieval church with "sensual apprehension": "We do not know how completely we have lost all comprehension of even Mediaeval Christianity" with its *"mystery"*: "The same with the mystery of the Eucharist. . . . The profound, passional *experience* it was to the mediaeval Christian is beyond our comprehension. . . . Because we do not choose to admit the sensual apprehension" (*SM* 221-22). And in "A Propos of *Lady Chatterley's Lover*" (1930), he sees "the old Church" as the guardian of the rare marriage that retains "blood-sympathy" and "blood-contact" in spite of the cerebral modern age (*PII* 503-9).

Because so many of his images involve Christian tradition, it is important to distinguish Lawrence's own beliefs from orthodoxy, reviewing some of the familiar details about his religious background and outlining some of his critics' understanding of these as influences in his literature. Next, it is necessary to explore his attitudes toward medieval arts and thought in more detail than I have already done. Lawrence's engagement with Christian sources is well known, discussed as his "quarrel with Christianity" nearly half a century ago by Graham Hough and more recently by James Cowan and others.[49] In an extreme form, this "quarrel" informs the short fictions in which Kingsley Widmer identifies an "art of perversity" and demonism, "rooted in ancient heretical traditions of anti-Christianity."[50] Like Widmer, Janice Hubbard Harris sees in the short fiction "disparagement of . . . marytred Christ figures," who are contrasted with pagan or Pan-like characters.[51] And Sandra M. Gilbert finds in the major poetry collection of Lawrence's middle years, *Birds, Beasts and Flowers* (1923), a "deliberately anti-Christian" cosmology and "downside-up versions of Christian myths."[52]

Yet Lawrence has sometimes attracted defense from orthodox commentators, such as Martin Jarrett-Kerr's view, "specifically from the Christian angle."[53] In addition, Lawrence, both early and late, identifies some of his favorite characters with Christ—from Paul

---

49. Hough, *The Dark Sun,* and Cowan, *D. H. Lawrence's American Journey,* 34-44 ("Lawrence's Quarrel with Christianity"). See also Eliot, *After Strange Gods.*

50. Widmer, *The Art of Perversity,* 168.

51. Harris, *Short Fiction of D. H. Lawrence,* 192.

52. Gilbert, "D. H. Lawrence's Uncommon Prayers," 82, 91.

53. Jarrett-Kerr [Fr. William Tiverton], *D. H. Lawrence and Human Existence,* x.

of *Sons and Lovers*[54] through the resurrected protagonist of *The Man Who Died*. According to Vivian de Sola Pinto, this latter work "is a parable of a Christianity that might die and be reborn";[55] yet Evelyn J. Hinz and John Teunissen assert "the utter inappropriateness of trying to approach *The Man Who Died . . .* as a redefinition of the Christian myth."[56] Although Lawrence is sometimes labeled a "Puritan," his own attacks on Puritanism, as a historical movement, are sharp and scathing (*SM* 24-27; *TI* 39; *PII* 509, 573-74).[57] Harry T. Moore judged that, while Lawrence believed Protestantism was insolubly wrongheaded, he "had some hope" for Catholicism, "religiously though not politically."[58] The passages from *Quetzalcoatl* discussed earlier tend to bear out this assessment—but only in an unusual way. A fragmentary Lawrence essay of 1923 also states that, "on the religious fundamentals, there is no breach between me [Lawrence] and the Catholic Church" (*RDP* 385). The same essay asserts, in fact, that he has "no real battle" with Christianity but only with "nonconformity"—since, "at the depth," his "nature is catholic" (*RDP* 385).[59] Nonetheless, when Ramón, in *Quetzalcoatl* and again in *The Plumed Serpent,* tells a bishop of the church what "catholic" really means—inclusive of all deities—it is clear how little the novelist's spokesman understands the Catholic church.

Lawrence wrote that, in his boyhood, the Bible and its Evangelical interpretations became "soaked in" his consciousness (*A* 59). He grew up a Congregationalist and often witnessed the Primitive Methodist chapel's revivals near his Eastwood home (*A* 64). However, he lost his Christian faith as a young man, and his

54. See Hinz, *"Sons and Lovers,"* 49.
55. De Sola Pinto, "The Burning Bush," 230.
56. Hinz and Teunissen, "Savíor and Cock," 296.
57. Hinz, *"Sons and Lovers,"* 35-40, finds that *Sons and Lovers* deals favorably with the unpuritanical Catholic past. See also Hinz, *"Ancient Art and Ritual,"* 617-20, on the impact of Roman Catholic Italy on Lawrence.
58. Moore, *The Priest of Love,* 346.
59. See Michael Herbert (*RDP* lii), judging that this fragment may be from an early version of the *Adelphi* essay "On Being Religious," quoted above. The fragment states: "Perhaps there is a certain battle between me and nonconformity, because, at the depth, my nature is catholic. . . . I believe that Jesus is one of the Sons of God: not, however, the only Son of God. I think that the men who believe in the all-overshadowing God will naturally form a Church of God. That is, I believe in a Church. And I believe in secret doctrine, as against the vulgarity of nonconformity. I believe in an initiated priesthood, and in cycles of esoteric knowledge. I believe in the authority of the Church, and in the power of the priest to grant absolution" (*RDP* 385).

interest in the negative uses of Christian imagery intensified
during and after the First World War, when he claimed the complete
death-commitment of his society. In a poetic fragment, "Passages
from *Ecce Homo*" (1914), for example, a soldier faces death because
the late stages of Christendom have perverted love into a desire for
death and death-dealing.[60] Here, Lawrence uses a common iconographic image of Christ, the *Ecce Homo* —which traditionally
shows him mocked by the Jews at his trial before Pilate (a motif
probably suggested to Lawrence by Nietzsche's title)[61] —and presents, instead, the soldier's deadly exposure to the warring Christians. The association between Christ and the soldiers exists
elsewhere in poetry of the First World War, but Lawrence's poem
contains a typological implication that makes it particularly harsh.
The soldier refers bitterly to Christ's offer to embrace mankind
with "rest." Since women now admire only wounds, he gives up on
the hope of a wholesome love: "we go to visit / Our Bride among
the rustling chorus of shells," he states, ironically evoking the
mystic relationship between Christ as the Bridegroom and the
church as the Bride.[62] Of course, the allusion is less to the Song
of Solomon than to the Book of Revelation, in which the Bride, as
the New Jerusalem, appears "prepared as a bride for her husband"
at the end of the world (Revelation 21:2). The imagery of the
mystic Bride and Groom is contained in *The Rainbow* in happier
contexts; but in this war poem, though written in the same period
(and even earlier than last drafts of *The Rainbow*), it serves
Lawrence for a darker vision—that which dominates in his "war
novel," *Women in Love* (1920). In a later essay, he states that the
war meant the collapse of any vision of "the all-pitying and all-

60. This fragment (E113.2b in Roberts, *A Bibliography of D. H. Lawrence*)
is less a variant of "Eloi, Eloi, Lama Sabachthani" (which did evolve from
it) than it is an earlier and separate poem. (See Sullivan, "D. H. Lawrence
and *Poetry,*" 269–71.) Its use of the Bride and Bridegroom imagery is similar
to that in both the early and late "Crown," in which "the enemy is the bride"
and "we are the bridegroom, engaged with him" in destroying the bride (*RDP*
290, 476).

61. Lawrence spoke of Nietzsche as early as 1907 after going to Croydon
(Chambers, *D. H. Lawrence,* 120), but Nietzsche's self-portrait *Ecce Homo*
was not one of the books to which Lawrence had access at the Croydon
Central Library nor does he mention reading it later. In *Lawrence and
Nietzsche,* 100, Colin Milton sees certain similarities between Lawrence's
thought and that of Nietzsche in *Ecce Homo* but does not establish that
Lawrence read it. See also Widmer, "Lawrence and the Nietzschean Matrix,"
115–31.

62. See Schiller 4.1:101, 109.

helpful Woman," the Madonna, who had not saved men from their death: "For the man who went through the war the resultant image inevitably was Christ Crucified, Christ tortured on the Cross" (*PII* 572).

Preoccupied with this idea, he repeatedly identifies his civilization with a fallen Christus, like the roadside crucifix that presides over the death of Gerald Crich (pronounced as in "Christ") at the end of *Women in Love*. In "The Red Wolf," in *Birds, Beasts and Flowers*, for instance, he uses the metaphor of "a white Christus fallen to dust from a cross" (*CP* 403) to characterize the defunct European culture. As in *Quetzalcoatl*, he often depicts the world as awaiting a new dispensation that might return the Adamic man and metaphorically reinstate the tree of life in place of the tree of knowledge and the cross. Ironically, the idea of this reversal draws from the very sources it would seem to oppose—from Christian typology.

His own religious ideas are notoriously difficult to define, and texts exist to support various versions. In *Aaron's Rod*, a supposed Lawrence surrogate, Rawdon Lilly, claims that there is no God outside the individual (296). But in *Women in Love* and *Kangaroo* (1923), the Lawrence-like protagonists urgently seek beyond selfhood for nonhuman divinity. In an essay of 1923, Lawrence states, "God always is, and we all know it" (*RDP* 189), and the recently published *Apocalypse* fragments continue in this vein. For all his apparent pantheism on occasion—and he was the major figure in the revival of Pan in modern literature—he states, "The cosmos . . . is not God" (*A* 200). Above all, though, he exalts the "entirely religious" vision, in which the "idea" of God has not yet formed and "the tribe lived breast to breast, as it were, with the cosmos" (*A* 130). Philip Rieff, examining *Fantasia of the Unconscious* and *Psychoanalysis and the Unconscious*, finds Lawrence's religion "proudly anthropomorphic,"[63] but others, looking at a broader range of works, have claimed the opposite. It is precisely his nonhumanist strain, his elevation of "the unsearchable godhead" beyond anthropocentrism, that Scott Sanders has placed outside the mainstream ideas of western Europe "since the Renaissance,"[64] thus distinguishing Lawrence from many other modernists.

Lawrence's interest in the time before the Renaissance shows in the frequency with which he introduces medieval architecture

63. Rieff, "Introduction," xi.
64. Sanders, "D. H. Lawrence and the Resacralization," 166.

into his works, for he shares with Ruskin the idea that architecture can embody the spirit of an age. A famous argument on his taste in the style of Gothic cathedral arches shows that this building is sufficiently common in his works to attract not only attention but also controversy. *Sons and Lovers* contains Paul Morel's enthusiasm for the earthy round arches of Southwell Minster and Miriam's purported love of pointed Gothic arches, which to Paul represent the spiritual faculty.[65] This novel also sketches in a strategic historical background with a brief reference to a Carthusian monastery: Hinz has shown that this building evokes the pre-Puritan age that has been supplanted by an era of repression and hypocrisy.[66] Such locations form "architectural archetypes," such as Bettina L. Knapp has defined, structures of "sacred space."[67] Lawrence's "Study of Thomas Hardy," for example, refers to the "collective, stupendous, emotional gesture of the Cathedrals, where a blind, collective impulse rose into concrete form" (*STH* 65). *The Rainbow* makes Lincoln Cathedral a major setting, while naming, as well, Southwell Minster and Bamberg and Rouen Cathedrals; in *Women in Love,* the saving union between Birkin and Ursula occurs outside Southwell Minster; and *Aaron's Rod* distinctly celebrates Florence Cathedral and Giotto's Tower, while reflecting less favorably on Milan Cathedral. In the "Memoir of Maurice Magnus," which Lawrence wrote in 1922 as an introduction to Magnus's *Memoirs of the Foreign Legion* (1924), the abbey of Monte Cassino, though ultimately judged too backward looking, is a "quick spot . . . still not quite

65. *Sons and Lovers* is the text often cited to illustrate Lawrence's dislike of the pointed arch, but it is his character, Paul Morel, who, through the narrator, shows this taste while contrasting himself to his girlfriend Miriam: "He talked endlessly about his love of horizontals: how they, the great levels of sky and land in Lincolnshire, meant to him the eternality of the will, just as the bowed Norman arches of the church, repeating themselves, meant the dogged leaping forward of the persistent human soul, on and on, nobody knows where; in contradiction to the perpendicular lines and to the Gothic arch, which, he said, leapt up at heaven and touched the ecstasy and lost itself in the divine. Himself, he said, was Norman, Miriam was Gothic" (210). This statement, though it is frequently cited, needs more scrutiny, for the next sentence seems to cast some doubt on the claim: Miriam "bowed," says the narrator, *"even* to that" (210; my emphasis). The implication is that she need not have "bowed," that Paul's assertion may be questionable. See also Martz, "Portrait of Miriam," 73-91, challenging the narrative account of Miriam elsewhere in the novel. See also note 24 to chapter 2 below.
66. Hinz, *"Sons and Lovers,"* 37.
67. Knapp, *Archetype, Architecture, and the Writer,* viii-ix.

dead," a monument to the ages-long religious sense itself; it combines several eras: "all the wonder of the mediaeval past," the
prehistoric "sacred grove," the temples "before Christ was born,"
and the age of "the great Cyclopean wall . . . built even before the
pagan temples" (*MEM* 57).

Other significant church locations in Lawrence's works include
Metz Cathedral in "The Thorn in the Flesh" (1914), San Tommaso
and San Francesco in *Twilight in Italy,* Strassburg Cathedral in "The
Border Line" (1924), the country church in the last chapter of
Aaron's Rod, and churches in "The Last Laugh" (1924), *The Rainbow,* and *The Plumed Serpent.* In *Kangaroo,* his character Somers,
dreaming of an unnamed European cathedral, feels "sick" because it
is too massive and old (354), and in *The Plumed Serpent* the church
is completely emptied of Christian images — only to open, however,
in a more exotic, rather Italianate or even Etruscan guise. A place
"empty of God" (*PS* 287) is for Lawrence an unthinkable vacuum.

Thus when Rieff associates Lawrence with the "emotional and
intellectual boundaries of a church civilization,"[68] he points
precisely to the common situation of many of his characters.
Perhaps nowhere is this condition more literally evident than in
The Rainbow, in which the cathedral becomes progressively less
central, and in *Women in Love,* in which Southwell Minster is
physically in a peripheral position despite its symbolic significance.
The language and concepts of the "church civilization" persist
even when Lawrence produces centers of false worship and parodic
and ironic cosmologies that hollowly echo earlier systems of belief.
While writing some of his most biting assaults on Christendom, in
Birds, Beasts and Flowers, he nonetheless was seeking out "mediaeval Missals and Books of Hours and such" (*Letters* 4:124).[69]
Judith Wilt finds that Lawrence furthers more than one strain of
the Gothic mode in literature — that of vampirish terror and that of
longing for a lost medieval communalism.[70] His attitudes on
Gothic buildings are similarly complicated; while parodying "plaything" Gothic of the nineteenth century (*R* 399), he often shows
authentic medieval locations as continuing centers of worship.[71]

While Blake often seems his literary forebear, in temperament
and even in satiric approach, Lawrence's works also recall some of

68. Rieff, "Introduction," ix.
69. See chapter 5.
70. Wilt, *Ghosts of the Gothic.*
71. For a balanced look at Lawrence's interest in the medieval, see Verduin,
"Lawrence and the Middle Ages," 169–81.

the ideas and conventions of the Victorian Medieval Revival. With Ruskin, for instance, he has marked affinities,[72] and nowhere is the interconnection greater than in the somewhat nostalgic look back at the age of cathedral art. Lawrence and Ruskin saw the cathedral as an expression of a healthy society before modern disintegration, and both located the origins of the modern dilemma in the Renaissance. Even Lawrence's middle and late enthusiasm for the Etruscans, and his judgment that early "Christianity really rose, in Italy, out of the Etruscan soil" (*EP* 111), has its counterpart in Ruskin.[73] So, too, does his use of biblical typology, for which Ruskin is one more possible source.[74]

The Pre-Raphaelites, Thomas Carlyle, Thomas Hardy, and others, as well as Ruskin, all served to present Lawrence with aspects of the Medieval Revival.[75] Like Carlyle, Ruskin, and A.W.N. Pugin, he often contrasts the architecture of the Middle Ages with that of his modern setting so that a stock device in his works is a counterpoint between cathedral and colliery. In addition, he develops the Augustan dichotomy between neoclassic architecture and the more romantic Gothic, reviving some of the philosophical views of that controversy. As the neoclassic style represents Enlightenment and progress in a Renaissance tradition, it gives rise, says Lawrence, to industrial architecture; thus the cathedral-centered culture was the last really dynamic ambience in Europe, while the architecture and art that replace the cathedral are distinguished only by their negative qualities. In an early letter (1908), Lawrence seems to enjoy the "temples" of London, its commercial buildings (*Letters* 1:80), but he later completely reverses this view, somewhat echoed in a sinister key when attributed to the perverted Loerke in *Women in Love*. "Since churches are all

---

72. See Landow, "Lawrence and Ruskin," 35–50; Stroupe, "Ruskin, Lawrence, and Gothic Naturalism," 3–9; and Alldritt, *The Visual Imagination*, 70–96.

73. See *The Works of John Ruskin*, 23:203.

74. On Ruskin's use of typology, see Landow, *Aesthetic and Critical Theories*, 319–457, and Sussman, *Fact into Figure*, 3–31.

75. On Lawrence and the Pre-Raphaelites, see Alldritt, *The Visual Imagination*, 8–10 passim. On Lawrence and Carlyle, see Delany, "Lawrence and Carlyle," 21–34, and Alexander, "Thomas Carlyle and D. H. Lawrence," 248–67. On Lawrence and Hardy, see Swigg, *Lawrence, Hardy, and American Literature*, 58–80; Beards, "D. H. Lawrence and the *Study*," 210–29; Squires, "Scenic Construction and Rhetorical Signals," 125–45; and Langbaum, "Hardy and Lawrence," 15–38.

museum stuff, since industry is our business, now," says Loerke,
"then let us make our places of industry our art—our factory area
our Parthenon." Stating further that "art should *interpret* industry,
as art once interpreted religion," he reveals that the new artistic
theme is simply "mechanical motion" (*WL* 424). Needless to say,
this is the opposite of the mature Lawrence's thinking, for Loerke
is the high priest of the mechanistic modern consciousness.
Lawrence posits a sharp dichotomy between the cathedral-centered
"church civilization" and the industrial world, seeing little in
between. In an essay on Crèvecoeur, written in 1917, he notes that
"we have no architecture: we have only machines," for the world
lacks the communal "dark faith, or trust," in which "our mediaeval cathedrals were erected" (*SM* 61). *Fantasia of the Unconscious*
similarly praises the cathedral builders (60).

The desire to gain (or regain) a worldview animates his interest
in medieval art. In 1914, writing to his friend Gordon Campbell,
Lawrence advocates gaining a sense of "the Whole," which was
"how man built the Cathedral" (*Letters* 2:248). "At last," he writes,
"I have got it, grasping something of what the mediaeval church
tried to express" (2:249). To Lady Ottoline Morrell he characterizes "Giotto's and Cimabue's time" as one distinguished by the
"united impulse of all men in the fulfilment of one idea" (2:296). A
letter to E. M. Forster in 1915 continues in the vein of the first half
of *The Rainbow,* seeking to establish a comprehensive view such
"as the mediaeval men—as Fra Angelico" knew: a view "of the
beginning and the end, of heaven and hell, of good and evil flowing
from God through humanity as through a filter, and returning
back to god as angels and demons" (2:266).

Lawrence had observed to Campbell that "it is very dangerous
to use these old terms lest they sound like Cant" (2:249) and wrote
in 1915 to Bertrand Russell that he (Lawrence) had been "much
too Christian" (2:364). In spite of such admonitions to himself,
however, he never really expunges these terms from his vocabulary.
In 1919, while composing some of the essays now collected as *The
Symbolic Meaning,* he wrote Lady Ottoline that he was sketching
"a whole Weltanschauung—new, if old" (3:400), and the essays in
this group are indeed remarkable for their references to the Christian Middle Ages, an unexpected topic in a series on American
literature. A significant sequence of articles published in the
Adelphi in late 1923 and early 1924 also ranges into this topic.
The "foot of the Cross has shifted," Lawrence finds (*RDP* 190),
and Christianity has only "a past greatness" (200), but the monas-

teries of the Middle Ages are, nonetheless, the examples he gives of "perfect flames of purest God-knowledge," the monks having pursued the human adventure of establishing a "new way to God, to the life-source" (207); Lawrence praises "the lonely fortified monasteries, the little arks floating and keeping adventure afloat" (199).

Late in his life, too, Lawrence associates the "old Church" with the important lost human faculties of creativity and "blood-sympathy." The long essay "A Propos of *Lady Chatterley's Lover*" pointedly praises the process by which the medieval church accommodated itself to ancient pagan truths, thus forming a "quick spot" like that at Monte Cassino:

> The Early Christians tried to kill the old pagan rhythm of cosmic ritual, and to some extent succeeded. . . . But the Church, which knows that man doth not live by man alone, but by the sun and moon and earth in their revolutions, restored the sacred days and feasts almost as the pagans had them, and the Christian peasants went on very much as the pagan peasants had gone, with the sunrise pause for worship, and the sunset, and noon, the three great daily moments of the sun. (*PII* 509)

Apocalypse refers to the church in similar terms: "the early Catholic Church, as it emerged from the Dark Ages" had "adjusted itself once more to life and death and the cosmos, the whole great adventure of the human soul, as contrasted with the little petty personal adventure of modern Protestantism and Catholicism alike, cut off from the cosmos, cut off from Hades, cut off from the magnificence of the Star-mover" (75).

Although Lawrence has long been recognized as a cosmologist in the sense that "his matter is man's relation to the cosmos,"[76] the connections between his cosmic view and that of medieval typology have not previously been explored. Of course, "cosmology" is perhaps a pretentious word for his conception of the universe; certainly, he never offered a description of it as an astronomer or physicist would do. Although he entitled a chapter of *Fantasia of the Unconscious* "Cosmological," this effort is well described by Pollnitz as "a cosmogonic myth,"[77] and Vickery calls the work "a

76. Vivas, *D. H. Lawrence*, 238.
77. Pollnitz, " 'I Didn't Know His God,' " 8.

comic fairy tale."[78] But such mythology, often recalling archaic and medieval schemes rather than being Lawrence's invention, shows itself at times as a background even in his realistic fiction. Why else, for example, does Ursula seem to hear "the celestial, musical motion of the stars" (408)? What are the "the unseen hosts, actual angels . . . and good pure-tissued demons" mentioned by Birkin (128)? These references, though appearing in *Women in Love,* seem still to owe something to Lawrence's studies in angelology for *The Rainbow.* In 1914, his Christmas letter to Gordon Campbell refers to the orders of the angels of the spheres, "the Angels, and the Thrones, and the Cherubim," all *"absorbed in praise eternally"* (*Letters* 2:249). However archaic this language — apparently based on Jenner — it persists in his writings. In some of his very last work, *Apocalypse,* a similar passage appears: "These four great creatures [later the cherubim] make up the sum of mighty space . . . and their wings are the quivering of this space, that trembles all the time with thunderous praise of the Creator: for these are Creation praising their Maker, as Creation shall praise its Maker forever" (133).

In keeping with this celebration of a heavenly hierarchy is Lawrence's view that the lost sensuous consciousness includes a sense of natural aristocracy. The darker implications of this thinking are reflected with economy in the title *Lawrence's Leadership Politics and the Turn Against Women* (1986) by Cornelia Nixon.[79] While the novelist sometimes elevates characteristics of matriarchy, as in his praise of Pueblo life, much of his canon emphasizes patriarchal hierarchy.[80] Unlike many commentators,

78. Vickery, "D. H. Lawrence and the Fantasias," 167.

79. Simpson, *D. H. Lawrence and Feminism,* believes that Lawrence's early feminism ceased only at the end of the First World War, when he began to fear that women were gaining excessive power, but Nixon, *Lawrence's Leadership Politics,* states that the "turn" began earlier, in 1915. Storch, *Sons and Adversaries,* traces the triumph of "masculinity" in both Blake and Lawrence; and Ruderman, *D. H. Lawrence and the Devouring Mother,* gives a careful and informative account of the growth of Lawrence's "patriarchal ideal." But see also Siegel, *Lawrence among the Women,* placing him as an heir and transmitter of women's literary traditions.

80. On the Pueblo practices, see Tracy, *Lawrence and the Literature of Travel,* 15. Although Gilbert, "Potent Griselda," 141, terms Lawrence "famously misogynistic and, in rhetoric, fiercely, almost fascistically patriarchal," she shows the significance of matriarchal myths in some of his work. Gender issues may affect even his architectural imagery, for Dix, *D. H. Lawrence and Women,* 117, finds "matriarchal womb worship" throughout *The Rainbow,* not only in the rainbow itself but also in the arches at Lincoln

I see the latter tendency throughout his works, including early scenes of *The Rainbow*, interrelated with his frequent use of biblical patriarchs in typological patterns. Although Christianity, according to Frye, assumed the equal citizenship of both sexes and although typology itself led eventually to progressive social thought, Christocentric typology is by its very definition focused upon a male divinity whose precedent types are generally men.[81] Even the great vogue of the Virgin Mary, surrounded by her own typological motifs, does not reverse this tendency. Lawrence gains much mythic resonance from his use of such patterns, but he falls, too, into problematical politics.

Even the most controversial aspects of Lawrence's "leadership" views—long under attack for possible "protofascist" or even "fascist" leanings, as well as for antifeminist sentiments[82]—can be traced to his religious ideas, specifically to the medieval and Renaissance (as well as classical) great chain of being, although he does not quite call it that. The "ancient cosmic theories," those of paganism that "gave the true correspondence between the material cosmos and the human soul" (*SM* 176), says Lawrence, prescribed relationships among all living things. "The old aristocratic system at least recognised . . . the intrinsic and holy disquality between men," he states, but "was wrong" in basing it simply on birth (*SM* 84). Thus he asserts a natural hierarchy, further outlined in such essays as "Aristocracy" and "Reflections on the Death of a Porcupine" (1925).

Vestiges of such connections show themselves in *The Rainbow*, in the Brangwens' quasi-feudal world, but the proper ties between human beings and even humans and animals dissolve successively throughout the book. For example, Tom Brangwen, in his powerful youth, appears as a master of horses; but in his decline, drunk in the flood that ends his era, he is "apologetic to the horse" (*R* 227), a line that Lawrence added in his last revisions and there-

Cathedral; and Ruderman, *D. H. Lawrence and the Devouring Mother*, 139, comments that, during Lawrence's "leadership" period, he admires the pointed arch for suggesting "a culmination of society in the superior male individual."

81. Frye, *The Great Code*, 135, 86, 107.

82. On the issue of fascism, see Freeman's defense in *D. H. Lawrence*, 189–207, and Tindall's well-known discussion in *D. H. Lawrence and Susan His Cow*, 162–80. Nixon, *Lawrence's Leadership Politics*, 8–9, 183–85, considering him in the context of fascistic thought, states, "Lawrence denounced fascism itself; nevertheless, his views were similar in many respects to those held by some contemporary European intellectuals sympathetic to fascism" (5).

fore wished to emphasize (*R* 609). Instinctive "blood" relations
among masses of men—their "dark faith"—had built the cathedrals and would be necessary for any future creativity of similar
importance; and Lawrence's sense of the loss of such bonds appears
even in Birkin's desire for a deep contact with Gerald Crich, the
leader of industry in *Women in Love*. While Gerald's men unite
only in the motive of material production, they—and Gerald and
Birkin—might have had a warm, organic bond, instead. Often
seen as a homosexual desire, this lost option is more noteworthy
for its broader social implications. The natural hierarchy shows
itself in relations between men and women, even when Birkin
argues for "star equilibrium" with Ursula, and again, more insistently, when Somers in *Kangaroo* vainly asserts male dominance
over Harriet. Lawrence imagined the original Edenic condition as
one of perfect instinctive connections among all living things and
the cosmos. A lizard, he writes rather humorously, hears "the
sounding of the spheres" in its oneness with nature (*CP* 524). Art
can help one maintain all the true connections "between me and
another person, me and other people, me and a nation, me and a
race of men, me and the animals, me and the trees or flowers, me
and the earth, me and the skies and sun and stars, me and the
moon" (*STH* 172). Art can, in fact, both register this total view of
life and foster recognition of it.

It is now possible to see some of Lawrence's extensions and
adaptations of typology in a broader context than before. In the
most general sense, "typology" can be a belief in recurring types,
perhaps bringing with them all the shortcomings of a barbarous
past. In this regard, the most frightening novel Lawrence wrote
was undoubtedly *The Plumed Serpent* (discussed further in chapter 6), which raises broad questions about repetition of past
life-styles and modes of worship. "The more he asserted the fulfillment of preordained types," says Kermode, "the less he could
depend on that randomness which leaves room for quickness and
special grace."[83] But he grappled strenuously with the problem of
regression, for he did not believe that simple recurrence of earlier
ways could accommodate the human need to progress—to indulge
in the "thought-adventure," as he calls it (*RDP* 208). In *Women in
Love*, Birkin recognizes the danger of atavism, of lapsing back
into a previous level of development. Lawrence records how he
had told Magnus, who longed for the Middle Ages, "One can't go

83. Kermode, "Lawrence and the Apocalyptic Types," 25.

back" (*MEM* 56); and, in "Indians and an Englishman" (written in 1922), he rejects the life-style of the native American patriarchs ("old fathers"): "We do not need to live the past over again," he says. "I don't want to live again the tribal mysteries my blood has lived long since" (*P* 99). As early as "Study of Thomas Hardy," referring to Nietzsche, Lawrence takes issue with the idea of *Ewige Wiederkehr,* asserting that "each cycle is different" and ruling out "real recurrence" (72). And as late as *Apocalypse,* while insisting on the "pagan" idea that time moves "in cycles," not in a straight line, he explains that each new cycle is "not quite like the original one, but on another level" (97). In nonfiction like *Psychoanalysis and the Unconscious* and *Fantasia,* he outlines dual human imperatives — to regain old, supplanted faculties and also to employ them to move ahead in a form of cultural evolution. For all that, Lawrence often writes as if one can *almost* go back or, rather, as if the past can *almost* recur. I have referred to this view as a broadly "typological" one which allows, for instance, that the Pan type can be reborn, that "the living Quetzalcoatl" can return.

Biblical typology, however, as opposed to a more generalized system of returning types, is not a system of eternal recurrence but of additive process, as Northrop Frye suggests in his reference to "the forward-moving typological thinking of the Bible."[84] Such Old Testament types as Adam, Noah, Aaron, Moses, and David reflect only certain aspects of the antitype, Christ, who is the perfect consummation of these prefigurations. In that David was physically triumphant over Goliath, for example, he foreshadows Christ's triumph over death; in that Moses led his people toward the Promised Land, he foreruns Christ's salvation of mankind; in that Adam was physically the overseer of earth, he prefigures Christ's vicarage. Christ is the spiritual antitype, previously shadowed forth in imperfect physical ways, and he is the perfect spiritual sum of all the forerunners. Thus St. Paul can say that the "first man Adam" is "earthy," while the "last Adam," Christ, is a "quickening spirit" (1 Corinthians 15:45–47). Eve, as physical mother of the human race, is the imperfect type of Mary, the "new Eve," spiritual mother of the children of God. In his early poem "Eve," Lawrence shows his knowledge of the connection between the two women when, having eaten from the apple, "Eve walks into Sorrows" (*CP* 863). Of course, she will know the curse of

84. Frye, *The Great Code,* 82.

human pain, but she will also give place to the Mother of Sorrows. To the biblical exegete, this relationship suggests the redemption of man through the Crucifixion, and Lawrence's poem, although it fits the typology to his own purposes, comprehends this context. Similarly, the patriarchs yield to Christ, who becomes the fulfillment of Aaron's priesthood and of Moses' law; the son of David and King of the Jews; and the sacred Ark itself (though this is often the church as well). The progression is consistently from the old to the new, from the imperfect to the perfect, from the physical to the spiritual.

Precisely because of the perfection of the antitype, however, Lawrence senses stasis in this fulfillment in Christ. In his 1925 version of "The Crown," he states explicitly, "Jesus triumphant perished" (*RDP* 269). Bible stories that show the greatest activity of the physical types are, therefore, usually Lawrence's favorites: in "The Novel" (1925), he states that "the books of the Old Testament, Genesis, Exodus, Samuel, Kings" are "greater novels" than those of the New, though the Evangels are also "wonderful" (*STH* 181). "The Crown" casts the movement from sensual being toward mental consciousness in terms of typology: the senses belong to the Law (*RDP* 470) and are typified by one of the traditional messianic types, David: the flesh "develops to a great triumph, till it dances naked in glory of itself, before the Ark" (as David did in 2 Samuel 6:14-23),[85] but it can be joyous only because moving toward its opposite in "the procession of heroes travelling towards the ... white light, the Mind" (*RDP* 257).[86] That light force is the antitype—the Christian fulfillment. Elsewhere in "The Crown," the sensual and mental-spiritual directions are plainly defined, respectively, as "the Pagan, aristocratic, lordly, sensuous" and "the Christian, humble, spiritual, unselfish, democratic" (*RDP* 300). As I show in chapter 2, Lawrence believed that the pagan and lordly was at last overbalanced only at the Renaissance, the real triumph of the antitype. Theoretically, both type and antitype are necessary. In fact, however, Lawrence privileges the former, showing that the spiritual "Christ figure" needs to become again the type, the sensuous "old Adam," the patriarch, king, and champion. The presence of both in his texts, even in

85. While this passage remains in the 1925 "Crown," Lawrence's alteration of the 1915 version concerns David elsewhere in the essay, indicating a shifting attitude toward him. See chapter 1.

86. Although this passage contains a reference to a "goddess" of light, the same light imagery is, elsewhere in the essay, associated with Christianity.

this reversal, produces not only irony but also paradox, and he occasionally reworks his terms—as in a 1916 letter about his own marriage's need for "a new Adam and a new Eve" (*Letters* 2:662). But his fundamental preference for the "old" types is an abiding one.

The Cast of Characters

Sons of Adam, David, and Samson

1

The reader of Lawrence soon realizes a rich element of stylization in his work (including characterization) despite its captivating sense of life. Biblical typology's "historical" *figurae*, beginning with Adam and Eve, give him a cast of characters often underlying his own fictional men and women. I have already shown examples in his works of the other two categories of types—the Levitical and the prophetic—and all three will recur throughout these pages, but the "historical" types providing a "genealogy" of Christ are perhaps of most interest to him. Much has been said about Lawrence's innovation in characterization, which he described in a famous 1914 letter to Edward Garnett as presenting "another ego" than the personal one in the traditional novel so that his characters represent "some greater, inhuman will," falling into "the form of some other rhythmic form" (*Letters* 2:183-84). Because this letter contains references to Futurism and uses a chemical metaphor—Lawrence's fictional people will pass through various "allotropic states" of a single element—it may seem bold to suggest that he is, at the same time, outlining a system indebted to biblical typology. But P. T. Whelan has already identified the passage as a theory about archetypes and mythic entities, including the Mater Dolorosa. According to this line of thinking, Lawrence's "men and women reenact . . . ancient rites in their collective unconscious, swept by archetypal symbols into patterns of behavior in which their conscious mind has no part."[1] This is partly how he employs the biblical types.

Not archetypes, despite some overlap with them, the biblical types are bound to particular views of history and eternity; when Lawrence's characters incarnate them, they are involved in exact biblical contexts. In this scheme, the center of history is Christ, with his church and sacraments: "Before Christ," explains Landow, "all recorded Old Testament events serve as a lens converging upon His appearance; after His death and resurrection, all things simultaneously point backwards towards His earthly life and forwards to His second coming."[2] Because Christ is the fulfillment of all things, the *figurae* become interrelated in a highly complicated pattern, a kind of mosaic, so that they present not isolated figures but a complete view of earthly and cosmic events. This ability of the typological reference to serve as a form of synechdoche, to suggest "the entire Gospel scheme from a single image,"[3] accounts for some of the unexpected and even amazing effects in Lawrence's works.

Jung shows how images may be so common to human background as to constitute universal archetypes that people recognize at once in spite of diverse cultures; such images lie potential in human consciousness rather than in external codes or scriptures. Biblical typology may seem, in contrast, less fluid and comprehensive, while allowing sharpened specificity, but a biblical type can, and commonly does, coincide with an archetype. Lawrence may be said to move freely between the two forms, tapping into the archetype through the type; that is, he often takes up a typological *figura* to diffuse it, expanding it dynamically into a universal dimension. He may, for example, begin with an image of Christ and show how it also represents Adam or Pan or Osiris and the resurrected gods; or he may place the Christian and the pagan in ironic juxtaposition. Such eclecticism is not entirely foreign to biblical typology, as I mention earlier, for its restrictive or exclusive nature has often been honored in the breach—especially in some of the theosophical versions known to Lawrence. Always, even in his use of the biblical types, he is most concerned not with enforcing a preset system but with allowing "creative mutation," a

1. Whelan, *D. H. Lawrence*, 14-15, 37.
2. Landow, *Victorian Types, Victorian Shadows*, 40.
3. Ibid., 77, 179.

goal he set for his poetry (*CP* 182–83) and pursued in all his work. Even when his characters are based on Adam or Christ, they are living people, caught up, it is true, in specific patterns but also endowed with the spontaneity that can alter or reinterpret those patterns.

This chapter deals with both early stories and works of Lawrence's late "middle period," showing that his use of biblical typology begins early but develops significantly over time. The most obvious of his "historical" male types are Adam and David, forerunners of Lawrentian "Christ figures"—some of them negative martyrs, others "risen lords" based on the Christian pattern but, as James C. Cowan has put it, "de-Christianized."[4] In addition, Noah, Moses, Aaron, and Samson appear intermittently over a period of years. He can play with them rather sarcastically, as when he refers flippantly to "the Moses of Science and the Aaron of Idealism," or adapt them to familiar chatter, adding that "we are all Aarons with rods of our own" (*F* 62, 65). Beyond such casual allusions, however, these types usually have for Lawrence lordly, tribal qualities—and some have chthonic aspects.

It is natural to wonder why he would employ a system that, to most readers of this century, is little known. But writers on Lawrence have suggested before that his works contain esoteric levels of meaning, mythic or ritual patterns underlying the ostensible meanings. According to Gerald Doherty, for instance, *Women in Love* includes "a scheme, a kind of submerged narrative structure which, alien to novelistic convention, remains as opaque to contemporary readers as it certainly was to earlier ones";[5] further, *Lady Chatterley's Lover* and other works incorporate a complex system of *chakras* based on Hindu and esoteric sources.[6] Christopher Pollnitz locates in *Birds, Beasts and Flowers* alchemical references previously unrecognized and by no means necessary to a surface reading of "St. Matthew" and "Fish."[7] Howe is right, too, when she finds *The Rainbow* "constructed to invite the kind of allegorical interpretation long given the Old Testament,"[8] referring to four-level exegetical allegory like that of Dante. Leonora Woodman even finds the hermetic anthropos, or Adam Kadmon,

4. Cowan, "D. H. Lawrence and the Resurrection," 95.
5. Doherty, "The Salvator Mundi Touch," 54.
6. Doherty, "Connie and the Chakras," 72–92.
7. Pollnitz, " 'I Didn't Know His God,' " 39–40.
8. Howe, *The Art of the Self,* 35.

in his works.[9] Lawrence's extension of biblical typology is no more surprising or obscure than some of these elements. While it generally operates beneath the narrative surface, however, it often has a virtually subliminal effect that conveys meaning and supplies a cosmic scenario.

His biblical typology is complicated by its idiosyncracies, not the least of which is his aversion to abstract forms. As I mention in my introduction, his quarrel with the orthodox scheme arises largely from the very fact that the antitype—which he extends to include the modern "Christian" world—is more spiritual than the preceding types. He casts the dual faculties of "blood consciousness" and mental-spiritual knowledge in terms, respectively, of the Old Testament types and the New Testament antitype. Striving to emphasize the former because it is the lost or underprivileged faculty, he reverses the orthodox values by preferring not the antitype but the types, the more physical precursors.

I

By far the most prevalent types in Lawrence's canon are Adam and Eve. Often, he gives them the underlying mythic pattern of *Adamtypologie* —not only the fall in Eden but also its reversal on Calvary and Adam's resurrection through a savior (as illustrated in Fig. 3); in Lawrence's case, of course, the Christian or spiritual Adam must be saved by the "old Adam." This pattern is at its simplest in some early tales, growing in typological complexity in work of the 1920s—as shown, for example, by the reference to the "risen Adam" in *Quetzalcoatl.* To indicate the lines of development,

9. Woodman, "D. H. Lawrence and the Hermetic Tradition," 1–6. Such forms may sound suspiciously Platonist, whereas Lawrence assails Platonism unremittingly. Yet he sometimes skirts the idea of inherent or preexisting form, as when Lilly in *Aaron's Rod* catechizes Aaron about the "self-form" (295) or when the creatures in *Tortoises* bear crosses on their bodies as signs of universal realities. While Jung even traces archetypes back to Platonic ideas, I find Lawrence's primary interests far enough from such ideal forms, being centered in the immanent. (See Jung, *Archetypes and the Collective Unconscious,* in *Collected Works,* 9,1:4.) Of course, biblical typology rests firmly on the assumption that both type and antitype have historic reality. When Lawrence raises issues of Platonism, it is generally for ironic and even sarcastic purposes.

I begin with Lawrence's early focus on the Adamic element in sexual relations and in patterns of domination. I proceed to early works that more clearly contain but do not fully develop the theme of Adam's redemption; and I conclude with the 1924 story "The Border Line," which offers an elaborate example of the redemption pattern, albeit submerged beneath the surface events of the tale.

Lawrence was well informed by biblical and other literary sources dealing with Adam and Eve. In addition, he knew many graphic representations of the first couple—from cathedral figures on the west front of Lincoln Cathedral to famous paintings like the Titian *Adam and Eve,* which he wished to have near him "all [his] life," as he said in a 1929 essay (*PII* 611), to the full-scale depiction of *Adamtypologie* on the west front of Strassburg Cathedral, a setting of "The Border Line." He put Adam and Eve into a wood carving and a mural[10] and into paintings that stress the contrast between the encumbered modern and the free Edenic condition. His *Flight Back into Paradise* (1927) depicts a modern woman's desperate attempt to escape the entanglements of technology and to return to Eden with the help of a large, rudimentary Adam. Another painting, *Throwing Back the Apple* (1927–28), shows the first parents casting the apple of knowledge back at God, thus refusing "Christian" modernity (Fig. 4). In the poem "Paradise Re-Entered," they return to "the long-discarded / Garden" and "primal loam" by "the strait gate of passion," while the mind is "fused down like a bead" (*CP* 242–43). As in *Flight Back into Paradise,* which shows Michael in the background, they must fight their way back past the angels that guard the gate; as the fight with angels may suggest, they are "beyond good and evil" (243).

In his frequently expressed view that both "old Adam" and "old Eve" are more elemental, more emotional, more "natural" than their modern counterparts, Lawrence has much in common with a graphic-arts tradition, beginning at least as early as the Renaissance, in which "wild" couples, sometimes even with satyr features, may appear in the iconographic stances of Adam and Eve.[11] In the combination of the "wild man" with the iconography of Eden,

10. See Lawrence's description of a wood carving of the Temptation of Eve (*Letters* 2:597) and Luhan's account, in *Lorenzo in Taos,* 174, of how the Lawrences and Dorothy Brett, in 1924, decorated a door at the Del Monte Ranch near Taos, New Mexico, with a Garden of Eden, complete with snake, apple tree, and Adam and Eve.

11. Kaufmann, *The Noble Savage,* 36–41.

Fig. 3. Typology of Adam, on the central western tympanum of Strassburg Cathedral (detail): Crucifixion of Christ over the grave of Adam (bottom); Christ, holding the staff of Resurrection, with Adam and Eve at the harrowing of hell (middle); the Ascension (above these two levels). The foliage of the tree-cross appears on several levels.

Fig. 4. *Throwing Back the Apple*, watercolor painting by D. H. Lawrence (1927–28), whereabouts unknown.

the Adamic became more fully identified than ever with a primitive state of manhood (as illustrated in Fig. 5). Moreover, this iconography provides a link between Adam and mythological figures like the Pan and satyrs in the throng of Dionysus. (Of course, Pan himself was often depicted with a shepherd's staff, much like the rod of Moses and Aaron.)[12] In England, a variant of the "wild man" is the "Green Man" or "Jack in the Green," sometimes also associated with a staff, whose image survives in cathedral roof-bosses and capital sculpture[13]—and in a carving in the chapter house at Southwell Minster. But it is the direct association of the "wild man" with Adam that is most important for this discussion.

12. Merivale, *Pan the Goat-God,* 52, 162, notes the staff.
13. Clifton-Taylor, *The Cathedrals of England,* 144.

Fig. 5. Wild Man with a flourishing staff, in the iconography of Adam (detail), from a Hans Schäufelein illustration (1545), in the British Museum.

Fig. 6. Tree of Jesse, from a thirteenth-century English psalter, in the British Library (included in Jenner's *Christian Symbolism*).

Whether or not Lawrence was directly aware of such pictorial conventions in the iconography of Adam, his association of the Old Testament types with the primeval is somewhat similar. His 1911 short story "The Old Adam" concerns primitive emotions, spontaneous and passionate if unamiable, in two men—"essential brutes" (*CSS* 1:38). Its title undoubtedly plays, too, with the familiar term for unregenerate man, as in some baptismal ceremonies, in which the "old Adam" is to die and be replaced by the "new Adam," a typological scheme echoing the idea in biblical texts like Romans 6:6, in which "our old man is crucified" to forego sin.[14] Lawrence, of course, has revalued these terms.

"New Eve and Old Adam," two years later, emphasizes a man's difficult recognition of the potent, masculine "old Adam" in himself. In a similar vein, the essay "The Novel and the Feelings" (1925) refers to the "Old Adam" as "the true Adam, the mysterious 'natural man,'" associated with our own "primeval" sources (*STH* 204). In "Mother and Daughter" (1928), the younger heroine represents Lawrence's "new Eve," who is overly conscious and unsatisfied; but the "old Eve in her," reasserting itself, "will have nothing to do" with her mental and "nervous" modern life-style (*CSS* 3:814). In these tales, the types provide a shorthand terminology for Lawrence's projection of the early Adam and Eve as largely fortunate primitives before yielding to the "spiritual" antitypes, the modern, or "new," figures. Even in *The Man Who Died,* the Christ figure must lose his asceticism and regain sensuality—must, in effect, become more like the "old Adam."

The typology of the first couple is complex in itself, and Lawrence compounds the difficulties by associating it not only with primitivism but also with a system of dominance or hierarchy—a system that, he claims, has reversed itself in the modern world. Thus he asserts the degeneration of the powerful, free patriarch of the past—the Adamic man—into a neurasthenic martyr, tempted and dominated by the modern Eve. This shift, he suggests, is the real fall of man and his crucifixion. Though appearing even in early works, this view increases in his "leadership" period after the First World War—in tandem with a theme of male dominance, as Judith Ruderman shows.[15] What needs further emphasis, however, beyond the leadership theme, is the typological scheme in

14. Lawrence's "The Christening" implies, without stating, this context.
15. Ruderman, "The New Adam and Eve," 225–36.

which these references stand, a scheme in which all the Adam figures involve Christ—and all the Christ figures, Adam.

In *The Rainbow*, the men of the immemorial Brangwen past are associated with Adam, partly because of their traditional occupations of tilling the soil and mastering animals, standing as husbandmen within a natural hierarchy like that placed under Adam. Fairly early in the novel, however, men seem to have lost the old dominance that Lawrence associates with the "old Adam" —have been metamorphosed into the "new Adam," the martyred "Christian" man whose "new Eve" assumes an overbearing Marian role. *The Rainbow* provides the most famous example of Lawrence's habit of casting issues of male and female dominance in terms of Adam and Eve mythology. In Will Brangwen's wood panel of the Creation of Eve, she is "a keen, unripe thing" (112), while Adam, according to Anna, is "as big as God" (162). The relationship between the second-generation Brangwens will be considered in greater detail in chapter 2. For the present discussion, however, it is enough to point out that the panel reflects the troubled relations between them, based partly on the assertion of Eve's original dependence upon Adam in both the Genesis story and Will's carving.

Similar issues pervade "New Eve and Old Adam," a short story apparently written in 1912 just after the first draft of *The Sisters* (later *The Rainbow* and *Women in Love*). Although the title "New Eve and Old Adam" differentiates between the hero and heroine typologically,[16] one seemingly assigned to the old and one to the new order, their names, Peter and Paula, link both to the modern "Christian" dispensation, with its overbalance of the nervous mental faculties and its spurious assumptions of independence and equality. While one critic finds Peter's intellectual activity in his favor,[17] it is clear that his greater effort is to come to terms with the "old Adam," or "that dark, unknown being, which lived below all his consciousness in the eternal gloom of his blood"—the blood-consciousness of "the elemental male" (CSS 1:82).

In "New Eve," as the title suggests, Paula is preeminently the modern woman, far different in her free-form identity from Will Brangwen's carved Eve, who is still rising from the body of Adam. Paula "must live perfectly free of herself, and not, at her source, be

16. Lawrence's title suggests one by Rudolf Golm (pseudonym of Rudolf Goldscheid), *Der alte Adam und die neue Eva* (1895), a work Lawrence knew by 1910. He also knew Charles Doughty's *Adam Cast Out* (1908) in the year of its publication. See also Jules Bois, *L'Eve Nouvelle* (1896).

17. Harris, *Short Fiction of D. H. Lawrence*, 89.

connected with anybody" (1:82). Vestiges of the creation myth enrich the story, as in a suggestion of the wound left by the loss of the rib that became Eve: Paula's head presses "into [Peter's] chest where the hurt had been bruised in so deep," and he has a "slightly broken feeling" (1:91). Paula writes to her husband near the story's end, "Your idea of your woman is that she is . . . a *rib* of yourself" (1:93). Sexual strife, Lawrence says elsewhere, is "the invariable crucifixion" (*PII* 619). Thus even the Adam of "New Eve and Old Adam" never quite ceases to be of the "new" dispensation. His wound suggests both the mark of the fallen Adam—the mark of imperfection—and those of Christ; in his attempt to tap the "old" reserves, however, he at least approaches resurrection.

The trouble with Peter is that the natural hierarchy properly uniting him with his Eve is broken when she refuses his lordship; the story was, after all, once entitled "Renegade Eve" (*Letters* 2:38). Thus "he never felt like a lord" or like "a king," not even "when she was crowning and kissing him" (1:92, 93). Lawrence clearly sees the original Adam as a dominant leader. In keeping with this idea, the staff of the "wild man," in the iconography of Adam, indicates authority, even kingship. But the "new Adam" is no longer connected rightly to women, men, or the cosmos, and his redemption can lie only in reversing this loss. Other stories written in the same period, "The Prussian Officer" (originally "Honour and Arms") and "The Thorn in the Flesh" (originally "Vin Ordinaire"), both first published in 1914, also dramatize the loss of connection and contain beneath their surfaces some of the outline of a redemption pattern. The first has been associated with Adam mythology and the second, with Christian imagery. In fact, both involve Adam and Christ in a fairly simple typological pattern.

The young soldier Schöner in "The Prussian Officer"—the victim of his perverted officer—is an Adam in the tradition of Herman Melville's Billy Budd, for he is an innocent punished by a severe superior.[18] The story seems to contain a reenactment of the Fall of Man.[19] That is, the soldier, initially unthinking in his unison with his surroundings, is brought to consciousness by the sadistic officer, whom he is forced to kill; and his disorientation and separation from others and from his very surroundings constitute the fallen condition. We are left pondering the meaning of

18. See Humma, "Melville's *Billy Budd,*" 83–88.
19. See Anderson, " 'The Prussian Officer,' " 215–23.

something that is "lost in him" near the tale's end (*PO* 20), something he seems to seek in distant mountain heights. It is not simply innocence but also a sense of order and unity, for he has killed his Captain (Hauptmann). The very name identifies the officer as "the head man" — the representative of mind — and also the leader, however flawed. Although his rank may be only an artificial mark of dominance, his name and story raise issues about the relationship between authority and servitude, the Adamic and the Christ-like. Unlike "New Eve and Old Adam," this tale does not concentrate on male-female relations but on a more extended hierarchy, a particularly warped one, among men.

The Captain is evidently an instrument and a victim of the disintegrative phase of civilization described in "The Crown" and associated in it with Christianity (*RDP* 300). In fact, some 1915 passages of this long essay (those that Lawrence canceled before the work was finally published in totality in the 1925 *Reflections on the Death of a Porcupine*) bear particularly upon his character. Describing several kinds of men in late stages of their culture, Lawrence states that a "sensitive man, caught within the flux of reduction," will find no satisfaction with women and will turn to love of men in an apparent attempt to reverse his state of development. Being "too conscious, too complete," such a man wishes "to reduce himself back to the level and simplicity, the undevelopment, of a boy," to "the level of a lower type of man" (*RDP* 472). While it is hard to think of the Captain as a "sensitive" individual, he follows this pattern in significant ways, clearly fixating upon his orderly because of a twisted desire to share in his "lower," but healthier, condition. This is so even while he tries the more urgently to maintain his official superiority to the other man. In some ways, the Captain is the story's "Christian" as the orderly is its Adam, at the opposite end of the scale of development. While the two are potential saviors to each other, they remain locked in mutual destruction, and Lawrence's frequent pattern of death followed by resurrection is in abeyance.

This is not the case in "The Thorn in the Flesh," which also concerns a young soldier, Bachman. While he, too, might be likened to the Adamic Billy Budd, with the single flaw of humanity upon him (a fear of heights), his "thorn" is specifically related to St. Paul instead of Adam: he has the "thorn in the flesh," like the one that the apostle claims in 2 Corinthians 12.[20] He is a more

20. Black, *D. H. Lawrence*, 231.

advanced member of his culture than he at first appears. Although his setting is more clearly Edenic than is Schöner's, it becomes a garden of suffering recalling Christ's Gethsemane.

The site for military maneuvers is a garden with lime trees, vines, and poppies in "untouched stillness" (*PO* 24). Here Bachman is forced, during his training, to climb a ladder despite his fear, and his involuntary urination brings him to a crisis of manhood — an incident in which Michael Black finds "analogies with the Crucifixion."[21] The ladder Bachman fears to climb recalls one of the traditional *Arma Christi,* instruments of Christ's Passion. In painting, the scene with the ladder has two versions: sometimes Christ ascends voluntarily to the cross, and sometimes he is pushed up (Schiller 2:87) — as Bachman, too, is roughly aided, adding to his humiliation. The incident reveals his defect, the "thorn in the flesh" that he must ultimately accept as St. Paul had to accept the mark of his own humanity. The New Testament allusion makes it a true "stigma," one of the stigmata, perhaps even recalling Christ's crown of thorns.

Later, Bachman walks in a public garden, clearly cast as a sacred location. Just after viewing Metz Cathedral — "the lovely dark cathedral with its myriad pinnacles making points at the sky" — he sees "walls" of horse chestnuts, "lighted like an altar with white flowers" and, a short time later, in the country, vine trees that "rose up in spires" (26, 27). His progression is from the Christian monument to something like its pagan counterpart in nature — and the plot supports such interpretation, for he moves from the crucifixion experience to a Lawrentian rebirth. In the earlier version of the story in the *English Review,* he explicitly identifies himself with a crucifix (" 'It might be me,' thought the soldier" [309]); in "The Thorn in the Flesh," he retains his interest in it (30).[22] Even further associations with Christ are present. The story's original title, "Vin Ordinaire," alludes obliquely to the sacrament, referring to Bachman's translation from the victimized youth of the opening pages into the full-bodied man of the end — his conversion not into the spiritual host of the Eucharist,

21. Ibid., 226.
22. Cushman, *D. H. Lawrence at Work,* has demonstrated the close relationship between Bachman and a Christ-like Bavarian peasant described in "The Crucifix Across the Mountains," which became the first chapter of *Twilight in Italy.* "The language and symbolic structure of the story are taken over intact into the travel essay," says Cushman (171). See also the poem "Meeting Among the Mountains" (*CP* 224-26).

one of Lawrence's metaphors for modern man, but into a sensual being full of the wine of common life.

Bachman and his lover approach each other from opposite dispensations — he from the new, more civilized, more "Christian" epoch and she from the old, more primitive age. This story might almost, in fact, be called "New Adam and Old Eve." Unexpectedly, Bachman is rather genteel, "a gentleman in sensibility," while his Eve, the "paganly religious" and "primitive" Emilie, is seeking the higher life: "For her, a gentleman had some mystic quality that left her free and proud in service" (32, 31). In this quality, she resembles Paolo in *Twilight in Italy,* a character contrasted with his more modern, materialistic wife: "When Paolo was in relation to a man of further vision, he himself was extended towards the whole" and "fulfilled," writes Lawrence, because to him "the world was . . . divine in its establishment." Thus his attitude "was not servility" but had "the dignity of a religious conception" (*TI* 89, 88). Like Paolo, Emilie longs for "the service of real masters and mistresses" and needs "to be in subjection," having "no grasp on civilized forms of living" (31, 32). Despite this limited place in the world, she is in the creative phase of development, not, like Hauptmann, at its end.

Bachman's fear of heights, possibly a wholesome recognition of the danger to him of excessive consciousness, does not negate his acceptance of the natural hierarchy in which he and Emilie are connected. As he becomes her lord, the two enter "a new world" (36), and repeated references to their nakedness (four) recall the original Adam and Eve. Encountering her employer after love-making, Emilie reveals in her eyes "the dark, naked soul of her body" — a "dark, deep nakedness" — and Bachman has the "same naked soul" (39, 38). The emphasis upon the eyes comes from the incident in Genesis 3:7 in which Adam and Eve become conscious of their bodies: "Then *the eyes of both were opened,* and they knew that they were naked; and they sewed fig leaves together and made themselves aprons" (my emphasis). Lawrence means that his couple returns to the ancient mode of vision that preceded the "clothed vision," as he later terms modern consciousness (*CP* 286). The early poem "Elysium," in which Adam is severed from "the All" by Eve (*CP* 262), was originally entitled "The Blind," focusing on a preconscious period when nonvisual senses were preeminent.[23]

23. The holograph version "The Blind" (E113.3 in Roberts, *A Bibliography of D. H. Lawrence*) is in a notebook containing part of the *Women in Love* manuscript.

"The Thorn in the Flesh" contains two sacred centers. The features of the cathedral are repeated in nature as Bachman makes his way to the farm where Emilie waits, but the ultimate holy place is her bedroom, where he feels himself "in sanctuary" (30). Its Roman Catholic appointments make it a shrine, and one critic finds the girl's "southern" religion itself an important factor in the restoration that occurs there. Lawrence found such Catholicism "a mystery religion," says James F. Scott, one "grounded in . . . blood consciousness."[24] Through their sexuality, Bachman and Emilie share a blood communion allowing him to draw "the stigma from his shame" (37). Instead of finally resembling the crucifix, he is a resurrected man.

"The Prussian Officer" and "The Thorn in the Flesh" complement each other in their typological designs, for Schöner begins like a young Adam but suffers victimization, while Bachman begins with a metaphorical crucifixion and progresses to Adamic manhood. In the latter story, the pattern of redemption, depending on both an Adam and a Christ, is distinguishable; it lies potential but largely untapped in "The Prussian Officer" as well. But Lawrence's later uses of the myth of Adam include far more ambitious and complex typological schemes than do these early stories. *The Rainbow,* completed only slightly later than the tales, reveals the deepening implications of the Edenic pattern. And "The Border Line," written ten years later, presents a literal resurrection in terms of a major typological symbol for Christ's triumph over death — the renewed tree of life.

The early "Border Line" confirms the centrality of this tree: the first published version of the tale (in *The Smart Set* and *Hutchinson's Story Magazine,* both 1924)[25] shows the hero's return from the dead with "the limbs of the living tree," suggesting the "tree-cross," or living cross, common in southern Germany and well known, too, in Strassburg Cathedral sculpture (Schiller 2:130–36). This iconographic model presents the cross as a tree, frequently with stems and leaves, with Christ as the center and fruit of the tree; sometimes the foliage arms seem extremely animate, suggesting

24. Scott, "D. H. Lawrence's *Germania,*" 149.
25. Four years after the magazine publications, when Lawrence collected stories for *The Woman Who Rode Away,* he found that both his proofs and manuscript of "The Border Line" lacked the conclusion, so he wrote another. The standard collected version is the revised one. The full early version exists today in a manuscript owned by George Lazarus (E53b in Roberts, *A Bibliography of D. H. Lawrence*).

hands and feet. In the standard collected version of Lawrence's story (in *The Woman Who Rode Away* of 1928), the references to the tree of life are less overt than in the earlier one, but its meaning is still at the work's core. Both versions feature a man, Alan, returned to life again some years after his death in the First World War. He is likened to the "pitiless" tree of life, bringing death to another man, Philip, who has replaced him as a husband.

We must not be content with the standard readings of this tale—limited to its supposed satire on John Middleton Murry[26] or to the significance of the politically charged setting (between France and Germany).[27] To look beyond these details is to see a typological design in which Alan and Philip are virtual doppelgängers—the old and the new Adam, the dead and the resurrected man. Of course, the "border line" is, most deeply, the metaphysical one between life and death, "a weary *everlasting* border-line" (*CSS* 3:595; my emphasis). Philip, whom Harris has already termed one of the "martyred Christ figures" receiving Lawrence's "disparagement" in several tales,[28] represents the last failing presence of doomed, effete Christendom following the war; Alan obviously has played the part of a similar figure, killed in the war. In his rebirth, however, Alan is "reddish" like the "Adam of red earth" described in an essay, "On Being a Man," of the same year, 1924 (*RDP* 217); he is also like Strassburg Cathedral, with its red stonework, where he first appears to his wife as a remarkably palpable ghost—"a man who came from the halls of death" (3:597). The color links him to the patriarch, for Lawrence would have read Madame Blavatsky's claim that the name "Adam" translates *red* (*Isis* 2:465). He may also have known that James G. Frazer connects the name with both *red* and *earth*,[29] and he would have been pleased with

26. In *D. H. Lawrence's American Journey,* 45–50, Cowan, for example, like most other commentators on "The Border Line," includes it in a group of lampoons of Murry. No doubt the tale is partly inspired by a real-life romantic triangle (Murry, Frieda, Lawrence) and by Lawrence's trip across the Marne country from Versailles to Baden-Baden in February 1924, when he first wrote it.

27. For the political importance of the story's "border-line" between France and Germany, see Scott, "D. H. Lawrence's *Germania,*" 142–64. On other forms of "duality" in the tale, see also Hudspeth, "Duality as Theme and Technique," 51–56.

28. Harris, *Short Fiction of D. H. Lawrence,* 192.

29. Frazer, *Folk-Lore in the Old Testament,* 1:29.

C. G. Jung's association of the name "Adam" with a Hebrew word for *blood*. [30]

The reference to Strassburg provides a key to the entire story, for the cathedral's central western tympanum depicts the tree-cross (with foliage on several tiers) and the typological relationship between Adam and Christ (Fig. 3). The dead Adam (a skeleton), having eaten of the tree of knowledge, lies beneath the cross, which is made from the tree of life. [31] Above the Crucifixion is Christ triumphant over hell (at the harrowing of hell), where, with Adam and Eve, he bears the staff of Resurrection; above this is Christ's Ascension toward heaven. Thus the tableau shows, vertically, first the dead Adam (at the bottom), then the "new Adam" (Christ of the Atonement, at the center). At the top is the "new Adam"/Christ in ascent (Schiller 2:16). The Christ on the cross appears almost to stand on the skeleton of Adam, and, to some extent, the two can be seen in opposition to each other, although they are inextricably interrelated in the salvation scheme. Referring to similar iconography, Tennyson wrote an address to Christ in *In Memoriam:* "lo, thy foot / Is on the skull that thou hast made";[32] and, while this passage may remind some readers of the "survival of the fittest" theme introduced later in the poem, it refers in fact to the mystery of the Resurrection in the typology of Adam. [33] This is the pattern enacted, with the usual Lawrentian alteration, in "The Border Line," in which both Philip and the old Alan die, while the reborn Alan (apparently an anagram for Adam) lives. He is the savior, too, of the Eve-like woman: "a man . . . come back out of death to save her" from "the supreme modern terror, of a world all ashy and nerve-dead" (3:598).

Significantly, Alan's return is related to the reassertion of a natural hierarchy that has been lost: Philip is only "a little somebody," his wife realizes, while Alan, even before death, was "Lordly" (3:588). The entire postwar world is one without a lord: "The Somebodies with a capital 'S' were all safely dead" (3:588). And this decline is related to a larger, cosmic problem — the loss of "some supreme Somebody," for which Paris with its cathedral and museums seems waiting — as does Strassburg Cathedral. Alan returns as a lord "with strange silent authority," bringing with

30. Jung, *Mysterium Coniunctionis*, in *Collected Works*, 14:406.
31. See the *Legend of the True Cross*, discussed in my introduction.
32. *The Poems of Tennyson*, 2:316.
33. See Mattes, *'In Memoriam': The Way of a Soul*, 96–97, referring to medieval paintings to interpret these lines.

him "his peace" (3:596, 598). Through such description, Lawrence represents the death experience as having conferred some kind of earthly as well as chthonic power on him. Alan is clearly one of the "lords of death," who will be considered further in later chapters.

Perhaps most curiously, he is likened to the cathedral. Before death, he had "asserted himself like a pillar of rock, and expected the tides of the modern world to recede around him" (3:589). The cathedral, "standing gigantic" with its red stonework gleaming, is "like a great ghost" but seems to possess, nonetheless, "an ancient, indomitable blood" (3:595) like the phallically potent Alan. It, too, has become transformed, "blotting out the Cross it was supposed to exalt" (3:596), a change that appears demonic to most critics.[34] But this change is linked closely to a statement in Lawrence's essay "Resurrection," written only a few months later—"the Cross is again a Tree" (*RDP* 234), a reference to the typology of the Resurrection, retrieving life from death. The rebirth in "The Border Line" is also in keeping with Ramón's affirmation (discussed in my introduction) of the "redeemed Adam" in *Quetzalcoatl*, written only a year before this story. The full-scale *Adamtypologie*, including crucifixion and resurrection (Schiller 2:130–32), under-lies the tale—as it does the essay and the novel.

II

After Adam and Eve, the most significant typological figure in Lawrence's works is David, to whom his attitude changed remark-ably between 1915 and 1925. David's place in typology justifies the complexity of Lawrence's shifting response. The shepherd king of Bethlehem represents the rustic simplicity and the monarchical splendor of his descendant, Christ; while Lawrence lost some of his sympathy with David, he first finds him an admirable power figure as when, in *Twilight in Italy*, he praises the "Churches of the Eagle" as those of "the Spirit of David" (19), powerful and sensual, and refers to "the Davidian ecstasy" as opposed to humble self-sacrifice (71). The typology of David furnishes Lawrence with the

34. On the "demonic" cathedral, see Widmer, *The Art of Perversity*, 54; Scott, "D. H. Lawrence's *Germania*," 161–62; and Harris, *Short Fiction of D. H. Lawrence*, 180 ("Lawrence imagines this edifice as a blood-dusky monster about to . . . destroy the very force that built it").

significant concept and image of the Jesse tree, a graphic "family tree" that springs from David's father, Jesse, and burgeons with his later progeny, including David, Solomon, Mary, and Christ. Lawrence would have known the Jesse tree from an illustration in Jenner's *Christian Symbolism* (Fig. 6) and doubtless saw it rightly as a version of the tree of life.

Early passages in his works support the view of George Panichas that Lawrence's David represents living pride and fulfillment.[35] But the novelist had changed his mind by 1925, when he revised "The Crown" for *Reflections on the Death of a Porcupine*. To begin with, he sees David as a representative of the senses and "the glory of power and might," the lion as opposed to the unicorn, one who is in touch with "the God Almighty who has established Creation upon poles of Law" (*RDP* 470). He even faults David for being too sensual, associated with "too much of darkness" (*RDP* 470). But in the revision, this figure is contrasted to powerful earlier "warrior kings" and is "the small man slaying the great": "David slaying the preposterous Goliath, overthrowing the heroic Saul" heralds an age of petty egoism (*RDP* 268). Indeed, "the flood of vanity [earlier, "flood of darkness"] set in after David, the lamps and candles began to gutter" (*RDP* 269). In both versions, Lawrence tells the story—also incorporated into *The Rainbow* and the drama *David*—of David's dance before the Ark of the Covenant while his wife Michal jeers so that David never again acts as a husband to her, leaving her childless (2 Samuel 6:14-23). Lawrence originally judges that David's problem is "the unfertility of the spirit giving utter supremacy, absoluteness to the flesh" (*RDP* 470) but later finds his seed "too egoistic" (*RDP* 268). In both versions, he sees David somewhat in the wrong, but only in the second does the Old Testament king lose his primitive splendor. The reason for the change—a shift already obvious in a 1919 essay on Michelangelo's statue *David*—is that Lawrence focuses increasingly on David's role as a typological precursor and ancestor of Christ, one who inclined toward the spiritual faculty and thus dispossessed the old dispensation of the flesh, now represented by Saul. This idea is at the heart of the drama *David*, written in 1925.

Lawrence had long known the typology of David, probably from many sources but certainly from Jenner.[36] In this scheme, to be sure, David prefigures Christ the King (Schiller 1:4), whom

35. Panichas, *Adventures in Consciousness*, 136.
36. Jenner, *Christian Symbolism*, 155.

Lawrence prefers to Christ the meek and self-sacrificing martyr. By 1919, however, both Pryse and Blavatsky may well have influenced his developing view that this king foreran the modern desacralization of life. Pryse casts David as the "adolescent," or middle, figure between Adam and Messias, with traits of "the spiritual man."[37] Blavatsky, though terming David the "Israelitish King Arthur" (*Isis* 2:439), nevertheless places him at the *end* of the "silver age" in a scheme beginning with the "golden age" of Adam and Abraham (2:443).[38] She also attributes to David the first use of a specific name for the Almighty (2:297); to Lawrence, this would be an anthropomorphic shift away from a primal sense of oneness between the worshiper and the sacred cosmos. Late in his life, in *Etruscan Places,* he acknowledges that the Psalms of David contain a great cosmic vision "half-transmuted" but complains that "with David the living cosmos became merely a personal god" (50). In *Apocalypse,* Lawrence claims that, before David, the old power religion prevailed, when the worshiper did not distinguish between self and Jehovah and other gods; with David, however, the modern "Christian" orientation, seeing the world in terms of "other," began. "The Jews of the post-David period have no eyes of their own to see with," Lawrence writes. "They peered inward at their Jehovah till they were blind: then they looked at the world with the eyes of their neighbours" (82).

In his essay on Michelangelo's *David,* Lawrence points to its unpleasant "corpse-like" quality despite his general admiration for the statue, containing, as it does to him, the antique pagan touch of Dionysus and representing the "one moment" of Renaissance balance between physical and spiritual (*P* 63). In *Aaron's Rod,* this statue is precariously balanced between the "old" and the "new" as the "adolescent" figure seems to take a first step out of the physical life (the Old Testament tribal life as well as the medieval period preceding Michelangelo). In the same novel, a Bandinelli statue, in an archaized style (though not actually earlier than Michelangelo's), "with a heavy back and strong naked flanks," contrasts with David, "so much whiter," newly "self-conscious" and seemingly aware of his separation from the physi-

---

37. Pryse, *The Apocalypse Unsealed,* 109.

38. Blavatsky had offered enlightenment, too, on the episode in which David danced before the Ark, stating that the dance "denoted the motion of the planets round the sun" (*SD* 2:460). But Lawrence does not follow this lead in his 1925 revision of "The Crown," attributing the dance to David's personal vanity.

cally powerful men of the past (*AR* 211).[39] The young man, stepping free from his surroundings, somewhat recalls the early Brangwen men who first distinguish themselves from contiguous elements early in *The Rainbow*. In "Fireworks in Florence" (1926), Lawrence finds the *David* statue "the incarnation of the modern self-conscious young man, and very objectionable," while, however, he can still admire what the Bandinelli forms represent (*P* 124)—the primitive condition of the "old Adam." A parallel forms in these works between the progress from medieval to modern forms and the shift from Old Testament tribesmen to New Testament antitype, from Adam to Christ—a shift in which David is the pivotal figure. In keeping with this movement, Lawrence B. Gamache finds that, in the play *David*, Saul represents the "Dionysian" old religious order, while David suggests the more "Apollonian" Christian one.[40]

Some of the most noteworthy features of Lawrence's drama may result from his likely knowledge of G. F. Handel's *Saul* (1739). Keith Cushman points to Lawrence's use of an aria title from Handel's *Samson* (1743)—an oratorio in the same series with *Saul*—in the story title "Honour and Arms" (later "The Prussian Officer") and his reference to it in "A Modern Lover" (written in 1912).[41] It is thus quite possible that Lawrence was familiar with the popular *Saul*. Like Lawrence, the composer makes Saul the central character and puts his lively daughter Michal, David's wife, in prominent focus. In addition, the sixteen scenes of the play, in an unusual tableau-style arrangement, recall the shifting scenes of the *Saul* oratorio, and a chorus is an important feature of both Lawrence's and Handel's works. Even the pronounced typological pattern in *David*, albeit an inverted one, could owe something to the Handel oratorios: although *Saul* possesses little of this Christology, *Samson* contains elements of it from its source, Milton's *Samson Agonistes*.

Michal is an especially important figure in Lawrence's play because she is cast as an ironic version of the Virgin Mary. Likened to a "young pomegranate tree" and "the rose of Sharon" (*Plays* 127, 128), both associated with Mary and Christ, she is further connected with Sorrows (87). Her separation from David is like "a thorn in the heart" (88), and her barrenness is more

39. Lawrence has obviously made free with the facts that this *David* sculpture is a copy and that the Bandinelli forms are really later in date than *David* though they do intentionally evoke an earlier age.
40. Gamache, "Lawrence's *David*," 244.
41. Cushman, *D. H. Lawrence at Work*, 209.

explicitly linked to Mary's being pierced "as with a sword" by the death of her son: "The spear of this vexation . . . pierces my womb," she says (137). Despite Marian and Christian imagery, however, Michal will never be an ancestress of Christ. She laments, "So sure as it is springtime in me, and my body blossoms like an almond tree," an "evil wind" destroys her fertility. The fact that she will not bear David's children recalls Lawrence's earlier statement in "The Crown" that "it was David who really was barren" (*RDP* 268). The tribal strength and sensuality of the daughter of Saul are thus lost to the Christian heritage.

David is himself "a son of God" and "twice begotten" (102, 132), one whose Bethlehem home is emphasized as the setting in which a sacrifice and feast foreshadow the concluding scene at the place of atonement—and both scenes look forward to Christ's sacrifice and the celebration of it in the Eucharist. While the prophet Samuel partakes of the feast in Bethlehem, he feels the need of greater meaning in life: to "eat bread" does not fulfill the desire for God, and "wine will not heal my bones," he says (74), but the viewer or reader is aware that both the bread and wine will have more than physical significance in another era. Anointing David, the prophet uses "the oil from the body of Him" (75) in an evident sacrament of ordination. Echoing the young Christ of John 2:4 ("Mine hour is not yet come"), David states at the Bethlehem feast, "My day is not yet come" (82). Other biblical language abounds. For instance, Jonathan echoes John 21:15-17 when he asks, "Lovest thou me, David?" (91). David's thighs, likened to "the pillars of His [God's] presence" (81), recall the Song of Solomon 5:15, describing (to some biblical exegetes) Christ the Bridegroom: "His legs are as pillars of marble."

David is, according to Jonathan, "the young lion of Judah . . . the young eagle of the Lord" (106)—as in the iconography of Christ's royalty and triumph (Schiller 3:127)—and Saul himself calls him the "young King-bird" (108). Lawrence, however, knew a medieval illustration of David with a dove rather than the royal eagle (in Jenner's *Christian Symbolism*), and it is possible that this depiction first suggested a "Christian" David to him (Fig. 7). The dove, which he associates with the churches of humility (*TI* 19), is a traditional feature of the Jesse tree, which often bears doves in its branches to signify the gifts of the Holy Spirit in the Christian church (Schiller 1:16-17). While Lawrence still identifies David with the churches of the eagle in *Twilight in Italy* (19), the later drama is partly ironic in its reference to the "King-bird." As

Gamache has remarked, it is Saul who is more consistently associated with tropes of power, like the burning bush, while David is identified (by Saul) with flowers.[42]

Even more striking than this imagery is the introduction into the drama of Aaron's (and Moses') rod or staff (shown in Fig. 8), a prefiguration of the Nativity (Schiller 2:136). The staff is also related to the raised Brazen Serpent, that type of the Crucifixion and Resurrection discussed in my introduction. In the play, a character mentions the staff, referring to an occasion "when Moses held the rod for God uplifted in his hand" (68). Although she speaks of another context, a particular battle, the uplifted stave is still more famous as the Brazen Serpent. This device, which Moses held up before the Israelites to deliver them from a plague of vipers, is the type of crucifixion to which Christ himself refers in John 3:14: "And as Moses lifted up the serpent in the wilderness, even so must the Son of man be lifted up [on the cross]." In Lawrence's play, David asks, "But who am I to be suddenly lifted up?" (106) A herdsman prophesies rather humorously of David in terms recalling Aaron's flowering rod: "As I plant this driving-stick in the soft earth, so hath the Lord planted David in the heart of Israel. I say: Stick, may thou flourish! May thou bud and blossom and be a great tree" (124).

Lawrence is evidently referring in the play not only to Aaron's rod but also to the Jesse tree (Fig. 6), itself often related to the flowering staff in Christian iconography (Schiller 1:15). The meaning of this tree, one of the favorite motifs of biblical typology, is explained by Schiller: "As before in the person of David, so again would a king come from the house of Jesse and the spirit of Yaweh would rest upon this second David [Christ] too" (1:115). The Jesse tree in Jenner's book elaborately displays not only Christ and Mary but also eleven other descendants of Jesse. Since Michal in *David* will have no place on such a tree, poignant irony surrounds the description of her "like a young tree in full flower, with flowers of gold and scarlet" (127) and David's statement to her that she "shall blossom in the land" (128).

In Lawrence's drama, the coming "great tree" does not suggest royalty but the vast assemblage of Christendom—probably the democratic masses so often the target of Lawrence's ire—here ironically heralded by a bare stick. Gone is the giant Goliath, "out of the old days, before the Flood" (94), and gone, too, is the tribal

42. Gamache, "Lawrence's *David*," 239.

Fig. 7. King David with a dove on a scepter-staff, from an eleventh-century English manuscript, in the British Library (included in Jenner's *Christian Symbolism*).

Fig. 8. Aaron with the flowering rod, detail from a fourteenth-century German *Biblia pauperum,* in the Österreichische Nationalbibliothek.

monarch Saul, who has foreseen the modern era: "men in myriads, like locusts, / To this the seed of David shall come" (117). Samuel has expressed the Lawrentian predilection for a natural aristocracy as opposed to democracy: "When a people choose a King, then the will of the people is as God to the King. But when the Lord of All chooses a King, then the King must answer to the Lord" (91). The old king has noticed in David the characteristics of the coming age: somewhat surprisingly, the spiritual young man appears "shrewd" and "canny," a materialist gathering spoil into his own tent (102), "smooth-faced and soft-footed, as Joseph in the house of Pharaoh," a "weasel" (114). All of these unpromising qualities come to mind when the tree image looks forward to David's numerous progeny, including Christ, who would indeed be "lifted up" in ways the play's David does not guess.

The motif of Moses' or Aaron's rod is one of Lawrence's favorites. He uses it extensively in *Aaron's Rod,* which will be discussed in chapter 4, in connection with the flowering cross, a variant of this tree imagery. Although the pole on which Moses raised the Brazen Serpent is distinct from the rod, it is usually closely associated with it, prefiguring crucifixion and salvation (Schiller 2:125–26), and it proves unexpectedly important in *Birds, Beasts and Flowers,* which will be discussed in detail in chapter 5.

III

A third Old Testament character, Samson, has particular significance in the Lawrence canon, where, like David, he undergoes change over time — but in the opposite direction. While David grows increasingly spiritual in the novelist's scheme, Samson continuously gains sensuous underworld power. The shifting depiction of him needs careful discussion because it illustrates the development of Lawrence's "dark gods" from characters originally based loosely on typological figures — in this case, Samson, whose life was held to prefigure events in the life and death of Christ (Schiller 1:50). In the poem "The Revolutionary" (written in 1920), Samson is clearly the model for a "Lord of the dark and moving hosts" (*CP* 289) — a far cry from the paltry Samson figure in "Delilah and Mr. Bircumshaw" (written in 1912 but not published until 1940). An intermediate work, the 1917 short story "Samson and Delilah," though seemingly something of a potboiler, reveals new depth and complexity in the depiction of Samson and his surroundings. Although these two stories are not among Lawrence's best, their biblical allusions give them special importance here. Because they have never been interpreted in this way before, they require detailed analysis.

The original Samson represents to Lawrence, even early, the old order of heroes and patriarchs including King Saul. The familiar story of Samson is that of a man robbed of his strength by a woman. Delilah sought the secret of his power — his uncut hair — in order to destroy him, as she did when she cut it, allowing him to be enslaved and blinded by the Philistines. In addition, other incidents in his life prefigure, in biblical typology, Christ's descent into hell and triumph over death. These include a youthful amatory adventure and his death, both at Gaza. In the former incident, he was detained in a house with a Philistine woman while his enemies lay in wait, but Samson burst through the trap, carrying with him the gates of the city. Later, at the end of his life, when he pulled down the Philistine temple upon himself and his enemies, Samson died but triumphed in death, signifying typologically Christ's later victory over death and hell. Both the woman's house and the Philistine captivity sometimes correlate in Christian iconography with Christ's three days in the underworld, in the harrowing of hell. Lawrence eventually uses all three of these main stories about Samson.

The first story is particularly present in "Delilah and Mr. Bircumshaw." Not at all like Samson the tribal hero, Mr. Bircumshaw more closely resembles Lawrence's weak and unsympathetic "Christ figures," though the "old Adam" rears up in him intermittently. Of course, Bircumshaw is only rather ludicrously related to Samson — an "ignoble Samson" (*PII* 86), as his wife and another woman see him — and he is clearly suffering from a loss of patriarchal identity, being victimized by the modern society in which his Delilah has features of a malign madonna. The religious context is firmly established by the opening situation, for Harry Bircumshaw and his wife have just attended a church pageant. Lawrence early informs the reader, too, that the man has "vague, sensuous, religious feeling, but . . . lacked a Faith" (84). The women mock his pageant performance, in which he has portrayed one of the Magi — a role putting "the light of the Star in his eyes" and reminding his wife of a comical "Abraham setting out to sacrifice" (85). This mixture of Old and New Testament elements reveals the trouble with Bircumshaw, for the old role of male mastery is perverted in him by the prevailing new epoch so that he resorts to mean bullying of the women supposedly in his control, his wife and daughter. In the essay "The Real Thing" (1930), Lawrence discusses how such a ruined man tries "to *impose* himself" on others because of the collapse of his faith: "Tortured and cynical and unbelieving, he . . . remains a shell of a man," and this is when the conflict comes between man and woman (*P* 200).

Bircumshaw lacks the heroic identity of an Abraham or a Samson and, though he seldom appears with "his mouth fairly sweet with Christian resignation" (as in the pageant), he is a product of the repressive "Christian" era (*PII* 85). He is identified with Christ when he feels "virtue depart from him" (90), ironically echoing Luke 8:46 and Mark 5:30, in which Christ feels the "virtue" of his healing power going out to a woman he cures. This is the same Bible incident from which the story "You Touched Me" (1920) takes its name. In that tale, a woman gives a man an unforgettable sensual touch, bringing the two to a new life together. But in Bircumshaw's case, a woman has deliberately robbed him of power: by mocking him, his wife has "clipped a large lock from her Samson," and "another lock" falls just as he feels the "virtue depart" (90). Lawrence means to suggest, though, that dominating women in general have brought him to this condition; thus his wife's friend joins in the whispering against him, and even his daughter is likened to "a little Virgin by Memling," one with a "wilful, imperious way" that is evident even in sleep (90). Bircumshaw lives in the shadow of a lopsided "trinity" (90) consisting of the mother and child but not himself, for he cannot enter this sacred circle. Since the Adamic patriarch is unable to emerge in him, Harry's perverse manner well exemplifies the slang term referring to the "old Adam" as a "mean streak." And his first name suggests that he is a decrepit version of the devil, the Old Harry. The story's types are of a simple kind, yet they share some features with the greatly complicated typology surrounding the second-generation Brangwens in *The Rainbow*. [43]

Lawrence's next story based on the same Old Testament figures, "Samson and Delilah" (written in 1916 and published in 1917 in the *English Review* and the *Lantern* of San Francisco), was originally named "The Prodigal Husband," apparently from Christ's

---

43. Harris, *Short Fiction of D. H. Lawrence*, 75–76, sees connections between the characters Bircumshaw and Will Brangwen of *The Rainbow*, but not in typological roles.

parable of the prodigal son.[44] Its connection with Samson typology seems, at first reading, remote. A Cornish miner returns
sixteen years after deserting his wife, now the owner of an inn. In
retaliation for his desertion, she sets soldiers upon him to bind
him and throw him from the inn, but she is still attracted to him
and later allows him to come back to her.

Despite these generally domestic events, the story's opening
scene suggests the larger gravity of the occasion. Lawrence sketches
a cosmological motif into the outdoor Cornish setting, for Willie
is following the Pole Star, whose significance to the later Lawrence
is great. In times of changing epochs, "the pole-star no longer
stands on guard at the true polaric centre" and people are "dis-
orientated," says Lawrence in the 1923 essay "On Being Religious";
specifically, this happens when a new central symbol replaces the
cross — when "the pole of heaven shifts" (*RDP* 192, 190). This
essay projects the return of a pagan epoch of male power after
Christendom. Lawrence further unveils this epoch in the rhap-
sodic essay "Resurrection" of 1925, projecting "lords among men
again" (*RDP* 234).

It is very unlikely that Lawrence intends *all* of this context in
this earlier story, but elements of it — the star-guided journey, the
seemingly powerful wanderer — deserve attention they have not
received. Other details further the setting's slight but significant
removal from the everyday. Willie, the story's Samson, travels a
vaguely ominous region, strewn with towering ruins from tin mining; while these are no doubt the marks of the punishing industrial age, they nevertheless appear like "remnants of some by-gone
civilization" (*E* 108). The story, dealing with ambush and escape,
partly justifies the rather portentous presence of that Pole Star.

Willie enters a disquieting interior milieu, first focused on the
queen of spades in a game of cards. The inn, ironically named
"The Tinners' Rest," is not initially a haven at all but the scene of
the violent assault on him.[45] The physical struggle that forms the

44. In the holograph entitled "The Prodigal Husband" (E352.7 in Roberts,
A Bibliography of D. H. Lawrence), the present Samson design already
existed under this title.

45. In 1916, Lawrence actually stayed in an inn called the Tinners' Arms
(*Letters* 2:560–81). But his interest in the tinners may have been heightened
by a curious Cornish saying that he would have known from Jenner's *Christian
Symbolism*, 63: linking the Cornish tin miners with Joseph of Arimathea and
even with Christ, it held that "Joseph was in the tin-trade." Another version
of this legend makes it Christ who was in the tin-trade, as reported by

story's center is a grim one, almost suggesting a sacrificial rite. His wife, Alice, likened to "an Amazon" (115), subdues him with the aid of the soldiers, who tie him while she pins him down. Willie's tied body, with its "strong back bound in subjection," reminds her of "a calf tied in a sack in a cart, only its head stretched dumbly backwards": seeing this image, "she triumphed" (118). The scene seems to recall Judges 16:18-21, in which the biblical Delilah, after cutting Samson's hair and thus rendering him vulnerable, betrays him to the Philistines, who confine him and make him a slave in the mills of Gaza. Although Willie has only ordinary braces bound on his feet, these parallel the "fetters of brass" on those of Samson (Judges 16:21). Willie, firmly locked out of the house after being thrown into the street, looses his bonds and returns, gaining an apparent welcome.

After his capture, the parallel with the familiar Bible story seems to break down. But Lawrence borrows from more tales of Samson than this. The earlier incident at Gaza, in which the hero leaves the Philistine woman's house and bears "the doors of the gate of the city" before him (Judges 16:3) — prefiguring Christ's triumph over the doors of death (Schiller 2:127, 130) — seems present beneath the tale's surface, even informing a curious focus on the inn door. As Alice announces closing time at the inn, the door is mentioned three times, and the sounds of "locking and barring the door" are emphasized during the ejection.[46] Yet the door is open when he tries it a short time later. On an obvious level, she simply closes and opens the "door" of the relationship with her husband, but Lawrence's fondness for biblical analogy suggests a more ambitious meaning. If the inn can be likened to the house of the Philistine woman (and the door to the gate of death or hell, as in the typological pattern), it is particularly dismaying that Willie walks straight back into it upon his release.

The question of whether Willie is likely to be an ultimate victim or victor is a difficult one. As a kind of Samson, he is suitably described as a strong man, even something of a giant, "a tall, well-built man, apparently in the prime of life," who towers over the Cornish miners like Gulliver among the Lilliputians and who

---

Cavendish, *King Arthur and the Grail,* 182. Joseph, who gave his tomb to Christ, is also associated in legend with a flowering staff like that of Aaron and Moses (Cavendish, 181).

46. First Alice Nankervis states, "I'm shutting the door"; she next stands "holding the door" and then shuts it decisively (112-13).

stoops slightly as if from excessive height. This first view yields to
a realization that his shoulders are "square and rather stiff" (108),
a condition later explained as a consequence of the mining trade:
"The rather rigid look of the shoulders came from his having had
his collar-bone twice broken in the mines" (114). Despite his
apparently free and powerful existence, he has the mark of victimization from an industrial "Christian" age, and his wife clearly has
the upper hand in the attack on him. Appropriately, therefore,
his hair is cropped, like Samson's when Delilah betrays him.
Just before Alice's assault, he is "spell-bound" and "bewitched" by
her — a binding he does not escape at the end despite his apparent
release.

Still, Lawrence intends him to be something of a power figure,
too. The revised version of the story, prepared for the volume
England, My England (1922), gives Willie "a sense of mastery
and of power in conflict" on the opening page (108). A further
addition alludes obliquely to the strength and danger potential in
Samson's hair. Willie's "close black hair" seems oddly alive in the
story's later version, for Alice regards it "as if it would bite her"
(121).[47] This suggestion of snake imagery does more than
express the conflict between the two, contributing something,
also, to his air of potency. His readmittance to the inn after
untying himself clearly promises a sexual triumph.[48] If anything,
the mutual peril in the couple's physical magnetism makes their
union the more impressive, as Lawrence shows a wounded modern Samson willing to brave the doors of doom for this attraction.
The implicit inversion of resurrection typology serves his customary celebration of the sensual consciousness, but the power struggle between man and woman seems unresolved.[49]

It is only in "The Revolutionary," in *Birds, Beasts and Flowers,*
that Samson emerges with his fuller typological identity. One of
Lawrence's sources is almost certainly Handel's *Samson,* with its
libretto based on Milton's *Samson Agonistes.* One of its arias —
although not the one from which Lawrence took the title "Honor

47. Some other changes emphasize his dark eyes, not blind but rather
uncannily "jewel-like," like "bright agate" (112, 121).

48. Lawrence frequently uses Resurrection imagery to refer to sexuality,
as seen above in "The Thorn in the Flesh." It has particularly strong typological implications when it involves a character based on Samson.

49. Critics have long felt the ambiguity of the story's "open ending."
According to Cushman, "Achievement of *England, My England,*" 35, it points
to a general, and perhaps continuing, struggle "for domination."

and Arms"[50]—has particular significance for this poem. In it, Samson, blind and enslaved at the mill in Gaza, refers to his condition:

> Total eclipse! no sun, no moon,
> All dark amidst the blaze of noon!
> . . . .
> Sun, moon and stars are dark to me.

The lines reproduce features of Milton's drama, hinting that Samson is a solar hero in eclipse. His name in Hebrew is related to the word for *sun*,[51] and Milton apparently uses and revalues the hero's connections with pagan solar figures to strengthen a typological identification between Samson and the true light, the Son of God. Samson's triumph in his hellish darkness prefigures Christ's harrowing of hell and triumphant emergence from the underworld (as well as his ultimate victory, at the Apocalypse, over the forces of darkness). This typological pattern underlies the oratorio's choral passages, reversing the imagery of darkness to affirm immortality:

> Then round about the starry throne
> Of Him who ever rules alone,
> Your heavenly guarded soul shall climb;
> Of all this earthly grossness quit,
> With glory crown'd forever sit,
> And triumph over Death, and thee, O time!

As one critic describes Milton's hero, he seems to move "under the world like the sun at night, back to the place of its rising."[52] This passage is sure to remind Lawrence's readers of the novelist's own fondness for the "dark sun" and the "dark gods." Like Blake, whose Los is indebted to Samson,[53] Lawrence is drawn to the apocalyptic tradition, the eclectic mythology, and the theme of resurrection surrounding the biblical hero. It is not surprising, therefore, that his own poem on Samson gives the character this

50. See Cushman, *D. H. Lawrence at Work,* 209. Lawrence had also attended the opera *Samson et Dalila* by Camille Saint-Saëns in 1911 (*Letters* 1:306).
51. Krouse, *Milton's Samson in Christian Tradition,* 78.
52. Frye, "Agon and Logos," 145.
53. Tannenbaum, *Biblical Tradition,* 261–72.

cosmic stature. Sandra M. Gilbert comments that the speaker in
"The Revolutionary" is "like someone other and larger than simply the Samson of biblical and Miltonic legend," and she associates
him with Lucifer, Osiris, and Dis/Pluto.[54] But another explanation for his compelling air of grandeur lies in the standard biblical
typology of Samson's relation to Christ in the underworld (Schiller
3:61), a relation enriched by long-standing mythological ties between
Samson and Hercules, Samson and other pagan figures, and even
Christ and Hercules.[55] "Lawrence's Samson makes plot necessi-
ties [such as blindness] into mystical virtues," says Gilbert.[56] But
"The Blind" and other Lawrence works on the original Adam and
Eve also emphasize the significance of senses other than sight.
This Samson is thus associated with a state before conscious
eyesight, one that is a customary part of Lawrentian rebirth.

Even though the revolutionary's hell is the "paleface" European
civilization and his heaven a realm of glamorous darkness, the
scenes depend for their allusive power upon the typological
underpinning. While the biblical Samson is enslaved in the Philistine temple, Lawrence's hero is enclosed within the repressive
European civilization. His enemies are symbolized by the "pillars"
of the temple-prison, "Pale-face authority, / Caryatids." Curiously,
the imagery suggests a cathedral: the revolutionary perceives himself "as among a forest of pillars that hold up the dome of high
ideal heaven"—indeed, of "the high and super-gothic heavens"
(CP 287). He refers to Christendom. In the 1915 version of "The
Crown," Lawrence stresses the similarity between the dilemmas
facing the biblical Samson and modern man: "For we shall be like
Samson, buried under the ruins" (RDP 305). In the 1925 version
of this essay, the analogy is extended by an addition: "And moreover,
if we are like Samson, trying to pull the temple down, we must
remember that the next generation will be none the less slaves,
sightless, in Gaza, at the mill" (305). He means that it is better to
allow spontaneous new creation than to strain at the old structure;
thus, immediately following this reference to Samson, Lawrence
likens a really new age to a chicken in an egg, breaking its shell
because of desire and not animosity. He stresses the necessity to
"move under a greater heavens" (305).

54. Gilbert, "D. H. Lawrence's Uncommon Prayers," 85.
55. On some Renaissance correlations between Hercules and Samson,
see, for example, Allen, Mysteriously Meant, 66, 105, 222; on the connection
between Hercules and Christ, see 222.
56. Gilbert, "D. H. Lawrence's Uncommon Prayers," 85.

In the poem, he is reworking temple typology, in which Solomon's temple not only mirrors creation itself, to some minds,[57] but is also the type prefiguring the antitypical temple of the New Jerusalem, the church. In standard typology, not the Philistine temple but the Temple of Solomon looks forward to the Christian church in the way that Eve precedes Mary and the church (Schiller 1:24, 4,1: 89–90).[58] Thus Saul has foreseen sadly in *David* that "the seed of David" (immediately, Solomon) will "put the Lord inside a house" and "enclose Him within a roof" (149). In Lawrence's poetic parallel, however, the Philistine temple is the counterpart of the contemporary world. It is a false temple, concealing much of reality; built from its own superconscious bias, it eliminates the sensuous "dark" world of experience. One is reminded of Lawrence's statement in *Twilight in Italy* that an ugly scene is like "a fabrication, like a dull landscape painted on a wall, to hide the real landscape" (145). In such a falsified world, the revolutionary's blindness is, indeed, an advantage, allowing him to "see" with his sensuous faculties beyond the "ponderous roofed-in erection of right and wrong"; an immortal, he will be "Lord" when the world "is in ruins" (*CP* 289). As in Handel's *Samson,* he will "triumph over Death and . . . time" in resurrection. According to another poem in the same volume, "Grapes," "Our pale day is sinking into twilight" (*CP* 286) to renew a condition "before eyes saw too much" (285). Although this latter state recalls the primordial past, the revolutionary's triumph is based, in part, on a less remote pattern of dying and reviving gods, including Christ—the same pattern governing Alan's reappearance in "The Border Line."[59]

Despite the debts of such figures to Christological models, however, Lawrence also revises typology to harken back to those earlier days "before eyes saw too much." Opposing such ancient power epochs is modern Christendom, which, to him, threatens the values of hierarchy, sensuous awareness, and life itself. Seeking a renewal of those lost values, he sometimes invokes classical, pre-Hellenic, or unrecorded Atlantean time. One critic sees Pan as the major influence on Lawrence's dark gods or heroes,[60] and

57. Von Simson, *The Gothic Cathedral,* 37–39.

58. See also Rosenau, *Vision of the Temple,* 39.

59. As early as the 1915 manuscript of *The Rainbow,* Ursula terms the resurrected Christ greater than Bacchus or Iacchos, Apollo or Jove, because, having risen from the grave, he is a lord of death whose lover can say, "I lay with death" (*R* 630).

60. Merivale, *Pan the Goat-God,* 217.

another proposes Nietzsche's Dionysus as their principal source.[61]
But biblical figures have at least equally strong claims. One remarkable example, recalling the dark Samson of "The Revolutionary,"
appears near the end of *The Boy in the Bush* (1924), in a section
of the coauthored work that is confidently attributed to Lawrence.[62]
The hero imagines a "Lord, as dark as death and splendid with a
lustrous doom," who will make him "earth-royalty, like Abraham
or Saul" and open "the black wonder of the halls of death ahead"
(337–38)—a lord explicitly derived from the God of Abraham and
from the Old Testament patriarchs and heroes, whom the character valorizes. Sometimes Lawrence turns to the "essential days" of
Genesis, such as Ursula recalls in *The Rainbow:* "There were
giants in the earth in those days," when, even aside from Adam,
there were "Sons of God" (*R* 257). Often, however, he evokes the
more familiar biblical types. Thus many of his characters must be
termed the literary sons of Adam, David, and Samson.

61. Pollnitz, " 'Raptus Virginis,' " 120.
62. See Paul Eggert's introduction (*BB* xlv–liii) and Rossman's *"The Boy
in the Bush,"* 187–88.

The Time Scheme

Typological Time in *The Rainbow*

2

In Lawrence's works, history has a structure related to that of biblical typology; this is especially evident in *The Rainbow,* containing both Old and New Laws and gesturing toward a further age in its concluding rainbow vision.[1] Among many possible sources for the novel's typology, Jenner's *Christian Symbolism* is evidently the most immediate, but graphic-arts models must also be singled out. In her chapter "Old Testament Types," Jenner relates typology to cathedral iconography and makes the Ruskinian statement that "such monuments of medieval symbolism as the carvings of Chartres and Rheims cathedrals" demand attention to nearly forgotten meanings: "Such a minute knowledge of Scripture does not obtain [in the early twentieth century] . . . as in the days when the Bible was taught and fixed in figures of stone and blazoned in colours on walls and windows."[2] One modern writer who did have such "minute knowledge" of the Bible was, of course, Lawrence, who, in addition, could not have helped noticing

1. Kinkead-Weekes, "The Marble and the Statue," 384, sees a tripartite division in *The Rainbow.* On the other hand, Reeves and Gould, in *Joachim of Fiore,* 286, 288–89, cast *The Rainbow* as an expression of one epoch (Old Testament) in a Joachimite time scheme (with *Women in Love* and *The Plumed Serpent* completing the design). See also Kermode, "Lawrence and the Apocalyptic Types," 14–38.
2. Jenner, *Christian Symbolism,* 168.

typological elements in the medieval monuments he frequented —
such as Southwell Minster and Lincoln Cathedral, described in
rich detail in *The Rainbow.*

Cathedral sculpture is commonly arranged to reveal, visually
and structurally, an entire historic sequence in which the Old
Testament patriarchs, prophets, and kings precede the New Testament figures and saints of the church. For example, the southeast
porch of Lincoln Cathedral juxtaposes Synagoga (a personification of the temple of the Old Law) and Ecclesia (a woman
representing the Christian church of the New Law),[3] sculptures
that Lawrence must have known. Often the cathedral presents a
porch of patriarchs or prophets (of the Old Law) through which
one passes toward the altar, the realm of Christ and Mary (of the
New Law). Similarly, the reader of *The Rainbow* first encounters
the Brangwen patriarchs of Marsh Farm and moves progressively
toward more individualized "Christ figures" of the modern world.

Meaningfully, the chapter "The Cathedral" emphasizes the
ornamented west front, the porch, and the altar at Lincoln. In
keeping with the structural symbolism of the building, these are
seen as stages in a progression, a journey, toward Christ — or, in
Lawrence's thinking, a journey from the old tribal consciousness
to the mental awareness and individuality of the Christian era.
Will Brangwen arrives "eager as a pilgrim" (186). He has loved to
"go through the great door and look . . . towards the far-off, concluding wonder of the altar" (191) until Anna shows him that "the
altar was barren, its lights gone out" (188). In the 1915 manuscript version, even more stress was laid on the movement toward
the altar: "the stately, mystic march of the pillars down the nave"
reminds Anna of a journey in which "far down there, should be
the altar" (592).[4] Because she thinks the "goal," the altar, no
longer houses deity, she fears her journey is "at an end" (593). In
the published novel, as in the earlier version, she rejects the
impasse, resisting "the lift and spring of the great impulse towards
the altar" and focusing, instead, on the individualized carvings
that suggest to her "a shrewish woman" and enmity between a
husband and wife (189, 190).[5] To Lawrence, this shift reveals, in

3. Anderson and Hicks, *Cathedrals in Britain and Ireland,* 71.
4. On the manuscript and the typescript of *The Rainbow,* see footnote 3
to my introduction.
5. Lawrence states elsewhere: "There was . . . in the Cathedrals, already
the denial of the Monism which the Whole uttered. All the little figures, the
gargoyles, the imps, the human faces, whilst subordinated within the Great

part, an ultimate, negative stage of Christianity and not simply the healthy human drive to differentiate the self from its surroundings. Despite the nominally Christian background of all the earlier Brangwens, in their virtually medieval life-style, it is not until mid-novel that the objectionable Christianity arises—a form self-condemned by its lack of essence, even in Will, after "The Cathedral."

Lawrence's old order, of course, is that of pagan "blood consciousness" and sensual awareness, while the new order is that of mental and spiritual knowledge. Just before entering Lincoln Cathedral, Anna explicitly repudiates "blood-relation" in favor of "her mind and her individuality" (185). Sometimes Lawrence presents the dialectic simply in terms of Eden and the fall from Eden—conditions over which the original Adam and the modern Eve (the Madonna), preside respectively, for the Edenic condition is patriarchal, while the fallen condition of the modern world is dominated by woman. Sometimes Lawrence alludes more diffusely to Old Testament figures when he sketches in the old order of Adam and Noah, Moses and Aaron, David and Samson, as discussed in chapter 1. As mentioned earlier, *Twilight in Italy*, written in the same period as *The Rainbow*, distinguishes two kinds of churches that are categorized by the faculties they suggest, not by chronological time. The churches of the eagle celebrate power and triumph. As they "stand high, with their heads to the skies," they embody "the Spirit of David" (19), the heroic and royal side of the Old Testament warrior and monarch; more broadly, they represent the senses, "the Dionysic ecstasy" (37). But the churches of the dove stand for submission and excessive spirituality. The eagle churches, Lawrence finds, are still predominantly pagan, predating dove churches, regardless of actual chronology. Lincoln Cathedral is, significantly, related to both (186).

He often further translates the dichotomy into more specific historic theory, in which an old order prevails until the late Renaissance. In the Middle Ages, he writes, Christian Europe seems to have been "striving, out of a strong, primitive, animal nature, towards the self-abnegation and the abstraction of Christ"

Conclusion of the Whole, still, from their obscurity, jeered their mockery of the Absolute, and declared for multiplicity, polygeny" (*STH* 66). Although such figures may seem to Anna in *The Rainbow* to represent forces "left out" of the cathedral, they are, in fact, pointedly present. See also Pinkney, *D. H. Lawrence and Modernism*, 72–73.

so that the balancing of flesh and spirit created "a triumphant joy
in the Whole" (*TI* 34). This is a progression very much like that
suggested in the Brangwens' experience of Lincoln Cathedral. As
modern abstraction won out in northern Europe "at the Renaissance" (71), the movements of technology and industrialization
began their long route to prevalence: "Hence the active worship to
which we were given at the end of the last century, the worship of
mechanised force" (40). In "Study of Thomas Hardy," Lawrence
declares absolutely, "It was after the Renaissance, Christianity
began to exist. It had not existed before" (77).[6] In the 1925
version of "The Crown," he states, "He who triumphs, perishes"
(*RDP* 269), and this is undoubtedly how he even earlier saw the
post-Renaissance victory of spirituality over sensuous paganism.
Somewhat like Yeats, therefore, he depicts the Renaissance as
both a glorious culmination and the beginning of the end. The
shift from the medieval to the post-Renaissance experience — with
little transition between the two — is dramatized in *The Rainbow,*
and its tragedy is the failure of an adequate *renascence,* a genuine
new direction, when it should have occurred.

Alternatives to this arrested development fascinated and even
tormented Lawrence throughout his life. In his essay "Nottingham
and the Mining Countryside" (1930), he discusses how Italian hill
towns — like Siena, the famous art center of the thirteenth and
fourteenth centuries — remain models of beauty so that they form
striking contrasts to the mining towns of England, part of the
mechanistic north as opposed to the more sensuous south (*P* 134,
139). Similarly, the early Florentine Renaissance had produced
enduring monuments that still, in the twentieth century, capture
the attention of the protagonist in *Aaron's Rod* (1922). This potential of the Renaissance to have taken a better path, its significance
at the crossroads into modern time, the necessity of such renewal
to produce a new epoch: these points are emphasized in *The
Rainbow.* In *Fantasia of the Unconscious,* pointing to the necessity for man to advance and put "something wonderful" into the
world, Lawrence mentions one of the great monuments to such
labor: the cathedrals (60). But when the cathedral fails in *The
Rainbow,* nothing replaces it but the "monstrous superstructure"
of modern London (179), the "chaos" of Wiggiston (321), and the
"plaything" Gothic of Ursula's university (399).

6. In this essay, he divides the church more specifically into "the Protestant
Church, the Church of the Son" and "the Roman Catholic Church, the
Church of the Father" (*STH* 80–81).

I

The typological scheme in *The Rainbow* is amazingly complex. The book's familiar division, a bifurcation that has been both deplored and defended,[7] reflects and alters the two main orders of standard typology. The first half begins with intimations of Eden on the Marsh Farm and proceeds through associations of main characters not only with Adam and Eve but also with Noah (Tom) and Moses and David (Anna). Anna even likens her child Ursula to the Hebrew youths in the fiery furnace, one of the allusions causing George Ford to see Ursula as a prophetess to lead mankind through a wilderness experience toward the new Promised Land.[8] In addition, a particularly complicated set of motifs connects the young Will Brangwen both with the patriarchs and with Christ. The novel's second half features modern Christendom, with its overriding cerebration and rampant mechanization. The division exists on the several levels of Lawrence's mythic and historic time frame—as Eden and the Fall, as Old Testament and New, as patriarchy and matriarchy, and as medieval and post-Renaissance time.

The men of an immemorial past on the Marsh Farm are, like Adam, exposed by their Eves to knowledge, but this tendency toward mental abstraction does not overwhelm the old sensual awareness until the time of the novel, when first Tom Brangwen and then Will lose masculine mastery and enter a world of increasing matriarchy.[9] Although religious iconography conditions characters' thinking even in the opening pages, it is meaningful that they do not consciously recognize it, so deeply imbued are they with its tradition. I have argued earlier that Will, the most obvious advocate of Gothic ecclesiastical art, still loves the religious images "in his *blood* and *bones*" (159; my emphasis), but this is before his mid-novel disillusionment. As sterile mental knowledge triumphs over the old "blood consciousness," Anna—whose name recalls

7. See, for example, Rosenzweig, "Defense of the Second Half," 150-60; Michael Ross, " 'More or Less a Sequel,' " 263-88; and my article "Will Brangwen and Paradisal Vision," 346-57.

8. Ford, *Double Measure,* 129-30. Lawrence would have known this type as a prefiguration of the deliverance of the Christian saints, as recorded in Jenner, *Christian Symbolism,* 170.

9. See Miliaras, *Pillar of Flame,* 188, who, unlike commentators who find matriarchy in the early *Rainbow* society, sees in it the centrality of the father as leader and nurturer. See also Heilbrun, *Towards a Recognition of Androgyny,* 102-10, on Ursula's emergence from patriarchalism.

St. Anne, the mother of the Virgin Mary—assimilates to herself references to figures of male power like Moses and David. Ursula's life is typologically announced by allusions to Old Testament prophets,[10] and this is not so positive a fact as it may at first seem. Ford acutely sees Anna's celebration of pregnancy as "a modern Magnificat,"[11] and this is not entirely the joyous occasion it sounds, either, but rather is a phase in the troubled new order.

The patriarchal stage, though represented by Tom, is at least partly ushered out by him, as well, in his role as an early and all but unnoticed adherent of the machine age (a role carried on through Anna); he is a latter-day Noah who drowns in the flood of modernism. Will, too, a representative of the age of handicrafts and blind but vital faith, "falls" into consciousness in Lincoln Cathedral, where Anna is his serpent (189). This fall is ironically associated with the Christianity that claimed to redeem the Fall but that, in this case, is the very embodiment of fatal knowledge, of a "crucifixion" into consciousness of the self's fragmentation.

On a social and historical level, *The Rainbow* depicts the medieval agrarian world as it comes to a Renaissance juncture, when the young artist Will might have provided new and beautiful forms for the future rather than losing his "blood" connection with the old ones. As he carves his wood sculpture of Adam and Eve, the figures remain stiff, based on conventional iconographic patterns, rather medieval (112-13), but he can envision their development toward more rounded form, "tender and sparkling" (138). Will and Anna, of course, are the Adam and Eve of their time; and, while Will begins with some characteristics of the Old Testament patriarch—like his sensuous consciousness—he becomes more like the typological "new Adam," Christ. It has been easy to blame Will for his personal and public failings,[12] but he has yet to be evaluated in the light of this typological framework.

Because my reading of the relationships between Anna and Will

---

10. Ford, *Double Measure,* 131.

11. Ibid.

12. See, for example, Daleski, *The Forked Flame,* 97 ("the conflict between Will and Anna derives, ultimately, from *his* imperfections"); Moynahan, *The Deed of Life,* 58 ("Will's defeat condenses into a few agonized moments the historic decline of Christian faith during the past century or so," but "Lawrence is on the side of Anna"); Clarke, *River of Dissolution,* 45-53 (Will's value is as a representative of "disintegrative" energy); and Kinkead-Weekes, "The Marble and the Statue," 391-93. Kinkead-Weekes states in his essay "The Marriage of Opposites," 30, that Will and Anna each have "half a truth."

is revisionary, it is important to consider in some fullness the disputes involving them in their early married life. Indeed, Lawrence's alterations in these scenes in the manuscript and typescript versions of the novel, although studied elsewhere,[13] still justify such detailed lingering over these characters. The common view of the young couple is represented by Howe's assertion that Anna is the pagan, while Will is "a Christian."[14] But exactly the reverse is the case. "He was no Christian," Anna feels (160); and Lawrence defines through Anna what "Christianity" means in this novel — it means the intellectualized, self-sacrificing creed of the modern world. Thus it is Anna who gains from church only certain rules of morality and a humanism centering on "the welfare of mankind" and "certain acts conducive to the welfare of mankind" (146), while Will, to her rage, ignores "the greatness of mankind," wanting "a dark, nameless emotion, the emotion of all the great mysteries of passion" (147). Anna has only "the *thought* of her soul," even rather envying the "dark freedom and jubilation" of Will's soul (148; emphasis mine). Increasingly, she clings "to the worship of the human knowledge" (161), while Will long continues a kind of symbol-thought.

Until the last revision of the typescript of *The Rainbow*, the condemnation of Anna was even more blatant: of all the Brangwens, she was "most in accord with the vulgar clamour" of modern humanism (615), but ultimately, in the published novel, she is "most careless of the vulgar clamour" (256). In the 1915 manuscript, Anna has an explicit crucifixion experience suggesting the one she instigates in Will: during visits to Lincoln Cathedral, she remembers when "her hands and feet had been nailed at the summit of self-realisation" and recognizes the loss in this condition: "Was it at an end? Was it indeed at an end, her journey" (593). At this point, she even feels nostalgic for the superseded cosmology filled with angels: "They flickered on the outer circle of the Most High like altar flames, they quivered in flames of praise. And she knew in her dream, that beyond these were the fiery, stately Archangels, and beyond these the fiercely bright circle of the Cherubim" (593). But she dismisses this "dream" for being literally false.

13. See Kinkead-Weekes's introduction and notes to *The Rainbow* and his essay "The Marble and the Statue," 371–418, as well as Charles Ross's "Revisions of the Second Generation," 277–95, and *The Composition of* The Rainbow *and* Women in Love: *A History.*
14. Howe, *The Art of the Self*, 44.

I do not believe Lawrence's fundamental conception of her character changed greatly in rewriting. He must have felt, though, when he revised this section (in "The Cathedral"), that Anna's religious disillusionment was evident without these reveries. He allows the reader to realize it through the imagery surrounding her courtship and marriage, an imagery of angels (often in her consciousness) that falls off gradually. In the published account of the early marriage, it is meaningful that she can still sometimes see divinity in her husband: "he stood in the upright flame . . . transmitting the pulse of Creation" (158). Indeed, she has been "subject to him as to the Angel of the Presence" and "waited upon him and heard his will" and "trembled in his service" (158). Anna's loss of the religious sense—and of the built-in hierarchy suggested by the quoted passages—greatly affects the way she views her husband, making her attacks on his faith particularly devastating. The two represent separate but overlapping epochs, hers just in advance of his. "The Crown" of 1915 also presents two such epochs in imagery like that of *The Rainbow:* one of fiery Creation, presided over by "the ruddy choirs, the upright, rushing flames, the lofty Cherubim that palpitate about . . . the Source"; one of misty or watery dissolution administered by "the tall, still angels soft and pearly as mist, who await round the Goal . . . the last Assumption" (*RDP* 271). These represent the pagan and the Christian, the "Origin" and the "Goal." In the novel, Will originally belongs to the first order and Anna to the second. Water has female significance to Lawrence, as to most writers, and the triumph of the water pattern in *The Rainbow* fittingly appears, in passages on Will and Anna, before the famous flood that finally drowns the old epoch. Will's "fire was put out, she [Anna] had thrown cold water on it" (150), signaling the age of flood to come.

Although Ford has rightly noticed the "Dionysian" element in Will's religion,[15] this is not a common view of it. The religiosity with which most commentators charge the character does undoubtedly exist in his later years. But he is early identified with the phoenix (108), a symbol associated with immortality in both pagan and Christian contexts (Schiller 2:136).[16] An iconography of the

15. Ford, *Double Measure,* 47.

16. According to Lawrence, he adopted the phoenix symbol in late 1914 (*Letters* 2:252). On the phoenix, see (besides Schiller) Jenner's *Christian Symbolism* (150); Cowan, *D. H. Lawrence and the Trembling Balance* (167-77); and a special issue of the *D. H. Lawrence Review* (5 [1972]) devoted to the phoenix.

Creation radiates through the account of his courtship, both before and after the specific description of his wood carving of the Creation of Eve. He himself is like Adam, almost newly made from the hand of God: "The hand of the Hidden Almighty, burning bright, had thrust out of the darkness and gripped him" (112). This passage, suggesting such scenes of the Creation of Adam as Michelangelo's in the Sistine Chapel, is directly related to the description of Will's wood carving: "Adam lay asleep as if suffering, and God, a dim, large figure, stooped towards him, stretching forward His unveiled hand" to create Eve (112). Will even acts as Creator to Anna after a quarrel, when, "dim with pain," he reaches out his own hand to her and "the hand that touched her shoulder hurt him" (144). The reconciliation somewhat resembles the act of love in the poem originally entitled "Eve's Mass" and later "Birth Night" (written in 1912), in which the birth of Eve, during lovemaking, is not from Adam's rib but from his veins—from the blood so significant in Lawrence's metaphysic. As Anna weeps, Will feels that "his heart and all his veins would burst and flood her with his hot, healing blood" and "his blood seemed very strong, enveloping her" (145). The idea of transmitting his own life force to her by touch and even transfusion often informs their early scenes. In fact, Anna comes to realize and to resist this aspect of "blood-relation," in which "he seemed to lap her and suffuse her with his being, his hot life" (185–86).

In their famous quarrel about the Adam in his wood carving (discussed above in chapter 1), it is clear how female dominance comes to shape the marriage. Because Will has carved the patriarch God-like in size while Eve is doll-like, Anna objects that woman is the more important because "every man is born of woman" (162), and Will actually burns his artwork. At last, driven to a virtual crucifixion of the vital man in him, he becomes content to serve "the little matriarchy" of his family (193). He has even become "glad to forfeit from his soul all his symbols, to have her [Anna] making love to him" (151).

His shift from an Adamic young man to a tortured and submissive "Christ figure" is foreshadowed in his early association with the *Agnus Dei* and the *Pietà,* images of the crucified Christ. The lamb in Cossethay church, holding the banner of the red cross, is the *Agnus Dei,* the lamb of God, frequently connected with the Eucharist because Christ as the sacrifice replaces the lamb with himself in the bread and wine (Schiller 2:117–21). The banner is one of triumph, and the *Agnus Dei* is a frequent motif in art depicting the Resurrection.[17] The *Pietà,* portraying the wounded dead Christ in the arms of the Virgin Mary, is similarly connected with the Eucharist, as Will himself points out—"it means the Sacraments, the Bread" (149). Both images cause him ecstasy because he sees with emotional, not intellectual faculties (to Anna, "he was like a man whose eyes were in his chest") and focuses not on crucifixion but on resurrection. Even to Anna, the lamb momentarily conveys something of his experience: "the power of the tradition seized on her, she was transported to another world" (149). When Will explains, "It means the triumph of the Resurrection," she has again a glimpse of "something dark and powerful" (150). Looking at pictures of cathedral sculpture from Bamberg Cathedral, "he celebrated his triumphant strength and life and verity" (153). In an addition to his manuscript, Lawrence added (and retained) at this point, "He was again a bright lord" (154), emphasizing a short-lived triumph in the struggle with female dominance.

Will's early raptures in church are not responses to words but to symbols. Lawrence notes, "He preferred things he could not understand with the mind" (153). To Anna's rationalistic mind, though, symbolism does not exist: a lamb is only an animal and *Pietà*s only "those bodies with slits in them, posing to be worshipped" (149). It is she who asserts the identification between Will and the sacrificed Christ, and it is she who, in effect, turns him into "a Christian" in this sense. "It's *you,*" she insists of the *Pietà* (150). Disdaining her husband's capacity to gain satisfaction from symbols, she wants "to destroy it in him" (148). After the passages on the lamb and the *Pietà,* he begins to resemble the dead Christ, being "cold with corpse-like anger" (151). After their major battle over the Marriage at Cana, "He went out, dark and destroyed, his soul running its blood. And he tasted of death" (160). Lawrence labored over these sentences in manuscript, adding "running its blood" instead of "bleeding" (ms. 255). The resulting image suggests the iconography of the Crucifixion, in which blood issues in a running stream from Christ's breast, often sprinkling the bystanders (Schiller 2:205), an image related to the "smitten rock" of Horeb. The association is the more likely because Lawrence's 1915 manuscript refers not to the *Pietà* but to pictures

17. Frank Kermode, *D. H. Lawrence,* 46, associates the lamb with Christ's ultimate victory in the Apocalypse, but Will's own explanation is typologically valid. See also Manicom, "An Approach to the Imagery," 474–83, and Thomas, "Somewhere Under *The Rainbow,*" 57–65.

of the Sacred Heart, Anna objecting to their showing "hearts in bodies, as if the chest were open" (581). The Sacred Heart is often shown with the issue of redeeming blood (Schiller 2:195–96).

Since the Marriage at Cana is itself a symbolic representation of the Lord's Supper, as Lawrence would have known from Jenner,[18] it is clear that these painful religious arguments further a complex eucharistic motif and that Will himself is the sacrifice. As he is goaded to deny Christ's translation of water into wine, "his blood was up," for "in his blood and bones, he wanted the scene, the wedding, the . . . red wine" (159). It torments him, too, that his own marriage, like the Bible story, is losing the sacred quality he originally found in it. His blood is mentioned four times in a few lines about the wine. His symbol-thought, his "blood knowledge," is impaired and his soul "running its blood." Still, thinking again of the "best wine" of the wedding, his life force is resurgent and his heart knows not only "a craving" but "a triumph," while even Anna realizes that he has "something real" (160). In the past, after a quarrel, he could offer his living blood to re-create or "restore" her. But his shift from the full-blooded young man to the man who bleeds in death is far advanced by this time. A crucifixion, states Lawrence in the essay "On Being a Man," involves the conflict between the surface self and "the self which darkly inhabits our blood and bone" (*RDP* 216), the self which bleeds in Will. In the same essay, this crucifixion is interrelated with conflict in marriage. It is, therefore, especially fitting that, in the climactic argument in Lincoln Cathedral, the couple eventually contemplates not the altar of communion but carved figures of marital strife.

The sacrifice of Will is greatly furthered in Anna's famous Davidic dance, a ritual specifically designed "to annul him" (170). Seeing her husband's attempt to regain his patriarchal pride, Anna considers him "like Saul proclaiming his own kingship," and she herself takes on the role of David, the typological figure for Christ as King, dancing as David did before the Ark of the Covenant. In Lawrence's manuscript, "All the time she ran on by herself, *being David*" (585; my emphasis). The reference to Saul identifies Will with a "king-warrior"—as Lawrence later calls the Old Testament figure (*RDP* 268)—who lost his power. A similar reference, discussed above in chapter 1, relates Saul to Harry Bircumshaw, the failed patriarch in the earlier short story "Delilah and Mr. Bircumshaw." To be sure, Will has lost his power over the

18. Jenner, *Christian Symbolism*, 170.

wife who once "trembled in his service": the old power relationship has reversed itself. As previously noted, an earlier passage
gives his passionate soul "six wings of bliss" (R 158), a depiction
probably based on an illustration of one of the cherubim (Fig. 1),
among the highest angels in the heavenly hierarchy; but Will is no
longer described in such terms after the most serious quarrels.

Lawrence's conception of Anna's dance seems somewhat in
keeping with Blavatsky's pronouncement that the biblical counterpart was a " 'circle-dance,' said to have been prescribed by the
Amazons," a "Bacchic frenzy" (SD 2:460).[19] Anna knows well
that this ritual of female domination is to Will's "nullification";
thinking of herself as David the warrior in battle with the enemy,
she wills her husband "delivered over" and recalls the rousing war
cry in 1 Samuel 17: "Thou comest to me with a sword and a spear
and a shield, but I come to thee in the name of the Lord:—for the
battle is the Lord's, and he will give you into our hands" (170).
The Ark of the Covenant, according to Blavatsky, contained "the
germs of all living things": it is a "female symbol" (along with
Noah's Ark) and, in diverse cultures, similar objects served ancient
goddesses of "generative powers" (SD 2:461, 463). Thus it is very
much in keeping with Anna's assumption of kingship as she
celebrates her fecundity. She herself is the ark over which she
exults. Will feels "as if he were at the stake" and "being burned
alive" (171). Yet Anna is "the ark" in the flood to him (173). She is
shown, too, with her child sucking her breast in one of the
traditional stances of Mary, a crowned Madonna: "Anna Victrix."
A major iconographic stance, Maria Victrix (Schiller 4,2: 152,
174-77), is the model for this scene and for the title of the novel's
sixth chapter. When the Madonna is nursing the child, as in this
case, she is also designated Maria Lactans.

In an inversion of the earlier Creation of Eve imagery in which
Will appears as creator, he is himself eventually "born for a second
time, born at last unto himself" in his separation from Anna and
from "the vast body of humanity" (176), and we are too inclined to
consider this a change for the better. While it does place him in
the modern tide of individualism, this event actually details the
loss of the kind of "blood consciousness" by which the early

---

19. Although we do not know that Lawrence had read *The Secret Doctrine* before 1917 or *Isis Unveiled* before 1919, nonetheless he sometimes
seems to echo Blavatsky even as early as the 1915 version of "The Crown," in
which the "Bacchic delirium" (*RDP* 257) of David's dance before the Ark
recalls its "Bacchic frenzy" in *SD*.

Brangwen men felt themselves part of the cosmos. As I have shown in chapter 1, Lawrentian "crucifixion" is precisely this isolating process, this enforced recognition of the divided, separate self. Lawrence often presents this experience as a universal and necessary one—and, to some extent, a welcome one because of the human imperative to advance and to balance mental with physical faculties. But he writes, too, of "the great *counterfeit* liberation" when man loses "his primary faith in himself and in his very life" so that he is "tortured and cynical and unbelieving" (*P* 197, 200): "It is when men lose their contact with this [creative] eternal life-flame, and become merely personal, things in themselves, instead of things kindled in the flame, that the fight between man and woman begins" (*P* 202). While it is sometimes dangerous to cross-reference Lawrence's works from two different periods (*The Rainbow* and this essay, "The Real Thing," of 1929), the novel itself bears out such a meaning.

Will faces his disillusionment in two ways. First, he turns to voluptuous fulfillment, trysting briefly with a warehouse girl and then engaging with Anna in "all the lust and the infinite, maddening intoxication of the senses, a passion of death" (220)—this novel's version of the sexual revel after the fall of Adam and Eve.[20] Both partners are now mentally conscious, and their lovemaking is never again rendered in terms of the blood-conscious religious sense. Will's other release, often praised in him, is his late work as a crafts teacher and his continuing labor in the church even after his loss of faith; far from showing the creativity that once seemed potential in him, this work simply entrenches that which needs replacing in both school and church. Just as the "great, involved seed" of the cathedral (187) turns in his eyes to "dead matter" with no more florescence in it (190), Will himself looks "vacant," having inner "buds" that will not ripen and "folded centres of darkness which would never develop and unfold whilst

20. This judgment is at variance with the usual view that the couple's contrived sexuality is useful, releasing Will to public activities. See, for example, Kinkead-Weekes, "The Marble and the Statue," 391-93; Charles Ross, "Revisions of the Second Generation," 282-95; and Spilka, *Love Ethic of D. H. Lawrence,* 104-5. (But see, too, Butler's opposing view in *This Is Carbon.*) In *Psychoanalysis and the Unconscious,* Lawrence notes that the fall of man came when "we got our sex into our head" (121) and takes the first parents to task on grounds that seem applicable to Will and Anna: "when they [Adam and Eve] discovered that they could deliberately enter upon and enjoy and even provoke sexual activity in themselves, then they were cursed and cast out of Eden" (8).

he was alive in the body" (195). In his manuscript, Lawrence labored over the last words of this passage (ms. 317), and they have a far more conclusive ring than does the subsequent mention of Will's teaching, though it is itself an even later addition.[21] He stands as a depleted Christus such as Lawrence describes in a later essay: "the self-aware-of-itself, that pale Galilean *simulacrum* of a man" (P 770). He is the character most exemplifying the failure of the Lawrentian social program, by which men should rise from sexuality inspired to rebuild the world, to give it "something wonderful"—as medieval men, in their time, had done when they reared the cathedrals.

Oddly, he is shown to be aware of the problems of his civilization, for he sees London as "the ponderous, massive, ugly superstructure of a world of man upon a world of nature" and, reflecting that "the works of man were . . . terrible," meditates almost in the vein of Ursula's final rainbow vision or of Birkin's most radical speeches in *Women in Love:* "Sweep away the whole monstrous superstructure of the world of today, cities and industries and civilisation, leave only the bare earth with plants growing and waters running, and he would not mind" (179). In this passing recollection of an Edenic condition, he is, at least, no slave to the man-made world "that he did not believe in" (179). Returning late to his art, however, "now he had knowledge and skill without vision" (330), and his work in the world shares this lack.

Anna's domination is both furthered and caused by this failure in him, and her recognition of his weakness occasions a curious change in the religious imagery of her thinking. In the manuscript version, she meditates that she needs her husband to lead her on the journey of human progress: "The sun knew, and the moon knew, that she could not go alone, save the man took her, as Joseph took Mary to Egypt" (588). The references to sun and moon (generally male and female to Lawrence), appearing repeatedly at the end of the chapter "Anna Victrix" in both drafts and published novel, suggest an eternal order of things: I interpret the quoted line to mean that, according to the rules of the cosmos, the man should lead (or so she now assumes). As Anna's journey reaches its stalemate—without God or man to guide it—she adopts Old Testament power figures into her imagination, and the ulti-

21. Nixon, *Lawrence's Leadership Politics,* 32, finds this addition to the text incongruous with the earlier writing, issuing from a different impulse in Lawrence than that in which he wrote most of the novel.

mate omission of Joseph and Mary is in keeping with this pattern. I have mentioned earlier how she identifies herself with David, and the typological figures proliferate at the end of chapter 6. "From her Pisgah mount" (181), she sees herself as Moses, unable to enter the Promised Land but able to envision it for her children; she further imagines herself as a kind of Noah, receiving the rainbow promise—though in a diminished form—since she conceptualizes "a faint, gleaming horizon, *a long way off,* and a rainbow like an archway, a *shadow-door"* (181; emphasis mine).

Most remarkable of all is the strange fantasy of the three Israelites in the fiery furnace (Daniel 3): "The child [Ursula] she might hold up, she might toss the child forward into the furnace, the child might walk there, amid the burning coals and the incandescent roar of heat, as the three witnesses walked with the angel in the fire" (181).[22] The only explanation for this passage lies in biblical typology. In the Book of Daniel, three young men (Shadrach, Meshach, and Abednego) are cast into the furnace for refusing to worship a gold statue, a false god, but they are preserved by a fourth figure, appearing with them in the flames—a figure "like the Son of God" (Daniel 3:25), typologically identified with Christ in his later triumph over death and hell (Schiller 1:13, 153). Only in her childbearing can Anna be in touch again with the imagery of fire and angels once associated with her husband. This example, however, suggests not only creative fire but also purgative fire, no doubt forecasting Ursula's harrowing experiences and eventual hope of triumph. Surprisingly, Anna, the initial bearer of sterile modern Christianity, has taken refuge in the types from the Old Testament.

In doing so, she seems to appropriate the masculine identity, but the final paradox of Lawrence's treatment is that she is, at the same time, "Anna Victrix," unmistakably a Madonna. Based on iconography going back to classical depictions of deities and victorious warriors, the *Maria Victrix* image (Schiller 4,2: 174-77) is related to several standard views of Mary in triumph and Mary as the apocalyptic woman "clothed with the sun" and with "the moon under her feet" (Revelation 12:1). Although Lawrence eventually had some fondness for the latter image, in which he could see a splendid pagan goddess, he knew well that she had "suggested many pictures of the Virgin Mary" (*A* 120). The cosmic images of Sol and Luna are standard ones in Christian iconography—often flanking the venerated cross—symbolizing power over the universe

22. See Ford, *Double Measure,* 129-30.

(Schiller 2:8, 111). At the end of the chapter "Anna Victrix," it is significant that "dawn and sunset were the feet of the rainbow," and
"still her doors opened under the arch of the rainbow," reflecting "the
passing of the sun and moon" (181, 182). Both heavenly images are
particular symbols of Mary (Schiller 4,2:169, 198) and, despite her
failure to "journey" with them and to fulfill her destiny fully, Anna is
seen between the two and upon a mountaintop (her Pisgah) like Mary
on the mount of paradise. She is the Magna Mater in a Marian guise.

In her marriage, she has a solitary individuality: "She did not
turn to her husband, for him to lead her" (181). In her "long trance"
of motherhood (328), she alone forms her marriage unit—"she was
a door and a threshold, she herself" (182), whereas Tom and Lydia
had formed a full human arch, or rainbow, "the pillar of fire and
the pillar of cloud" that met "to the span of the heavens" (91) in
the earlier generation. An elaborate imagery of arch, cathedral,
rainbow, and ark, unfolding throughout the novel and suggesting
associations with biblical typology, is particularly complex in relation to Anna and eventually Ursula, who, in one of her corrosive
experiences, resembles a "pillar of salt" (297) like the one formed
by Lot's wife when she looked back on her doomed home in Genesis
(19:26). Indeed, Kinkead-Weekes argues that Ursula sojourns,
metaphorically, not toward the Promised Land but into the wilderness and the desolation of the "cities of the plain" like Sodom.[23]

The rich ecclesiastical iconography in the earlier *Rainbow,* in
both church and love scenes, is largely absent from the second
half. When Ursula enters a little church with her sweetheart
Skrebensky, she finds "the immemorial gloom full of bits of falling
plaster and dust of floating plaster, smelling of old lime, having
scaffolding and rubbish heaped about, dust cloths over the altar"
(275). Anachronistic Gothic form often characterizes merely barren civic buildings, such as the brutalizing St. Philip's School,
"imitating the church's architecture for the purpose of domineering,
like a gesture of vulgar authority" (343), or Ursula's university,
with Gothic forms that "looked silly" next to the modern squalor
(399). Nevertheless, at Rouen Cathedral, which Ursula visits with
Skrebensky, she responds as if to "something she had forgotten,
and wanted" (422). Otherwise, the arches, doorways, and arcs
surrounding the earlier characters are replaced only by the
"amorphous" and angular in the later world.[24] It is nothing

23. See Kinkead-Weekes's notes (*R* 532–33).
24. Unlike most commentators, I see vital values attaching to all of the

simple that is gone in the third generation, for an elaborate complex of meaningful interrelationships centered in the cathedral.

To many biblical exegetes, the Ark of the Covenant, before which David danced, and Noah's Ark are both types looking forward to the church, the true "ark" of the New Law (Schiller 1:139; 2:123). This is why Noah's Ark is frequently found in church sculpture, as it is in a frieze on Lincoln Cathedral's western front.[25] Schiller describes one such artwork: "The Ark on the mountain of water is depicted as the castle of God, meaning the Church" (1:139). In "The Cathedral," the church is seen not only as a sacred vessel but as a vehicle of journey, like an ark. The focus on its altar indirectly relates the cathedral to the Ark of the Covenant, for the altar, even more specifically than the church itself, is the direct New Testament counterpart of the Old Testament Ark (Schiller 2:123). The Tables of the Law were eventually housed in the synagogue's Holy of Holies, as Christ was believed to be housed at the church altar in the Eucharist. This is why Anna's view that "God burned no more in that bush [the altar]" (188) is such an apt one, recalling another reputed location of deity — the bush from which God spoke to Moses (Exodus 3:2-4). The cathedral, "spanned round with the rainbow" (187), suggests the covenant

---

arch imagery in this novel, including that of the cathedral. In the 1980s, an old controversy over the meaning of the arches reasserts itself. Millett, *The Vultures and the Phoenix,* 28-32, has renewed the longtime claim that, in Lawrence, a pointed Gothic arch symbolizes an unacceptable lack of sensuality, while a rounded Norman arch suggests physical fulfillment. This view has often been assumed ever since Mark Spilka's well-known chapter "The Shape of an Arch," in *Love Ethic of D. H. Lawrence,* 93-102, asserted the different connotations of the two forms. By such readings, adherents of the Gothic style, like Will, represent abstract spirituality at odds with earthy Lawrentian faculties. Sagar, in *The Art of D. H. Lawrence,* 53, has called Lincoln Cathedral Will's "substitute for sensual experience"; but he has since shown, in *D. H. Lawrence: Life into Art,* 134-35, that the 1915 revision of the chapter "The Cathedral" increases the structure's genuine appeal. Howe, *The Art of the Self,* 49, finds that Will's love of the *rounded* Romanesque and Norman arch leads him to excessive "physicality," while, in contrast, Ursula's encounter with the pointed Gothic arch at Rouen Cathedral is life enhancing, teaching her "that she must not remain sunk in the past or sensuality." Nixon, in *Lawrence's Leadership Politics,* 73, retorts that the arches in the interior of Lincoln Cathedral, which Will especially loves, are pointed and Gothic, not rounded as on the cathedral's west facade. Thus the argument on "the shape of an arch" comes full circle. In fact, Lawrence, in the 1929 "Introduction to These Paintings," seems to scoff at the claim that Romanesque form is preferable to Gothic (*P* 566). See also note 65 to my introduction.

25. Cook, *English Cathedral through the Centuries,* 157.

made by God to Noah after the great flood; for the bow, promising mercy, was typologically a prefiguration of the New Law of Christ.[26] All of these associations, though nowhere detailed in *The Rainbow*, converge in Lawrence's creation of the sacred effects in chapter 7 ("The Cathedral"), and all become detached at this time from their interconnections with life.

It is no accident, however, that Will has viewed the cathedral as "a world . . . a reality, an order, an absolute" (190-91), for it radiates an entire worldview, long affecting the general life-style around it. All that has been said of the cathedral can also be said of the marriage units in the earlier *Rainbow*. It is well known that descriptions of the Lincoln Cathedral experience resemble accounts of the second-generation honeymoon. In the manuscript version, the association between the bedroom and the sanctuary is even more explicit in one respect than it is in the published novel. Both housed deity, for the honeymoon's revelation to Will of a "bush blazing with the Presence of God" (579) is directly echoed in the "sacred bush" of the cathedral altar (593). To Lawrence, as to Blake,[27] the altar has sexual significance, and its barrenness has repercussions in the couple's marriage. The cathedral arches recall the human arch of marriage formed by Tom and Lydia early in the novel, when "the house was finished, and the Lord took up His abode" (91). The arch even recurs in an altered form in Anna's view of herself as a "doorway." One recent critic, citing Jewish mysticism, even relates the novel's marriage arches to the pillars of Solomon's temple.[28] Early in *The Rainbow*, houses, too, are like microcosmic sanctuaries, arcs, or arks. In the "original" *Rainbow* manuscript, when Tom tries to get to safety during the flood that kills him, he calls his home an "Ark" (609), later a "homestead."

Underlying the many associations between ecclesiastical and erotic imagery in *The Rainbow* is the biblical allegory, based on the Song of Songs, of the Bridegroom (Christ) and the Bride (the church). The novel contains more than one biblical scene (like the Marriage at Cana) interconnected with this typological rela-

---

26. Landow, "The Rainbow," 346-47.

27. See Tannenbaum, *Biblical Tradition*, 161, 245-46, and Miner, "William Blake's 'Divine Analogy,' " 46-61.

28. Whelan, *D. H. Lawrence*, 119. Although he states that "only the Jewish mystical tradition" could have provided the "symbolic vocabulary" to relate marriage to temple imagery, biblical typology embraces the same sources, extending the meaning to the New Jerusalem.

tionship. Another is that in which Christ addresses Jerusalem, wishing to embrace it—a scene recalled by Ursula in her young womanhood: "Oh Jerusalem, Jerusalem—how often would I have gathered thy children together as a hen gathereth her chickens under her wings, and ye would not—" (265). Christ's watch over Jerusalem (Luke 19:41-44) was a popular subject for paintings and prints, as well as evangelical sermons, in the nineteenth and early twentieth centuries; and a pictorial element is present in Ursula's visualization of the buildings and people of Jerusalem, as it is again present in her final rainbow vision of Beldover. While she feels an erotic element in the Bible passage, she knows "that Christ meant something else: that in the vision world, He spoke of Jerusalem, something that did not exist in the everyday world" (266). That "something else" is the mystic marriage between Christ as the Bridegroom and the church as the Bride, the New Jerusalem. The combination of the erotic and the sacred in Ursula's fantasies is only partly misplaced, for the novel allows—and abounds in—correspondences between the two levels. Such a combination is even present in Tom's famous wedding speech about marriage as the creation of an angel that can rise at the Judgment Day "praising the Lord" (129). Here he states the novel's central theme, that "on earth there *is* marriage, else heaven drops out."

After "The Cathedral," these interpenetrations between religious and sexual spheres are increasingly absent or strained, as exemplified in Ursula's shamed desire for Christ's sensuous love, in her inability to find an object in her own life for the sacred passion. The "Sunday world" and "weekday world" are now sundered so as to cause confusions that were absent in earlier sections of the novel. The Brangwens themselves lament the desacralized life-style: "Alas, that Christmas was only a domestic feast, a feast of sweetmeats and toys! . . . Where was the fiery heart of joy, . . . the star, the Magis' transport, the thrill of new being that shook the earth?" (260) The failure of marriage, like that of the holy days, now advances in *The Rainbow* and *Women in Love* to the accompanying decline of sanctuaries in general, including the home—no longer an ark or rainbow-like arch, it is the dreary "little grey home in the west" avoided by all protagonists (*WL* 374).[29] While Anna, at the end of "Anna Victrix," is seen "settled in her builded house, a rich woman" (182), Ursula as an adult opposes all that is

29. This is Ursula's reference to the title of a popular song of 1911, "Little Grey Home in the West."

"hemmed in" and house-like. The reference to the parable of the rich man (Matthew 19:16-30), a tale pondered more than once by Ursula, allies Anna's house with materialism and makes it as remote from the Kingdom of Heaven as from the Promised Land.

II

The most obvious typological context for *The Rainbow* concerns Noah's flood and the rainbow itself. A lengthy canceled section in the 1915 manuscript deals with the flood, and one of the titles for *Women in Love* was once *Noah's Ark* (*Letters* 3:183). Noah appears again in Lawrence's essay "Books" (1924) and in a late drama fragment, *Noah's Flood.* [30] In Genesis, of course, God punishes "all flesh" on earth by destruction in the great flood, which only Noah and his family (and pairs of creatures) escape in the floating ark. Afterward, Noah receives God's pledge of the rainbow as a sign of reconciliation and mercy: "And I will remember my covenant, which is between me and you and every living creature of all flesh: and the waters shall no more become a flood to destroy all flesh" (Genesis 9:15). In *The Rainbow,* four full verses of the biblical account of the rainbow (Genesis 9:12-15) appear in the chapter "First Love," along with significant passages on God's charge to Noah and his sons to maintain natural hierarchy and dominion over the creatures.

It is important that Tom Brangwen, before his drowning, two chapters earlier, identifies himself with Noah. "Which of us is Noah?" he asks an acquaintance at the tavern where he has been drinking. "Ducks and ayquatic fowl'll be king o' the castle at this rate," he says, "—dove an' olive branch an' all" (227). The final six words affect the allusion in an odd way: Tom, in his whimsical but prophetic state, foresees another flood despite the dove and olive branch that showed Noah the flood's end and God's mercy. Tom's drowning in the rising waters at Marsh Farm ends the old patriarchal era just as the matriarchal rises (soon after "Anna Victrix")

---

30. By 1917, Lawrence would have recognized a connection between Noah and Adam: in a version related by Blavatsky, Noah was the bearer of Adam's body in the ark among the "germs of all living things" (*SD* 2:467-68). Seven years after reading her, Lawrence, in "Books," echoes Blavatsky's language: "But for the living germ of Noah in his Ark, chaos would have redescended on the world in the waters of the flood" (*RDP* 200).

and ushers in a pattern of water imagery continuing even into *Women in Love.* (Examples include the "clayey" world in which Winifred and Ursula swim in *The Rainbow,* and the deadly "Water Party," mud flowers, and ice images in the later novel.)

To Lawrence, water and fire epochs alternate, a view he develops as early as the 1915 "Crown."[31] While both are necessary, the fire era is one of creation and the water era one of disintegration (*RDP* 270-71).[32] *The Rainbow* clearly follows such a pattern, opening with the hot sun of creation and closing with the cloudy rainbow after the flood of decline that sets in with "The Marsh and the Flood." It is worth remembering that, to Blavatsky, Noah's flood was a reenactment of Adam's fall, both signifying the same descent, and David's reign was a subsequent falling off from the silver age (*Isis* 2:423, 443). Whether or not Lawrence had read her when he wrote *The Rainbow* (and evidently he had not), he also conflates imagery of all three falls. At Lincoln Cathedral, Anna is not only Eve but the serpent, to which Will responds with the new, painful knowledge that means loss of faith. In the same general period, too, Anna has David's role and Tom has Noah's. Rather oddly, neither of these types is associated at this time with male power, and both, in fact, presage modern decadence.

According to Lawrence's version of biblical and later history, there had been more than one great flood: metaphorically, a "flood" followed David: "the lamps and candles began to gutter" (*RDP* 269). The Renaissance resulted in yet another age of water. In his essay "David," discussed above in chapter 1, he also projects the time after the Renaissance in terms of water: "A new flood. . . . The fire put out, or at least overwhelmed. Then Luther and the North" (*P* 63). The consequences are "equality, democracy, the masses, like drops of water in one sea" (*P* 63) — the modern, industrialized world.

In his changing time, Tom Brangwen, like Will, has felt himself a failure, giving no new cultural gesture to the times but marking his awareness of them by buying all the latest gadgets for Anna. The tide of household "machines" forms a minor but significant

31. The 1925 revision of "The Crown," written after Lawrence had read Heraclitus's ideas, makes the "flux" of the water era still more explicit. On Lawrence's uses of Heraclitus, see Kalnins, "Symbolic Seeing," 173-90. Whelan, *D. H. Lawrence,* 8, discusses Lawrence's use of a Heraclitean "scale" of dry and moist.

32. On useful aspects of the disintegration, see Kinkead-Weekes, "The Marble and the Statue," and Clarke, *River of Dissolution,* 45-69.

motif in *The Rainbow,* proceeding from Tom's purchase of "handy
little things" for Anna (122) through Anna's preoccupation with
the sewing machine in "Anna Victrix" and showing up again in
the "latest improvements" in *Women in Love* (48). In *The Rainbow,*
the old order passes in the flood, just as it had done, according to
Lawrence, at the Renaissance, when Puritanism, dreary moralism,
and leveling democracy overwhelmed the earlier pagan values:
"Christ, with his submission, universal humility, finding one level,
like mist settling, like water. A new flood" (*P* 63). The dance by
Anna/David in *The Rainbow* is an early warning of this shift,
conveying her dissatisfaction with patriarchal power. Ursula's entry
into a sterile civilization comes in the chapter "The Man's World,"
an ironic title: men, having left all their mistakes in place, have
lost their creativity as well as their mastery. "Woman is in flood,"
states Lawrence in his essay "Matriarchy" (1928), about the modern world (*P II* 550). Thus water and moon images continue to be
prominent in Ursula's section of the novel.

It is she who meditates in church on the Genesis passages
about Noah's flood, fantasizing not about the judgment of the
wicked but about the possible survival of ancient mythological
beings: "It pleased Ursula to think of the naiads in Asia Minor
meeting the nereids at the mouth of the streams, where the sea
washed against the fresh, sweet tide, and calling to their sisters
the news of Noah's Flood" (302). As a nymph, Ursula "would have
laughed through the window of the ark, and flicked drops of the
flood at Noah" (302). In passages from the *Rainbow* manuscript,
she thinks about another biblical destruction by water (Matthew
7:27; Luke 6:49): "And the rain descended and the floods came and
the winds blew, and beat upon that house; and it fell; and great was
the fall thereof" (629). But literal floods seem less dire to her than
the threat of her own age, destruction by excessive prudence and
materialism: "But the rain descended and the floods came and the
winds blew, and beat upon that house which the prudent man had
builded upon a rock; and the house stood; and the man within that
house rotted amidst his shelter and security and his having, and
gradually he fell, and petty was the fall thereof" (629). The passage,
revealing that mistrust of houses already mentioned above, under-
lines the idea that the "flood" in *The Rainbow* is a long process of
cultural disintegration.

In a reverie upon a variety of Bible verses, Ursula not only goes
over the passages about Noah's flood but also reviews the charge
of mastery given to Noah and his sons, which prove to have great

significance for this part of *The Rainbow:* "And the fear of you and the dread of you shall be upon every beast of the earth, and upon every fowl of the air, upon all that moveth upon the earth, and upon all the fishes in the sea; into your hand are they delivered" (301). This statement of natural hierarchy comes just as such an order has broken. Tom, whose ancestors "drew the heaving of the horses after their will" (10), must be humble to the horse the night of his death, "ashamed" of driving drunk (227). In Ursula's famous encounter with horses at the novel's end, the equine motif continues, showing the vital animals without masters, gone wild, "running against the walls of time" (452) in a time of broken contacts.

In this world of late Christendom, Ursula repudiates crucifixion in her attachment to a risen Christ of flesh.[33] In fact, the unattributed voice ending chapter 10 ("The Widening Circle"), a first-person appeal of Christ for resurrection, is at least arguably in Ursula's consciousness: "Can I not, then, walk this earth in gladness, being risen from sorrow?" (262). The possibility that this is Ursula's voice is especially compelling in light of the typological precursors of Christ that have heralded her birth. At times, however, she seems to turn to the pre-Christian past even more radically than her mother had done. When her lesbian lover Winifred favors "enlightened" religion and denigrates religions of "power," Ursula can "not help dreaming of Moloch," for God to her is "neither Lamb nor Dove" but "the lion and the eagle" (317), suggesting the churches of the powerful eagle that Lawrence contrasts with those of the meek dove in *Twilight in Italy.* Winifred has identified the followers of Moloch as "ancient worshippers of power," and Ursula is doubtless attracted to them on this account. Thus the two women are divided on the important issue of power, or hierarchy, that becomes an even more prevalent theme in later Lawrence works. In *The Rainbow,* it is clearly interconnected with religious ideas and even with particular kinds of worship.

Of course, Moloch, a condemned pagan god in 2 Kings 23:10 and a demon in Milton's *Paradise Lost,* lies outside both kinds of Christian churches and outside biblical typology. But Lawrence relates Moloch to Jehovah, "the dread Lord" of "the unutterable name" (*CP* 264) in the poem "Manifesto" (drafted in 1916), pos-

33. In the final form of the novel, she strays far from Will's understanding of the *Agnus Dei,* discussed above; for she imagines herself as a lamb held in Christ's bosom, and "she wanted Jesus to . . . take her sensuous offering, to give her sensuous response" (267).

sibly informed by Madame Blavatsky's reference to the two gods together (SD 1:463).[34] Both are employed in the poem to celebrate the power and sacredness of sexual desire, and this meaning is likely in *The Rainbow*, as well, differentiating Ursula's deepest desires from Winifred's and accurately forecasting their parting and Ursula's later experimentation with Skrebensky. For the *Rainbow* reference, Lawrence must have been thinking of Moloch's association with fire, for Milton, following the Bible, describes how the god's sacrifices "pass'd through fire / To his grim Idol," also termed a "burning Idol" and a "furnace."[35] This description forms a strange parallel to Anna's typological fantasy about the child Ursula in the fiery furnace, an image that is echoed when, with Skrebensky, Ursula sees the moon "incandescent as a round furnace door" (443) and offers to sacrifice her lover to it. Such images, I believe, have the alchemical sense of calcination by fire (in this case, by sexual desire) to prove the value of the sacrificed object, as the Hebrew youths in the furnace pass into fire before manifesting their immortality along with the Christ-like figure among them. The furnace motif in *The Rainbow* ranges from Christian to pagan but retains this preoccupation with death and rebirth. Skrebensky's failure with Ursula is not only from some unspecified sexual inadequacy (not necessarily physical) but also from his incapacity to prove himself the powerful immortal of Ursula's expectation. It is a failure related to the fact that Rouen Cathedral proves threatening to him (though inviting to Ursula), and, in another writer, it might be termed spiritual.

Something from Ursula's girlish feeling for Christ carries over into her abiding desire for the Sons of God who, in Genesis, mate with mortal women (Genesis 6:1-4). She is quite conscious of her position in a Judeo-Christian culture, and, in a lengthy passage in the manuscript version, she even calls Jesus "the only perfect lover"—greater than the Greek gods—because he is twice born and familiar with death as well as life (630). In the published novel, however, a similar contrast with the same gods elevates not Christ but the Old Testament "Sons" for whom Ursula, "no Grecian

34. Lawrence's meaning here is almost the opposite of Allen Ginsberg's, whose litany about Moloch in *Howl* is an assault on materialism.

35. Milton, *Paradise Lost* and "On the Morning of Christ's Nativity," in *Complete Poems and Major Prose*, 221 (Book 1, lines 395-96) and 49 (lines 207, 210). Blavatsky, too, describes the fiery sacrifices to Moloch (*Isis* 2:11).

woman," waits: "Not Jove nor Pan nor any of those gods, not even Bacchus nor Apollo, could come to her. But the Sons of God who took to wife the daughters of men, these were such as should take her to wife" (257). Attracted to the prelapsarian world, she thinks that these "unhistoried, unaccountable" sons may have escaped the Fall of Man (257). No doubt their standing as patriarchs is significant, too, for their children were "mighty men . . . men of renown" (257). In her longing for the "essential days" of these sons, she sees the rainbow vision at the end of the book, but even it is not unmixed with a strong element of Christian typology.

Before the final scene, each "shining doorway" has led to a new disillusionment for Ursula, and even a "Pisgah" sight seems to elude her: "Always the crest of the hill gleaming ahead under heaven; and then, from the top of the hill, only another sordid valley full of amorphous, squalid activity" (404). But the rainbow unites the novel's imagery of arcs, arches, and architecture: "The arc . . . arched indomitable, making great architecture . . . its arch the top of heaven" (458). This scene is also the culmination of the symbolism of the Bride and Bridegroom, for it connects with Ursula's previous reliving of the scene in which Christ addresses Jerusalem, wishing to gather it to him. "It was not houses and factories he would hold in His bosom," she knew, but "something else" (266). The Bridegroom's apocalyptic role in the Book of Revelation is appropriate to the final scene's situation, in which a new age is foreseen. As Ursula overlooks Beldover, with its "dark blotches of houses" spread over a hillside, and as she foresees the "new architecture" (458, 459), one is reminded of the earlier passage on Jerusalem. Ursula has some of the role of Christ and is also closely associated with the Bride of Christ. The church before her—"the old church-tower standing up in hideous obsoleteness" (458)—is not the Bride, of course, but a new city is to come as mysteriously as the New Jerusalem.

Lawrence had ample sources for the rainbow, chief among them the Book of Genesis, from which Ursula reads the Noah story. Milton's version in *Paradise Lost* of "a Cov'nant never to destroy / The Earth again by flood"[36] has been particularly influential, and it treats Noah explicitly as a prefiguration of Christ: God makes his covenant because "such grace" in "one just

---

36. *Paradise Lost,* 453 (Book 11, lines 892–93).

Man" causes him to show mercy.[37] In the immediate sense, that
man is Noah, but ultimately, Christ. This typological context
remained in some English writing and graphic art well into the
nineteenth century and even underwent a renewed popularity at
that time.[38] Some Pre-Raphaelites, for example, particularly liked
the typological rainbow, as shown in Everett Millais' *Blind Girl* or
in the early private version of William Holman Hunt's *Scapegoat.*
In the latter, a rainbow surrounds the animal sacrifice, and both
the scapegoat and the rainbow prefigure Christ. (At least, the
animal stands for the Old Law sacrifice that Christ would replace,
while the rainbow signifies the New Law.) Cardinal Newman and
others also represent the rainbow as Christ.[39] J.M.W. Turner's
Day After the Deluge presents a vortex of swirling rainbow-like
colors, showing the reemerging world that, bringing a new epoch,
has Moses in its center with the Tables of the Law. It is likely that
Lawrence was familiar with some of these works, as well as with
medieval and Renaissance iconography, in which the triumphant
Christ sometimes appears in a rainbow-like mandorla (Schiller
2:207). Lawrence's own drawing of a rainbow surrounded by
squalid buildings and colliery stacks—a drawing announcing his
conclusion of this novel (*Letters* 2:299)—not only illustrates the
book's last scene but also suggests his knowledge of the graphic
tradition involving the rainbow.

To the nineteenth century, this image was "problematic," according to Landow, because it functioned in two traditions, one biblical and one secular and ironic. On one hand, says Landow, many
Victorians continued to see the rainbow "as part of an allegorical,
sacramental universe"; others presented it as an ironic image in
scenes of storm and disaster, "not of a universe in which God
rules, but of one in which Nature runs rampant."[40] The image
must have been at least as "problematic" to a writer of the twentieth century. Significantly, however, Lawrence's rainbow stands
within the older tradition, just as he clearly deals here and elsewhere with a "sacramental" cosmos. But he has not omitted the
chaotic "flood," man's wreck of the modern world, standing in
the rainbow's path. This world of man-made flood continues in
Women in Love, even when Ursula meets one of the "sons of

37. Ibid. (Book 11, lines 890–91).
38. Landow, "The Rainbow," 341–69.
39. Ibid., 347–48, 358.
40. Ibid., 348, 353.

God," her own bridegroom, who should be capable of reestablishing hierarchy—at least such as the sons of Noah had. But while Birkin, planning his marriage proposal to Ursula, sees Beldover "like Jerusalem to his fancy" (*WL* 255), this vision goes no further than Ursula's own passing view of the rainbow over the same ruined city.

The Sacred Center

Versions of Ecclesia
in *Women in Love*

3

Despite the enormous dissimilarity of tone between *The Rainbow* and *Women in Love,* the first with its final hope of a utopian order and the other with its numbing disillusionment, the two works are related not only by common characters but also by an increasingly dogged search for the sacred. Even the imagery of the church, already seen in typological contexts in *The Rainbow,* continues in curious forms in the later novel. Kermode has connected imagery and action in *Women in Love* with the apocalyptic New Jerusalem,[1] a parallel that must take its place in a broader typological design. Both novels are, in fact, informed by some of the underlying concepts of temple typology, in which Solomon's temple in the Old Testament prefigures the Christian church and the eventual New Jerusalem prophesied in the Book of Revelation. Associated with this scheme is the idea that God, in prescribing the dimensions of the temple, had revealed principles of the creation itself so that the earthly building could reflect the divinely appointed universe; such a view was prevalent among the cathedral builders of the Middle Ages.[2] Lawrence plays with this idea

1. Kermode, "Lawrence and the Apocalyptic Types," 25-26. See also DiBattista, *"Women in Love,"* 67-90.
2. Von Simson, *The Gothic Cathedral,* 37-39.

of the microcosm in Will Brangwen's view of the cathedral
as "a world," and the idea itself is not entirely dispelled by
the character's recognition that this "world" is an incomplete
one, with the vaster heavens outside it (R 189-91). Though
the old structure becomes an empty form in desperate need of
replacement—partly like Samson's "super-gothic" temple in "The
Revolutionary"—it has clearly been a great image of the cosmos,
"between east and west, between dawn and sunset" (R 187), and
has become obsolete only in the generation of Will and Anna.
Before this, it is fully if unconsciously integrated into life, as
shown in the imagery surrounding the first-generation Brangwens
and the courtship of the second generation. It is therefore never
quite the direct target it seems in "The Revolutionary." Surprisingly,
not even the profoundly pessimistic *Women in Love* quite dis-
penses with church iconography to signify the sacred, which is
evoked by a reference to Southwell Minster in the key chapter
"Excurse."

This novel does, however, present at least two invalid forms of
the church—one the superseded modern institution and one, far
more negative, the parodic colliery-as-church. The first of these is
well illustrated in shallow chatter at the old mansion, Breadalby. "I
must go to church to read the lessons," says one character,
disavowing faith but "keeping up the old institutions" anyway
(99). More surprising is the extent to which, ironically, ecclesiastical imagery informs the description of the Crich mines. A direct
counterpoint is set up between church and colliery, and both
stand in contrast to the awaited church of the future dispensation—
the New Jerusalem.

These contrasting churches suggest the typological motif of
Ecclesia and Synagoga, forms appearing on the Lincoln Cathedral
facade. In biblical typology, the Christian church is often represented
as a beautiful crowned woman, Ecclesia, while Synagoga (the Old
Testament temple in a malign guise after the Crucifixion) is a
blindfolded, sometimes even demonic woman (Schiller 2:110-12;
4,1:51-52, 101-9). While the latter is purported to suffer spiritual
blindness (being blindfolded), the former represents salvation.[3]
Ecclesia is the more complex of the two, functioning not only as
the earthly church but also as the New Jerusalem, the Bride of

3. Sometimes Synagoga is even associated with Christ's betrayer, Judas
(Schiller 4,1:52). That she is also "old Eve" greatly complicates the typology
surrounding her. Despite Lawrence's fondness for the "old" instead of the
"new" Eve, his heroine seems cast in the mold of Ecclesia, not Synagoga.

Christ.[4] In *Women in Love,* both benign and malign churches are embodied, on one level, in the major female characters.

With the entrance of Birkin as a version of Christ,[5] Ursula's own typological role, closely identified with the risen Christ in *The Rainbow,* largely shifts to that of Ecclesia. As Kermode has pointed out, the novel abounds in "sexual eschatology," centering on "two marriages at the end of a world"[6]—the redemptive one between Ursula and Birkin and the purely destructive liaison between Gudrun and Gerald. The combination of marriage and apocalypse is reflected even in the early titles for the novel, originally part of *The Wedding Ring* (with *The Rainbow*) and subsequently *The Latter Days, Noah's Ark,* and *Dies Irae,* for the early marriage theme continued even as the setting increasingly gained the dark coloring of doomsday crisis during the First World War.[7] The combination is especially fitting since, in the Book of Revelation (21:2), the final union between the Bride (the church) and the Bridegroom (Christ) comes at the world's end, when the church as the New Jerusalem descends from heaven in bridal raimant.

I

Irony, if not tragedy, marks the novel's references to this apocalyptic union of the Bride with the Bridegroom to usher in the new order. Too much can be made of this symbolism, for the novel has a surface of verisimilitude; but, since the underlying esoterica are its most neglected features, they need emphasis. These biblical types rightly seem "allegorical" at some level, but Lawrence has, in his usual fashion, fleshed them out creatively even while retaining something stylized and impersonal in the characters, something continually suggesting that they "mean"

4. The *Sponsa,* depicting the mystical bride of the Sponsus (based on the Song of Solomon), forms a particular iconographic model of its own; appearing in the twelfth century, she was early seen as Ecclesia but later was often represented as Mary (Schiller 1:24; 4,1:94–116).

5. See, for example, Doherty, "The Salvator Mundi Touch," 58–66, discussing Birkin in the tradition of Jesus and other seers.

6. Kermode, "Lawrence and the Apocalyptic Types," 20, 26.

7. See David Farmer, Lindeth Vasey, and John Worthen (*WL* xxiii, xxxi) and Lawrence (*Letters* 3:183).

more than their fictive roles explain. Kermode, too, has found that even apparently trivial details in the novel support an apocalyptic pattern.[8] Further complicating such allusions in *Women in Love* is the creative revision of them by which Lawrence achieves irony and paradox. Despite Birkin's claim at one point that Beldover looks like Jerusalem,[9] the novel opens with the signal failure of the New Jerusalem to materialize. A major early setting is outside the local church at a wedding in the Crich family (pronounced, after all, as in "Christ"). Will Brangwen plays the organ inside (and the reader of *The Rainbow* remembers him tending the organ, though he is "vacant" after his loss of faith), while Ursula and Gudrun witness the wedding party from a spot beside the churchyard. This graveyard location, combined with Ursula's first-page statement that marriage may represent not experience but "the end of experience" (*WL* 7), seems to cast a pall over the wedding activities.

Adding to the peculiarity of the scene is the repeatedly emphasized fact that "the bridegroom had not come" (15). Lawrence is playing allusively with the biblical story of the wise and foolish virgins awaiting the Second Coming of the divine Bridegroom at the world's end. As "the bridegroom tarried" in this parable of Christ, the foolish virgins slept, and their untrimmed lamps went out so that they were unready when "a cry" went up, "Behold, the bridegroom cometh" (Matthew 25:5, 8, 6). In Christian iconography, Ecclesia and Synagoga are sometimes paralleled with the wise and foolish virgins (Schiller 4,1:52). Ursula, in her "place of vantage," is like a watchful virgin who notices the groom's absence with great anxiety—feeling "almost responsible"—and hails his approach with "an inarticulate cry": she "wanted to warn them [the wedding guests] that he was coming" (17-19).

Standing in contrast to the responsive Ursula is the bridesmaid Hermione Roddice, the overintellectualized "villainess" of the novel, in her usual "almost drugged" condition, blinded (as if blindfolded)

8. See Kermode, "Lawrence and the Apocalyptic Types," 18, noting that "sometimes his [Lawrence's] allusions are so inexplicit that only if you are a naive fundamentalist (in which case you probably won't be reading Lawrence) or are on the lookout (in which case you are reading abnormally) will you pick them up."

9. Similarly, Lawrence's "Autobiographical Fragment," written in 1927, describes how, as a boy, he could see his native Eastwood as Jerusalem: "I had looked up and seen the squares of miners' dwellings, built by the Company, rising from the hill-top in the afternoon light like the walls of Jerusalem" (*P* 829).

by her affectation "not to see the world" (15). Whenever she is
separated from Birkin—who, as best man, is absent along with the
bridegroom—she is a figure "established on sand" (17) like the
biblical house that cannot stand because it is not built on the rock
(Matthew 7:24-26, Luke 6:48-49). In the exegetical tradition, the
rock is, of course, Christ, and the allusion sets up a correspondence between Christ and Birkin. This connection is furthered in
Hermione's idea that he could shelter her from "this fretful voyage
of life" and "make her sound and triumphant, triumphant over the
very angels of heaven" (17).

The description of this triumph recalls a standard iconographic
image of Ecclesia crowned in heaven (Schiller 4,1: 95-96), an
image suggesting a parodic identification between Hermione and
the church triumphant. In the manuscript version of this opening
chapter, she is "like an unlighted candle" (514), and it is not too
much to see her as an unwatchful virgin, without her lamp for the
Bridegroom's coming. This meaning remains beneath the surface
of the chapter's final form. Hermione, not quite asleep but "dazed"
during the ceremony, eventually leaves the church (with Birkin)
as a rather hellish figure, "like the fallen angels restored, yet still
subtly demoniacal" (21, 22). Hermione appears later in the novel
with her eyes "full of sepulchral darkness," "like a priestess,"
developing "a drugged, almost sinister religious expression" (89,
91, 106); she precedes Gudrun as the novel's malign woman,
Ursula's opposite. If she is not Synagoga, she is at least a peculiar
and inverted version of Ecclesia.

While the Crich wedding in the first chapter fails to relieve
Hermione's trance, it makes a far different impression on Ursula.
Hearing the bells, "Ursula wondered if the trees and the flowers
could feel the vibration, and what they thought of it, this strange
motion in the air" (22). This exaggerated impact of the ceremony
suggests its symbolic importance. On the realistic level, however,
the church ritual is conventional and trivialized. Afterward, one
character scoffs because another has wanted to discuss the immortality of the soul before the ceremony: "Oh God! The immortality
of the soul on your wedding day! Hadn't you got anything better to
occupy your mind?" (31) The exchange harks back to Tom
Brangwen's wedding speech in *The Rainbow* about the angel
formed by the married souls of a man and a woman, and the echo
deepens the irony in the later novel.

Birkin's role as "groom's man," easy to dismiss as an incidental
detail, is in fact as meaningful as Ursula's part as the watchful

virgin. Lawrence is employing a doppelgänger device, somewhat like that examined earlier in "The Border Line," so that
Birkin is a generally positive "Christ figure," while Gerald is a
negative one. Thus Birkin enacts a pattern of death and rebirth
in which his "marriage with [Ursula] was his resurrection and
his life" (369). At the same time, he helps to initiate her into
symbolic rebirth.[10] Sometimes it is hard to tell which of the two is
more like Christ and which like Ecclesia, for they are saviors to
each other.

Ursula identifies Birkin, albeit unflatteringly, with a famous
iconographic stance of Christ, the *Salvator Mundi,* often associated
with the symbolism of the Bride and Bridegroom (Schiller 4,1:57).
Ursula's allusion is a rather sarcastic one because she dislikes this
strain in Birkin—that of a would-be savior, a kind of "Sunday-
school teacher" (130); the term is doubly ironic because the
Salvator Mundi, the Savior of the World, stands triumphant over the
entire globe (Schiller 3:134), while Birkin is generally ineffectual.[11]
Another apparent irony lies in Ursula's flippant association of the
couple's love with the Ark of the Covenant, the typological prefiguration of the Christian altar that is so prominently incorporated
into *The Rainbow.* She mocks Birkin's desire to be the only one
who can mention love, who can "take it out of the Ark of the
Covenant" like a priest (130). Even references of this kind, however,
set off reverberations that are more than ironic, and not all references to Birkin's priestly office are so easy to dismiss. He is once
seriously likened to "a church service": "Gerald must always come
away from Birkin, *as from a church service,* back to the outside
real world of work and life" (232; my emphasis). Despite Lawrence's
quarrel with Christianity, his hero and heroine seem ultimately
linked to Ecclesia.

Meanwhile, although Birkin and Ursula are associated with
church imagery, it is the Crich family that most obviously suggests the negative main course of Christendom. The Crich mines
are strangely described as an ecclesiastical center, one in total
opposition to the religious faculty embodied in Birkin and Ursula.

10. See Doherty, "The Salvator Mundi Touch," 62–66, and Kermode,
"Lawrence and the Apocalyptic Types," 22. But see also Balbert, *D. H. Lawrence
and the Phallic Imagination,* 85–108, showing the importance of Ursula's
"female corrective" to Birkin's pretensions.

11. The globe beyond which (or on which) Christ stands as the *Salvator
Mundi,* the Bridegroom, sometimes has Jerusalem (the Bride) at its center,
where Golgotha was (Schiller 3:134), emphasizing the redemption.

The very names of Gerald's parents, Christiana and Thomas, signal their allegorical function. In this case, unlike that of the second-generation Brangwens in *The Rainbow,* it is the woman who suggests the older order in the church, the Dionysiac churches of power. Likened to a hawk and an eagle in her wild pride, Christiana has been tamed and caged by her husband, the doubting but pious Thomas, the mine-owner whose religious experience lies only in obsessive charity work. In contrast to his wife, he rejects the principle of hierarchy that goes with the churches of power—"churches of the eagle," as Lawrence calls them. "To move nearer to God," the mine-owner thinks, is to be close to his workers, and "he wanted to be a pure Christian, one and equal with all men" (215, 226). Seeing the mines as "primarily great fields to produce bread and plenty" for the workers, he is the dispenser of "great basketfuls of buns and cakes" to schools (224, 226)—apparently a decadent version of Christ's feeding the multitude (Matthew 15:32–38; Mark 8:1–9) or of Moses' feeding the Israelites with manna (Exodus 16:15–35)—New and Old Testament events that typologically correspond to each other, both looking forward to the Mass (Schiller 2:25).

Thomas Crich's abstract materialism on behalf of the masses evidently characterizes Christendom in a very late form, flaunting its shallow and undiscriminating beneficence while losing all sense of power and splendor. The next stage is that represented by Gerald's mechanization of the mines. The changes in the colliery system illustrate, therefore, the historic process discussed in *Twilight in Italy:* "The new spirit" after the Renaissance, says Lawrence, denied divine mystery while aggrandizing mankind as a social aggregate in which the individual must be self-sacrificing. Proponents of this view proceeded, however paradoxically, to erect the most "inhuman" object of which they were capable, the machine. Their "worship of mechanised force" was the ultimate expression of a "religious belief" (*TI* 40). In *Women in Love,* too, Thomas's mines embody "a religious creed pushed to its material conclusion" (225). Going even beyond this stage, Gerald's reforms carry out for the miners of his generation "the religion they really felt" (231). As Thomas's dispensation yields to Gerald's, even the humanistic sanctuary is replaced. The father can retain his "beautiful candles of belief" only "in the inner room of his soul" (229). Although he is not really likened to a church, he is perhaps something like a small, individual chapel. Such description plays upon a typological tradition in which the individual soul is a microcosmic temple,[12] but Lawrence means to show that a microcosm lacking contact with a macrocosm is an empty business.

The colliery takes on the character not only of a church but of an entire cosmology, complete with a new hierarchy, a degrading, monolithic form of twentieth-century feudalism. It inverts temple typology by which the sanctuary is a model of the cosmos; this counterfeit temple or church, by being itself an artificial cosmos, conceals the real cosmos rather than revealing it. The man-made machine—with its human cogs—is "the Godhead," and "the most mechanical mind" is "the representative of God on earth" (225). Beneath him are engineers, then managers, then colliers in the varying degrees to which they fit into the machine's productivity. In an essay of 1919 ("Fenimore Cooper's Anglo-American Novels"), written for the *English Review* while Lawrence was still working on *Women in Love,* he specifically deplores such a situation, even in contrast to "the old aristocratic system"; for the new ethos produces only "lords of material production," and false values become the only measure of stature: "Though no man is [considered] higher than any other man, intrinsically, still, some men are superior *mechanically.* Some men are more productive *materially* than others. . . . Let *money* rule" (*SM* 84, 85; emphasis mine). As the creator of such a new system in the novel, Gerald is likened to the sun of the solar system, with the workers as the satellite planets (227) and the motion of the machine as the turning of the universe:

> [Gerald] found his eternal and his infinite in the pure machine-principle of perfect co-ordination into one pure, complex, infinitely repeated motion, like the spinning of a wheel; but a productive spinning, *as the revolving of the universe may be called a productive spinning,* a productive repetition through eternity, to infinity. And this is the God-motion, this productive repetition ad infinitum. And Gerald was the God of the Machine, Deus ex Machina. And the whole productive will of man was the Godhead. (228; my emphasis)

The colliery is explicitly under a "high priest," a place of worship that represents "a new world, a new order" (231). In *The Rainbow,*

12. See, for example, Galdon, *Typology and Seventeenth-Century Literature,* 136–38.

too, the colliery at Wiggiston is the parodic counterpart of the cathedral — a "proud, demon-like colliery with her wheels twinkling in the heavens," a "monstrous mechanism that held all matter, living or dead, in its service" (*R* 324, 325).

As in *The Rainbow,* so the more insistently in *Women in Love,* the sinister colliery-as-church expands its offices outward into the world at large, as shown, for example, when Gerald surveys his kingdom like a feudal lord — or even like a parodic Christ looking over Jerusalem, perhaps counterpointing Birkin's view of Beldover (and Ursula's at the end of *The Rainbow*): "He [Gerald] looked at Beldover, at Selby, at Whatmore, at Lethley Bank, the great colliery villages which depended entirely on his mines. . . . Four raw new towns, and many ugly industrial hamlets were crowded under his dependence" (222). Just as industry has replaced the cathedral, technological skill has prevailed over creativity. Thus the degraded sculptor Loerke, in the novel's last tragic days, can blatantly assert the wholesale desacralization of architecture and art, stating that churches are only "museum stuff" and urging that the factory, therefore, be "our Parthenon" (424). The temple, the cathedral, the shrine are supplanted by such mechanistic centers of worship.

II

Opposing the false sanctuary, however, is a medieval minster that, placed in the novel's most significant context, recalls the cathedrals of *The Rainbow.* This is Southwell Minster, near which Birkin and Ursula first exchange their private vows before marriage. In the shop windows of the old cathedral town, "the golden lights showed like slabs of *revelation*" (312; emphasis mine), only one of numerous hints that the Bride and Bridegroom are uniting, as in the Book of Revelation. But the couple's encounter with the old religious structure, while an important one, is brief; the chapter "Excurse," describing it, is meaningfully entitled, for the two characters are simply driving past a monument that, though it brings them under a kind of spell, exerts little or no power in the world at large.

Nevertheless, here Ursula finds her religious background, so extensively detailed in *The Rainbow,* transformed and in some ways fulfilled. In the previous book, of course, she has longed for

"the Sons of God [who] saw the daughters of men that they were
fair" (R 256)—the otherworldly beings of the Book of Genesis. In
Women in Love, she recalls "the old magic of the Book of Genesis,"
Lawrence noting that "she had found one of the Sons of God from
the Beginning, and he [Birkin] had found one of the first most
luminous daughters of men" (312, 313). Less obvious, perhaps, is
the fact that Ursula's longing for Jesus in the earlier novel is at
least partly fulfilled in Birkin's similitude to Christ. At one time,
he looks down at her as if haloed, "with a rich bright brow like a
diadem above his eyes" (313), and, during their lovemaking, Ursula
gains "riches" derived "from the smitten rock of the man's body"
(314). This passage is already much analyzed for its anatomical
curiosities,[13] but it requires a more symbolic interpretation in
the light of biblical typology. The "smitten rock" is the one from
which Moses obtained water—prefiguring Christ, the rock from
which came water and blood, as celebrated in the Mass. The
couple's union is therefore likened not only to the apocalyptic
marriage but also to the Eucharist. In line with such imagery,
their contact reverses the expulsion from paradise, for Ursula
experiences "the knowledge which is death of knowledge" (319).
Both speech and sight yield to the sense Lawrence considers more
primal, touch: "She would have to touch him. To speak, to see, was
nothing" (319). Even beforehand, Birkin thinks of marriage with
her as "the Paradisal entry" (254). Later, as the two leave England,
her heart seems to glow with "the effulgence of a paradise unknown
and unrealised" (388), like paradise regained, identifying her with
the redemptive pattern for the "new Eve" even while developing in
her the instinctive qualities of the "old Eve."

Birkin, too, undergoes transformation through Ursula. She has
some properties of "the woman clothed with the sun" in the Book
of Revelation (12:1), a figure representing Mary or the church
(Schiller 4,2: 174-77). As mentioned earlier, Lawrence eventually
shows a certain liking for this figure, seeing in her, beyond the
Marian guise, a great cosmic goddess (A 120)—probably Isis, an
identity claimed by many comparatists, including Blavatsky (*Isis*
2:489). If Ursula is indeed like this divinity (and she is associated
extensively with light imagery), Birkin can be seen as "the initiate
into the mysteries of the goddess," as Sarah Urang believes.[14] But

13. Miles, "Birkin's Electro-Mystical Body," 194-212, sees Yoga as the key
to the puzzling passages. See also Knight, "Lawrence, Joyce and Powys,"
403-17, with the influential claim that the sexuality in "Excurse" is anal.
14. Urang, *Kindled in the Flame,* 64-66.

Ursula is presumably purged of the dangerous fires of the Magna Mater, which Birkin has attempted to stone in the image of the moon on water, and their most intimate moments are often associated with darkness, as when they seem embodiments of the night—"the night masculine and feminine"—during their union near Southwell Minster (320). In the sea passage to the Continent, too, when Ursula feels paradisal bliss, they are encompassed in soothing darkness.

They achieve a hierogamous marriage, one uniting vast symbolic opposites, the universal feminine and masculine, light and dark, earth and heavens, thus completing the cosmos between them.[15] According to Kermode, their conjunction synthesizes Old Testament Law and New Testament Love.[16] The minster setting is in keeping with such diffuse sacred significance. After Birkin gives Ursula three rings that, to Kermode, recall the jewels of the New Jerusalem in the Book of Revelation,[17] the two continue a countryside drive that leads eventually to an old inn. From the car, Ursula recognizes Southwell, where the bells play an evening hymn on "the blessings of the light," thus emphasizing the union of opposites, of night and day: "So, to Ursula's ear, the tune fell out, drop by drop, from the unseen sky on to the dusky town. It was like dim, bygone centuries sounding.... This was no actual world, it was the dreamworld of one's childhood—a great circumscribed reminiscence" (312). The density of the time perspective in the couple's transporting experience embraces not only Ursula's personal past (the childhood) but also that of her dreams (the primordial days of Genesis) and that of the cathedral, to which her upbringing as Will Brangwen's daughter has served to introduce her. This evocation of the past becomes even more complex as the couple enters Sherwood Forest, itself providing a religious ambience even more ancient than that of the minster; for, as in a Druidic grove, "the palish, gnarled trunks showed ghostly, and like

15. Hinz, "Hierogamy versus Wedlock," 900–913. See also Hinz's *"The Rainbow,"* 27, suggesting hierogamy in *The Rainbow.*

16. See Kermode, "Lawrence and the Apocalyptic Types," 20, discussing the new dispensation for the "elect": "A mark of this elect will naturally be the new man-woman relationship: for the woman was law and the man love, and just as these two epochal ethics will be transformed in the third, so will the two Persons, Man and Woman, be, under the new dispensation, merged in a new relationship, and yet remain distinct."

17. Ibid., 25–26.

old priests in the hovering distance, the fern rose magical and
mysterious" (319-20).

If the location is not precisely a church, yet it is clearly one of
the rare places that Lawrence elsewhere designates as "quick"
spots of the earth, sacred centers adapting themselves age after
age to successive expressions of religious feeling. Like the "quick
spot . . . still not quite dead" at Monte Cassino, discussed in his
1922 memoir of Maurice Magnus, these sites frequently accommodate Christian cathedrals or monasteries, illustrating how the
church adjusted itself, on occasion, to pagan centers of worship
like temples and groves. Thus the minster in *Women in Love* joins
the famous church centers of *The Rainbow* — Lincoln, Southwell,
and Rouen — to signify ongoing religious needs and faculties. While
these centers are shown to be outmoded, they are never replaced
by anything else as good, and they serve as qualified examples of a
vital cultural continuum. In *The Rainbow* and *Women in Love*,
they are, in fact, directly contrasted to the obscene counterfeit
churches of the collieries. Faced with a choice between a cathedral and a colliery, no Lawrence reader should long doubt which
to prefer.

This is particularly the case when one building involved is
Southwell Minster. In *Sons and Lovers*, Paul Morel had celebrated
Norman arches, like those at Southwell.[18] In *The Rainbow*, Will
Brangwen, too, with particular warmth, had touted Southwell's
sedilia, north porch, and main body, waxing especially appreciative of its Norman arches, earlier than High Gothic: "It's got
heavy, round arches, rather low, on thick pillars. It's grand, the
way those arches travel forward" (*R* 106). Ursula, as an adult, had
also visited Southwell. It fits well into Lawrence's celebration of
eclectic centers of worship because it contains features that suggest ties with pagan nature cults. According to the art historian
Alec Clifton-Taylor, Southwell is well known for its reproduction
of natural leaf forms in the sculpture of the chapter-house, "giving
the impression that the sculptors . . . stepped out into the surrounding fields and woods and came back with freshly gathered
branches to serve as their models" (141-42). Lawrence was probably aware, too, of the carving of a pagan fertility figure, the Green
Man, among these leaf sculptures; representing "the tree-spirit"
important in ancient fertility rites, the image was allowed to

18. See, however, note 65 to my introduction, where I point out that Paul's
preference is too readily accepted as one endorsed by the author.

flourish in cathedral decoration despite its pagan origins.[19] At any rate, the background minster has the curious effect, in *Women in Love,* of seeming almost like a ruin, allowing focus upon the nearby forest. The site is more than a romantic backdrop, however; it is also one of the main symbols highlighting the major characters' association with the Bride of Christ (the church) and the Bridegroom.

III

Birkin and Ursula do not live their lives, of course, on this high allegorical level, and we see their attempts to cope with the blighted world of their time. Between themselves, they arrive at some of the adjustments necessary to secure a modicum of cosmic order in their private lives. In *The Rainbow,* an important aspect of the Noah myth is God's charge to the sons of Noah to maintain the natural hierarchy, and *Women in Love* echoes the same biblical passage quoted in the earlier novel.[20] Discussing dominance over animals, Ursula states, "I must say that, however man is lord of the beast and the fowl, I still don't think he has any right to violate the feelings of the inferior creation" (143). Alluding to Genesis 9:2, she is commenting on Gerald's earlier abuse of his horse (forcing the sensitive creature to stand by a passing train), thus indicating how far removed he is from the true masters of earlier, unmechanized times. The idea that the horse has, as Ursula states, "as much right to her own being" as does a human (139) is related to Lawrence's view that each being that achieves its true individuality fills its place perfectly and is, in the cosmic context, "a nonpareil" and "beyond comparison," regardless of its relative rank—though it does have this rank (*RDP* 358).

Some of Birkin's speeches are closely related to several of Lawrence's essays, delineating a chain of being in which living things are related to one another in degrees of natural aristocracy. In the 1919 *English Review* essay on Fenimore Cooper, cited earlier, Lawrence approves the organic chain, calling each of its members "a term of godhead": "But the deepest social truth about

19. Clifton-Taylor, *The Cathedrals of England,* 144.

20. See chapter 2 above, quoting from Genesis 9:2, as incorporated in *The Rainbow:* "And the fear of you and the dread of you shall be upon every beast of the earth, and upon every fowl of the air."

men is that some are higher, some lower, some greater, some less, some highest, and some lowest, even in the sight of the everlasting God" (*SM* 84). This essay praises the old aristocratic system for acknowledging these distinctions but faults it for basing them on the purely hereditary principle. These statements clearly forerun Lawrence's later outline of natural hierarchy in "Aristocracy." Explaining relative rank according to "the degree of life," he represents a daisy as "more alive," less "torpid," than a fern; a bee as "more alive" than a daisy; birds as "higher than bees: more alive"; and so on (*RDP* 367). In somewhat similar fashion, in *Women in Love*, Birkin discusses with Ursula the status of daisies: "Don't the botanists put it highest in the line of development?" (131). But when he rather cynically identifies the daisy with democracy and the proletarian mob, Ursula protests this analogy with "hateful social orders," and he agrees: "It's a daisy — we'll leave it alone" (131).

These matters of dominance are very much in question at times in the novel. It is actually Gerald who refers to the "natural order" in connection with man's mastery of the horse (139), but he misunderstands the sources of this power. It is left for Birkin to trace the chain of creation to its ancient source in deity — a creative power that can foster or dispense with man's mastery altogether. "God can do without man" and can replace him with other life forms, believes Birkin, "just as the horse has taken the place of the mastodon" (478, 479). This antianthropomorphic view directly opposes the creed of the colliery-church, in which man is the godhead. Of course, it is Gerald who loses every vestige of his mastery in his own extinction, reminding Birkin of "a dead stallion" (480), while Birkin, on the other hand, survives yet finds it "consoling" that the universe does not depend upon man for its continuation: "The fountainhead was incorruptible and unsearchable. It had no limits. . . . To be man was as nothing compared to the possibilities of the creative mystery" (479).

The novel's issues of hierarchy also involve male and female relations, particularly in the "star-equilibrium" that Birkin advocates (*WL* 319) and that Ursula, not without justice, first sees as a scheme of master and follower. Whatever its shortcomings, this relationship is part of a complex dual view: on one hand is the uniqueness of individuals, balanced on the other hand by their necessary interrelationship. Birkin imagines the bond with Ursula as one "which accepts the obligation of the permanent connection with others, and with the other, submits to the yoke and leash of love, but never forfeits its own proud individual singleness" (254). When explaining the principle by which creatures wish to "resign [their] will to the higher being," he has mentioned how difficult it is "to domesticate even horses, let alone women" (141), and this line is only partly a joke. Birkin later, in the chapter "Mino," tries to instruct Ursula by getting her to observe how a female cat is mastered by a male. But the model for the relationship he wants is really biblical and patriarchal, and it thus affects the typological pattern I have already outlined in the couple's search for a restored Eden. When Ursula refers to Birkin, with some hostility, as the "old Adam," he accepts the epithet, replying, "Adam kept Eve in the indestructible paradise, when he kept her single with himself, like a star in its orbit" (150). While protesting this hint of the "satellite," Ursula does eventually accept some of her husband's views on the paradisal relationship, for she tells Gudrun that she and Birkin have a tie "out of the Unknown" that "isn't so merely *human*" as love (438). According to more than one critic, "star-equilibrium" is only a glorified term for the ugly subservience of woman to a male "higher being." In fact, however, it *is* more than this.

Women in Love is a significant text on matters of dominance because it shows that the uncomfortable "power" theme of later works like *Aaron's Rod, Kangaroo,* and *The Plumed Serpent* arises from a sense of metaphysical loss. Birkin clearly desires to supply the lack of old cosmological views, those perverted or lapsed in his world at large. This is why he refers to "the unseen hosts, actual angels" and "good pure-tissued demons" (128), somewhat recalling the world picture of Fra Angelico's *Last Judgment* in *The Rainbow.* Gerald's tragic failure to relate to Gudrun, to Birkin, and even to his workers is really his inability to find a place in the chain of creation. The natural ties Birkin perceives form the Lawrentian counterpart to the mechanical hierarchy already seen in the Crich mining system. The ultimate lack of relationship between Gerald and Birkin is multiply disquieting because Gerald has what Birkin as preacher and seer needs—a public structure, a church (for the colliery is now, after all, a church). The two men might have combined their complementary strengths; instead, however, the false priest presides over a false temple, while the truer prophet stands entirely outside of a sanctuary.

Besides presenting cathedral and colliery as the embodiments of rival religious views, *Women in Love* also manifests elements of temple imagery in the late section dealing with Loerke, Gudrun,

and Gerald. If Ursula represents the positive form of Ecclesia,
Gudrun is herself more like Synagoga—being cast as a shrine of
sorts, but a dangerous and malign one. As she shifts her interest
from Gerald to Loerke, Crich is "left behind like a postulant in the
ante-room of this temple of mysteries, this woman," while Loerke
can "find the spirit of the woman in its inner recess" (451). In "the
house of her soul" is something hellish: "a pungent atmosphere of
corrosion, an inflamed darkness of sensation" (451). Says Loerke,
"Between the *religion d'amour,* and the latest 'ism,' and the new
turning to Jesus, one had better ride on a carrousel all day"
(458).21 This remark is in keeping with his wish to turn the
machine and its locations, industrial centers, into the new temples.
He and Gudrun are finally worshipers of "the obscene religious
mystery of ultimate reduction" and "diabolic reducing down"
(452),22 and, as they seek to create their own world, they are "the
god of the show" (453) as Gerald is the god of the colliery. According to Doherty, Loerke is the anti-Christ or "pseudo-seer" to Birkin's
Christ.23

Even clearer and more tragic associations exist, however, between
Gerald and Christ. The strongest of these arises in his death scene
as he encounters a crucifix in the Alpine snows, "a little Christ
under a little sloping hood, at the top of a pole" (473), and gives up
his life in spite of the near presence of a Marienhütte that could
save him. This structure is Lawrence's own invention (in the
actual setting he describes, an inn is in its place),24 and he clearly
wishes to establish its symbolic importance. Christendom, or some
significant part of it, is at an end. Despite the saving setting of
Southwell Minster, therefore, the novel's picture of ecclesiastical
sites is in general a devastating one. The church setting of the first
chapter is conventional and hollow, the final shrine deadly. Neither Gerald's colliery nor the old, supplanted church institution
represents a New Jerusalem; faith is finally unhoused altogether,
having its centers solely in the lone hero and heroine whose only
contact with a sacred structure occurs on a passing excursion.

It is significant, nonetheless, that their retreat from the snowy
north is Italy—and that Gerald chooses to freeze beside the north-

21. Farmer, Vasey, and Worthen (*WL* 582) gloss "the new turning to
Jesus" as a reference to the French movement in neo-Catholicism.
22. Like the sex act in "Excurse," this "reducing" has often been discussed.
See, for example, Ford, *Double Measure,* 196–97.
23. Doherty, "The Salvator Mundi Touch," 67.
24. See Farmer, Vasey, and Worthen (*WL* 583).

ern crucifix rather than take the old Imperial Road that, like the Marienhütte, is near the site of his death. His rejection of a southern option is particularly fitting in view of the frequent meaningfulness of Italy in Lawrence's works. Ursula thinks of it as a fruitful relief from the frozen Alps: "towards the south there were stretches of land dark with orange trees and cypress, grey with olives" (434). Whatever else it is in Lawrence's works, Italy is a church center, and this role is emphasized in *Women in Love* by the combined details of the crucifix, the shelter of Mary, and the road of the old Holy Roman Empire. In *Twilight in Italy,* Lawrence states: "The worship of the Cross never really held good in Italy. The Christianity of Northern Europe has never had any place there" (136). At the novel's end, though, even Birkin wonders if it is "any good going south, to Italy," along "the old, old Imperial Road" (478). This doubt gives the conclusion an added pessimism, closing even a customary escape route for Lawrence's characters. *Aaron's Rod* more pointedly probes the Italian milieu for its life potential, revealing some remnants of inspiration in monuments of medieval and early Renaissance Florence — the cathedral and Giotto's Tower — but, on the whole, finding Italy lacking despite some once-vital sacred and civic centers.

Women in Love, besides sharing with *Aaron's Rod* a system of "embedded" ecclesiastical centers and their symbolism, has a secondary typological pattern in common with the latter novel — that of the tree of life. As part of his end-of-the-world negation of humanity, Birkin has lamented that people are "apples of Sodom," stating that, with mankind gone, "the real tree of life would then be rid of the most ghastly heavy crop of Dead Sea Fruit" (126, 127). The entire scheme of man's fall from Eden through the apple of knowledge, his continued sin (as in Sodom and Gomorrah), and his redemption (through the renewed tree of life) also looms large behind some earlier Lawrence works, already considered. Still more specialized tree imagery comes, though, when Gudrun is given a particularly Lawrentian feature of the tree of life: Loerke is able to contact "the central serpent that is coiled at the core of life" in her (451). This reference could recall a standard image of Synagoga, sometimes entwined in the folds of the evil serpent of the tree of knowledge (Schiller 4,1:51),[25] but it is more typical of

---

25. Another related image is that of the *Arbor mala,* tree of vices, associated with Synagoga and paired with the *Arbor bona,* tree of virtues, associated with Ecclesia (Reeves and Hirsch-Reich, *Figurae of Joachim of Fiore,* 25).

Lawrence's imagery of tree and serpent for the innermost life force, *kundalini,* already associated in criticism with the renovatory sexuality between Birkin and Ursula and employed in *The Man Who Died, Lady Chatterley's Lover,* and elsewhere.[26] In *Women in Love,* it is clearly ominous that the corrupt Loerke has access to this ultimate center in Gudrun. The image itself calls for our attention because it represents Lawrence's intensifying interest in variants of the tree of life, to be discussed in greater detail in chapters 4 through 6.

26. Lawrence knew of the inner "serpent," *kundalini,* in Yoga largely from Pryse's *Apocalypse Unsealed,* 39, 97 passim. See also Tindall, *D. H. Lawrence and Susan His Cow,* 149-57; Miles, "Birkin's Electro-Mystical Body," 194-212; and Doherty, "The Salvator Mundi Touch," 53-71, and "Connie and the Chakras," 79-92.

The Rituals

The Unflowering Staff
in *Aaron's Rod*

4

In the wake of the First World War, Lawrence's disillusionment deepened, causing him to assert with new urgency that Christendom had gone sterile—unflowering and unfruitful. *Aaron's Rod* takes its title from the rod, or staff, of Aaron and Moses that, in biblical typology, blossoms to herald the birth of Christ (Schiller 2:136).[1] It forms a special instance of Lawrence's symbolism of the tree of life, and he eventually equates it with Florence Cathedral, furthering his use of church sites in the major novels. But this is

---

1. Other analogues to this flowering rod include those of the Renaissance "wild man" and the pagan "Green Man," or "Jack in the Green," that often survived in church roof-bosses and other sculpture (as mentioned in chapters 1 and 3) and those in the legends of Tannhäuser and of Joseph of Arimathea. In the former tale, a knight of the Middle Ages cannot be forgiven his pagan liaison with Venus unless a clerical staff blooms—as it does, but too late to prevent his return to her. Lawrence knew and praised the version by Richard Wagner (*Letters* 1:99) and might well have been attracted to the tale's illustrated version by Aubrey Beardsley, *Under the Hill.* Joseph of Arimathea, said in legend to have carried the Holy Grail to England after giving a tomb to Christ, is associated with a flowering staff similar to that of Aaron and Moses or that of Joseph, the spouse of the Virgin Mary. See Cavendish, *King Arthur and the Grail,* 181. Lawrence would have been familiar with part of Joseph of Arimathea's story, though not the flowering staff, from Jenner, *Christian Symbolism,* 63.

only a past florescence, and Aaron Sisson's rod — his flute — proves futile to help renovate or replace that past. *Aaron's Rod* is Lawrence's most clearly typological title, and the novel fulfills the promise this raises, though in unexpected ways. In biblical typology and in medieval and Renaissance iconography, Aaron's rod is frequently associated with the Nativity, for it shares much with the Jesse tree (Schiller 1:15), depicting the human descent of both Mary and Christ; but it is a symbol of patriarchal power, as well. Beyond these meanings is its place in the *Eucharistia,* for it was in the Ark of the Covenant along with a golden manna-pot (Hebrews 9:4), both related typologically to the Mass. Throughout this novel, unlocalized eucharistic patterns, often but not always detached from the church setting, abound in irony and are partly replaced by a new pagan sacrament.

In the Old Testament, the staff of Aaron, Moses' brother, put forth the almond flower as a sign of his election to priesthood, and the exegetical tradition extended this incident into a type of the coming of Christ. Descending from the house of Levi, Christ was to be the fulfillment of the Passover sacrifice (Schiller 2:124-28).[2] The rod thus looked forward, it was claimed, not only to the Nativity but also to the Crucifixion. The description of the almonds in Numbers 17:8 — "Behold, the rod of Aaron for the house of Levi was budded, and brought forth buds, and bloomed blossoms, and yielded almonds" — is echoed in Hebrews 9:4, referring to "Aaron's rod that budded" among the most sacred objects in the Jewish tabernacle, where the high priest (beginning with Aaron) shed sacrificial-animal blood for the sins of all the people until Christ became high priest and offered his own blood, as commemorated in the Mass.

The staff is also associated with temporal power. According to rabbinic legend, Aaron's rod belonged to every ancient king of Israel and was "destined to be in the hand of the King Messiah."[3] This almond staff obviously has similarities with that of the Adamic Renaissance "wild man," discussed in chapter 1, for both suggest patriarchal authority. In addition, Aaron's (and Moses') staff provided the Israelites with power over their enemies by turning miraculously into a serpent that devoured the Egyptians'

2. See also Yarden, *The Tree of Light,* 40-43. For more details on the typology of Aaron and the rod, see, for example, Hoefer, *Typologie im Mittelalter,* 68-69, 170, and Schiller 1:15-21.

3. Yarden, *The Tree of Light,* 37.

own serpent-rods (Exodus 7:9-12);[4] by turning waterways to blood (Exodus 7:17-22); and by producing plagues of frogs (Exodus 8:5-7), lice (Exodus 8:16-18), locusts (Exodus 10:13), and thunder, hail, fire, and darkness (Exodus 9:23, 10:22). All these plagues led up to the smiting of the firstborn sons of Egypt, an occasion on which the Israelites were spared because their doors were marked with the blood from Aaron's animal sacrifice (Exodus 12:12-13, 21-27). Shortly after, Moses used the rod to divide the Red Sea and allow the Israelites to pass through toward the Promised Land, while the Egyptians drowned (Exodus 14:16). Still one more important use of the rod released water from the "smitten rock" of Horeb (Numbers 20:8-12), thus relieving drought and at the same time looking forward to the sacraments of baptism and the Eucharist, as discussed in my introduction.[5]

Because *Aaron's Rod* is a "leadership novel," in which Aaron frees himself from matriarchal bondage and his friend Lilly attempts to establish a male hierarchy, the rod's masculine aspect is paramount in it. In typology, however, its identification with Mary's virgin womb is even better known (Schiller 1:15), and Lawrence turns this symbolism, too, to ironic advantage. Isaiah 11:1 states that "there shall come forth a rod out of the stem of Jesse, and a Branch shall grow out of his roots," and that rod, through identification between *Virgo* and *virga* (rod),[6] is Mary, thus giving special prominence to the virgin birth. In medieval art depicting Christ's birth and genealogy, Aaron often appears with the flowering staff in his hand (Fig. 8). It is also related, iconographically, to a rod offered to God by Joseph, as a suitor for the hand of the Virgin Mary; this rod buds, often with lilies, suggesting the imminent coming of Christ. Lawrence could have known of this usage from his interest in Giotto's fresco cycle in the Arena Chapel, Padua. These paintings include the scene that Lawrence himself copied from a print, *Joachim and the Shepherds* (Fig. 9), depicting an incident in the life of Mary's father, and another, the *Marriage*

4. Although serpents have little place in *Aaron's Rod* (beyond Aaron's sense that his wife Lottie is snake-like), they are increasingly important in Lawrence's middle period, standing for male potency and earthy sensual consciousness.

5. The striking of the rock came to symbolize, typologically, the paradox of crucifixion and renewal (Schiller 1:130, 2:23). See also my introduction.

6. See Reeves and Hirsch-Reich, *Figurae of Joachim of Fiore*, 25. Not Bible genealogy but this similarity between words explains Mary's depiction on the Jesse tree.

of the Virgin, with a famous representation of Joseph's flowering rod (Fig. 10).[7]

In *Aaron's Rod,* the Nativity, represented ironically in the opening Christmas scenes, fails to develop. Even marriage and sexuality prove barren, for, Lawrence suggests, children do not contribute to a new life-style but only solidify the old. The time scheme posits a passage from Christmas to Easter, but the references to both holy days are all but lost in a tide of negativity and nihilism. Matriarchy is in full sway, and men lack leaders. The situation resembles that in Lawrence's later essay "Resurrection": "Since the War, the world has been without a Lord" (*RDP* 233). It is not surprising, therefore, that ironic eucharistic imagery is particularly prevalent—and particularly hollow—in this novel, in which death still blocks life.

I

Lawrentian typology informs *Aaron's Rod* in several ways. First, two Old Testament precursors of Christ, Aaron the priest and Moses, appear embodied in Aaron Sisson and Rawdon Lilly. Second, an even more prevalent motif of a secularized Mass bears out Theodore Ziolkowski's comment that the typological object, when divorced after the nineteenth century from traditional faith, often "takes on . . . essentially playful significance."[8] Finally, the tree or plant motif originates in the title and recurs throughout the novel. The flowering staff, Lawrence's metaphor for Aaron Sisson's flute, is an image that, along with references to the trees of Eden and to the cross, dominates the text significantly.

The fact that Aaron opens "his darkest eyes" and falls "from the tree of modern knowledge" (151, 164) identifies him with Adam, awakening to primal consciousness. Critics correctly see Lilly fundamentally as a Moses in relation to Aaron—a complex and

---

7. In John Ruskin's popular illustrated volume *Giotto and His Paintings in Padua,* in *The Works of John Ruskin,* 24:50–64, these two paintings are represented in woodcuts II and XI. Somewhat surprisingly, Lawrence did not seize the opportunity of including a shepherd's rod in his own copy of *Joachim and the Shepherds* despite the fact that the Giotto original contains one.

8. Ziolkowski, "Some Features of Religious Figuralism," 354.

Fig. 9. *Joachim and the Shepherds,* watercolor painting by D. H. Lawrence (c. 1915), apparently copied from a print of Giotto's fresco in Arena Chapel, Padua.

Fig. 10. *Marriage of the Virgin* by Giotto di Bondone (c. 1305), Arena Chapel, Padua.

shifting relationship discussed in detail by Paul G. Baker.[9] George Ford, for example, thus demonstrates persuasively that Lilly, rubbing Aaron's lower body with oil during an illness, "anoints" him in a curiously Lawrentian version of the biblical Aaron's consecration to the priesthood.[10] But Lilly's role as a kind of prophet should not obscure Sisson's more important typological association with Christ, for he is himself the "new Adam," in that he is the most prominent of several Lawrentian "Christ figures" suffering from postwar malaise and spiritual aridity. His biblical name, his age (thirty-two), his journey — all fulfill criteria for what Ziolkowski calls a "fictional transfiguration of Jesus";[11] but beyond these rather scattered details, a far more complex typological scheme unfolds for him. Although Lawrence abandoned his idea of sending the character to a monastery,[12] Aaron sets out on a Christmas Eve pilgrimage that takes him eventually to Lawrence's city of David — Florence, with Michelangelo's famous sculpture as its "genius." Here begins a process in which Aaron encounters or incarnates a series of typological figures directly reflecting his changing identity.

Significantly, his rod/flute ultimately fails. As John Worthen remarks, this novel manages to remind the reader of "all the things it ignores and perverts and glosses over,"[13] and nowhere is this more true than in the treatment of the rod. Aaron's flute and piccolo may parody the trumpets used by the Old Testament priesthood during public rites (Numbers 10:1–10), but it is part of the novel's ironic design that they gather no congregation, raise no general alarm, and inspire no social action. Rather, the flute forms a phallic image suggesting Pan and the wind instruments traditional to him,[14] for Aaron's most decisive success as a musician is in the conventional function of Pan as a sexual charmer. During his affair with a neurotic singer in Italy, the flute is repeatedly called a "pipe," underlining a change in his musical repertoire — from Christmas melody to the "quick wild imperiousness of the pipe" (253). This change partly reflects the increas-

9. Baker, A Reassessment, 46–60.

10. Ford, Double Measure, 135–36.

11. Ziolkowski, Fictional Transfigurations of Jesus, 223–27.

12. See Achsah Brewster, in D. H. Lawrence, ed. Nehls, 2:58–59, reporting Lawrence's intention of ending Aaron's pilgrimage at Monte Cassino, the Italian monastery the novelist visited in 1919.

13. Worthen, D. H. Lawrence and the Idea, 135.

14. On the connection between the flute and Pan, see, for example, Baker, A Reassessment, 90–91, 145.

ingly pagan identity he regains, but the romantic episode turns out to be a mistake, casting irony on the phallic references. The destruction of the flute late in the book, during an anarchist riot, is "symbolistic" (285) because it precludes any vital annunciation to the deadened culture and also because it implies the limits of the "love urge" even in its erotic form.

In spite of social and sexual losses, however, Aaron does gain a measure of personal rebirth. While his painful marriage has represented a kind of crucifixion, like that of Will Brangwen in *The Rainbow,* he ultimately avoids further martyrdom. His desertion of his wife, family, and job is the fictional dramatization of the author's idea that the modern Adam, domesticated and deprived of power, must "un-tame himself" (*STH* 205). After Aaron's original rejection of a walking death at home—"life-automatism" (162)—and a later battle with physical death (from influenza) in London, he journeys into Italy, where he begins to feel a new identity. Italy serves as the reservoir of a "spontaneous life-dynamic" (152), freeing him from the deathliness of mental-spiritual consciousness and reviving his deep instinctual faculties. This is where he falls from "the tree of modern knowledge," gaining Adam's faculty of "knowing, but making no conceptions" (164). In keeping with the author's partly mythic view (and a qualified view) that "the substratum of Italy has always been pagan" (*TI* 136)—relatively primitive, outside the industrialized world—the character must absorb aspects of his Italian setting and its past for his Lawrentian renewal.

In Florence, for instance, he meets a figural type face to face: David (by Michelangelo), "standing forward stripped and exposed and eternally half-shrinking, half-wishing to expose himself . . . the genius of Florence" (211). Marguerite Beede Howe's statement on this scene—"In the image of David, Aaron is recreated"[15]—takes on a new complexity when considered in terms of Lawrence's revisionary typology. I have shown that, in the play *David,* this biblical precursor of Christ is less representative of the "old Adam" than is the more primitive, Dionysian Saul;[16] and in *Aaron's Rod,* too, the archaized statues of Bandinelli, signifying "undaunted physical nature" (212), somewhat like the Renaissance "wild man" art, impress Aaron almost as much as David does. But the Michelangelo statue, subject of the essay "David" that Lawrence evidently wrote in 1919 while working on this novel, represents more to

15. Howe, *The Art of the Self,* 26.
16. See chapter 1.

him at this time than the Old Testament type *or* its antitype alone;
it embodies a fragile balance between flesh and spirit, paganism
and Christianity: "For one moment Dionysus touched the hand of
the Crucified" (*P* 63). Somewhat faulting the statue's "Christ-like
submissiveness," thus underlining its typological element, the
essay nonetheless finds the two great opposites "proportionate" in
the Florentine David (*P* 63). It affirms the potential for the "fulfilled
self," which must be syncretic—comprised neither of "the frail
lily" of Christ nor of "the clinging purple vine" of Dionysus but of
both together in "the full tree of life in blossom" (*P* 64). The same
paganizing touch of Dionysus (or Pan) comes for Aaron, allying
this novel with works in which Lawrence's preoccupation with
both Christ and Dionysus/Pan is more obvious: works from *The
Ladybird* (1923) through *The Plumed Serpent.*[17] Aaron, already
associated with Pan by his flute, now contacts Dionysian faculties
inherent in the *David* statue. These are in keeping with the
Davidian power mode that Lawrence had once admired in the Old
Testament king but later found lacking in him. Given the author's
eclecticism, it is no surprise to find him evidently playing with the
tradition of Pan as a pagan type of Christ as well as that of Pan or
Dionysus as a foil to Christ.[18]

In *Aaron's Rod,* orthodox and heterodox elements combine
with great complexity. After all, Florence Cathedral itself, representing the novel's one great social flowering, consists, says Lilly,
of "earth-substance, risen from earth into air: and never forgetting
the dark, black-fierce earth" (232). With the blossoming plant as
the book's central metaphor, it is noteworthy that only here does
Aaron encounter "fearless blossoms in air . . . the cathedral and
the tower and the David" (232). Aaron senses that the flowering
phase of the civilization, the moment when the Middle Ages
moved into the early Renaissance, was genuinely creative, and he
sees the buildings as monuments to the communal activity of
men: "Here [in the Piazza della Signoria] men had been at their
intensest, most naked pitch, here, at the end of the old world and
the beginning of the new" (212). While the flowering is that of an
earlier epoch, the old cathedral still retains some of its past power
for Aaron. Its sounding bell, "felt in all the air" (211), is the

17. Lawrence refers to Pan even in his first novel, *The White Peacock*
(1911), but his more complex usage occurs in a later "cluster," as traced by
Merivale, *Pan the Goat-God,* 194–219.

18. On Pan's relation to Christ, see, for example, Korshin, *Typologies in
England, 1650–1820,* 5, and Merivale, *Pan the Goat-God,* 12–47.

sensuous counterpart to earlier silent or unattended bells and signals his continuing growth as "a new man" (212).

Whether or not he fully succeeds at resurrection may forever be in doubt, but he goes far in that direction. Counseled at last, by the sermonizing Lilly, to locate the "Easter egg" (295) and the "Tree of Life" (296) in himself, Aaron, far more than his companion, seems likely to be doing so. Critics generally see Lilly as Aaron's leader or potential leader, and his very name seems to argue for his importance. The lily is the emblematic flower of Florence, and its cathedral is even termed a lily in the novel. Moreover, Joachim of Fiore used the lily to symbolize the coming third age of the Holy Ghost;[19] and, while Lawrence may not have known this rather obscure detail from Joachim himself, he could have encountered a nineteenth-century adaptation of it. In spite of Rawdon Lilly's own desire for a new age, however, I see irony in his auspicious name. A self-parody of Lawrence the preacher, he seems far more associated with the old Logos than does Aaron, who has explicitly escaped "the verbal" (152). The "wordless" faculty—"utterly previous to words"—is one particularly associated with Lawrence's Adamic strain (*STH* 205) as well as the Panic, in which "speech is the death of Pan" (*P* 27). Thus Aaron is a musician whose "very thoughts were not composed of words and ideal concepts" (164), a trait allying him with the Lawrentian image-thinkers and symbolists discussed in my introduction. Although Lilly hints that Aaron's "soul" will eventually make him a true disciple, the novel's problematical leadership question becomes almost moot when Aaron, apparently uncommitted, still speaks "rather sarcastically" to Lilly near the book's end (291).

II

Told in a brief outline, the story of *Aaron's Rod* sounds reasonably cheerful; in fact, it gives a bleak picture of its world. The knowledge that Aaron's rod is traditionally a harbinger of Christ's birth may puzzle the reader because the novel apparently presents no such fertility and lacks a sense of optimistic celebration. The barren Christmas Eve opening initiates a theme of the evident death of Christendom, at least in Aaron's English home. The

19. Reeves and Gould, *Joachim of Fiore*, 24, 162, 227.

Nativity bell, a mere tree ornament, "made no sound" (9). A blue heirloom Christmas globe, apparently symbolizing the world as mankind has long known it, is willfully destroyed, leaving "the curious soft explosion of its breaking"; and carolers come, "pouring out the *dregs* of carol-singing" (11; emphasis mine). Even when Aaron takes up the flute to play a Renaissance Christmas melody, the "finely-spun peace-music" only frustrates him (13). Like other features of his milieu, the melody is from a defunct epoch and thus simply establishes the discrepancies between his world and its origins. Like the Christmas tree ball, the world has exploded; yet, "the war over, nothing was changed" outwardly (11), and the old forms of society continue with dead automatism, joined now to a displaced war spirit among materialistic shoppers. The holyday eve, which the Brangwens of *The Rainbow* experienced with diminishing "ecstasy" (*R* 260), is now far more obviously reduced to a secularized occasion of avarice and barren tradition. The Nativity portends no real birth for society or its individuals. Rather, it recalls a cultural stillbirth like that described in Lawrence's essay "The Crown": "The war is one bout in the terrific, horrible labour, our civilisation . . . unable to bring forth" (*RDP* 290).

Despite two Christmas trees in the first three chapters—the Sisson tree and a lighted outdoor tree nearby—neither one embodies the flowering rod of nativity or the flowering cross of resurrection; reflecting the condition of modern Christendom, they may be associated metaphorically with the barren tree, the cross. This is in spite of the fact that the second tree recalls, ironically, Moses' burning bush,[20] a type of Christ's birth (Schiller 1:71), and the pillar of fire that led the Israelites on their trek to the Promised Land (Exodus 13:21–22). This column of "perpendicular" flame (33), which guides Aaron on the initial night of his pilgrimage, is the object of a dance ritual "to worship the tree" (32); however, its decadent celebrants try in vain to be "sufficiently naive" (31) and never succeed in recalling either its vital pagan origins or its Christian significance. Aaron's rod itself, metaphorically a branch belonging to the tree motif—"a reed, a water-plant" (285)—finally seems culturally stalemated. By the time the flute is bombed, even the casual reader recognizes the inversion of a creative ambience into one of emptiness and destruction. "The War was the Calvary of all real Christian men," Lawrence writes later, so that the "Lord" is absent on earth (*RDP* 233).

20. Baker, *A Reassessment,* 47.

It is, therefore, not surprising that, in postwar *Aaron's Rod,* the dead Christus has metaphorically replaced the more vital "Lord." The sole explicit mention of this crucifix image occurs when Lilly pronounces the body of Christian ideals "dead": "I'm sorry," he says, "for any Christus who brings him to life again . . . the beastly Lazarus of our idealism" (281). The Lazarus/Christus combination is assimilated throughout the book to eucharistic images. As successor to the rites over which the biblical Aaron had presided, the Mass is not only to expiate sin but also to instill new life in the believer; in this novel, its office pointedly fails. For instance, Jim Bricknell, an English mining heir, obsessively eats "hunks of bread" and drinks wine while professing sententiously, "I reckon Christ's the finest thing time has ever produced" and prating that "love and sacrifice are the finest things in life" (76–77). Precisely this ideal of self-sacrificing love is repugnant to Lawrence. Lilly protests to Jim that he, Lilly, does not really "believe bread's any use" for a person who, like Jim, feels himself continually "losing life"; and Lilly urges further, "You don't want crucifixions *ad infinitum.*" Jim's attitude, termed "modern Christ-mongery" (78), not only emphasizes the sacrificed Christ but also conflates Jesus with Judas, his sacrificer—and Jim proves, in fact, to admire Judas. As the modern advocate of the Christus/Judas/Lazarus figure, he insists that bread puts "something inside" him, to fill an apparently metaphysical void, and claims that only through burgundy or love does he now gain the "inrushes" of life once common to him (77, 80–81). Now "only love brings it [life] back—and wine" (80), in combination with bread.

Nor is this parody of the Eucharist an isolated feature of the novel. Later, in Italy, an effeminate young English Georgian—whose name is the Germanic Franz, anglicized Francis, now the Italianate Francesco—seems a latter-day St. Francis, rolling his eyes from the effects of "a bottle of Lacrimae Cristi" (189). Christendom, having passed through the northern Reformation and the Anglican via media, seems drawn, in the person of this young Oxford man, back to the earlier church center at Rome. But the pilgrimage of this minor "Christ figure," somewhat caricaturing Aaron's, is no more vital than effete sight-seeing, fashionable effeminacy, and wine tasting can make it.

In Milan Cathedral, an actual celebration of the Mass seems simply another tourist attraction—almost, however, recalling the eerie atmosphere of the absurd ritual in the chapter "The Cathedral" of Kafka's *The Trial:*

> Aaron came to the side altar where mass was going on,
> candles ruddily wavering. . . . All [visitors] strayed faintly
> clicking over the slabbed floor, and glanced at the flickering
> altar where the white-surpliced boys were curtseying and
> the white-and-gold priest was bowing, his hands over his
> breast, in the candle-light. All strayed, glanced, lingered,
> and strayed away again, as if the spectacle were not suffi-
> ciently holding. The bell chimed for the elevation of the
> Host. But the thin trickle of people trickled the same,
> uneasily, over the slabbed floor of the vastly-upreaching,
> shadow-foliaged cathedral. (182)

It should be portentous that the namesake of Aaron the high
priest here observes the direct representative of the antitype, but
the keynote of the scene is hollow disillusionment. The very
symbols of priesthood — the clerical garments, the bell, the sacrifice,
all originating with the biblical Aaron and forerunning those of
the later Christian ritual — should suggest the antitype's holiness
and majesty, yet precisely these qualities are lacking. The bell is as
futile as the toy one of the first chapter; perhaps recalling ironically the original Aaron's golden bell (Exodus 28:35) or his silver
trumpets used to summon people together, this bell is as ineffectual as the modern Aaron's rod. The Milan Cathedral setting is
noteworthy, for Lawrence was probably aware that it was the
supposed repository of Aaron's rod itself.[21] Whether he knew of
the relic or not, however, he shows the cathedral as a reliquary.
The city, too, has about it "a curious vacancy . . . something empty"
(180). The one really commanding procession goes on in the
streets in a violent clash between a mob of workers and the
trumpeting Carabinieri.

From his detached location of Italy, Aaron finally realizes that
he himself has been like a martyred Christus in his marriage.
Thus even his desertion of his wife proves related to the deadly
modern celebration of the antitype: "Why, of course, in our long-
drawn-out Christian day, man is given and woman is recipient. . . .
This is the sacrament we live by; the holy Communion we live
for" (165). While his wife has had the ostensible role of a
loving madonna, her will has actually been "like a flat cold snake
coiled round his soul and squeezing him to death" (161). Still,

21. See, for example, Evans, *Animal Symbolism in Ecclesiastical Architecture,* 287.

"she did but inevitably represent what the whole world around her asserted: the life-centrality of woman," for men "yield the worship to that which is female" or, contrariwise, "profane the god they worship" without breaking free of their bondage (159). In the later essay "The Risen Lord" (1929), Lawrence comments that the war shattered the image of the "all-pitying, all-sheltering Madonna, on whose lap the man was enthroned, as in the old pictures" (*PII* 572). This image has been irretrievably broken in *Aaron*.

His affair with an Italian marchesa proves especially complicated, for the two are locked in a conflict for gender dominance; and Aaron is also involved in idolatry like that practiced by his biblical namesake with a molten image, a golden calf (Exodus 32:4-6). The appropriately named Marchesa del *Torre* is described as a gilded monument, glistening "metallic" and seeming "as if she were dusted with dark gold-dust" (249). The "red Florentine lilies" of Aaron's "rod," a metaphor for his passion and rising potency, suggest to him "male godhead" (258), but this proves a dangerous identity. He finds again that a woman uses him with "amazing priestess-craft" in "terrible rites"; in fact, this accomplished femme fatale "would drink the one drop of his innermost heart's blood, and he would be carrion" (273). Such is the manipulative "new Eve," subtly combining, in this case, with Cleopatra, who "killed her lovers in the morning" (273), and with Venus, subject of the Botticelli painting Aaron discusses with the lady (250-51). The red lilies, besides denoting the official flower of Florence, probably suggest Adonis anemonies (called lilies), commemorating the violent death of Adonis — a death caused and mourned by Venus in a myth that Lawrence mentions in *The Lost Girl* (1920), commenting forebodingly on the "vindictiveness" of classical spirits in the Italian air (333-34); the allusion in *Aaron's Rod* increases the sense of danger for the protagonist as a "God and victim" (273). The image of the blooming rod also recalls a clerical staff that blossoms in the Tannhäuser legend, apparently offering forgiveness to a Christian knight for his sexual dalliance with the pagan Venus.[22] Of course, Aaron the priest was not condoned in his idolatry with the golden calf, and Aaron Sisson feels self-condemned in his destructive liaison. The "flowering" he has sensed is strictly ironic.[23]

22. See Hill and Woodberry, "Ursula Brangwen of *The Rainbow*," 274-79, on the Tannhäuser myth and a cognate to it in *The Rainbow*.
23. The version Lawrence certainly knew, Wagner's (note 1 above),

Aaron's difficult task is to avoid the doom of the dying gods while securing their potential for rebirth. Atypically for Lawrence, Aaron's renewal is not to be achieved through erotic experience but through repudiation of it. In this novel, it seems, the proper Adamic model is not only before the Fall but altogether before Eve. If the biblical Aaron's fault is to create and worship a mere statue in place of Jehovah, the modern Aaron's corresponding mistake seems to be to continue his love-worship of the false god, woman. Lilly has explained that the "love-urge" and the "power-urge" create and thrive on different kinds of relationships between man and woman. In the former, "the man is supposed to be the lover, the woman the beloved"; in the latter, however, "it is the reverse": "The woman must now submit—but deeply, deeply, and richly!" (298). The novel suggests that Aaron Sisson needs, in fact, to be more like his patriarchal namesake, more seated in the pagan "power-urge," which can be independent of woman. "Aaron's black rod of power" (258), which he feels when aroused by the marchesa, is not only a phallic image but also a reminder of the scepter-like staff by which Moses delivered his people from Egypt and assumed patriarchal leadership shared by Aaron the priest. Sisson, in turning his manhood only to phallic play, perpetuates the uncomfortable gender relations he has earlier escaped and makes no gesture toward a new age. Perhaps the most ludicrous hint of a Nativity scene occurs after Aaron's loss of his flute, when Lilly, as if midwifing him, accuses him of malingering "in bed like a woman who's had a baby" (290).[24] This curious passage refers to Aaron's need to give birth to himself anew after the loss of his sexual partner and the flute that had charmed her. It has no broader application, despite the worsening situation and greater need in the society at large. Thus Lilly still urges his own leadership, a claim that fails partly at the level of typological imagery: since the novel provides him with no tangible "rod" or staff at all, he lacks even Aaron's connection with the "rod of power."

The institutionalized Mariolatry of *Aaron's Rod* is linked to the excessive mental consciousness of the modern world. According to the Italian marchesa's husband, the church no longer fosters

---

separates the lovers but unites Tannhäuser with a more moral and orthodox match, certainly far from Lawrence's design for Aaron.

24. Howe, *The Art of the Self,* 92, sees a "couvade" in one scene in which Lilly aids Aaron during influenza.

women's old (submissive) role in relation to men—a role needed
"so that with their minds they [women] should not know, and
should not start this terrible thing, this woman's desire over a
man, beforehand.... *This is Eve*" (243; my emphasis). Thus,
what Lawrence calls sex in the head (*F* 169) unwholesomely
confuses man's ancient temptress with the "new Eve," leaving him
no identity but that of victim or "host" in "the holy communion
we live for." Aaron's troubled relationships with women show
his recoil from this final stereotype of himself, one that gives
new meaning to Judith Ruderman's reference to "the devouring
mother."25 Hence the pervasive death imagery of the Mass in
Aaron's Rod.

Perhaps the most striking example of such a death image appears
in his strange dream in the novel's final chapter. Supposing that
he is in an underground location like a mine, he witnesses a grisly
ritual: "In one of the great square rooms, the men were going to
eat. And it seemed to him that what they were going to eat was a
man, a naked man. But his [Aaron's] second self knew that what
appeared to his eyes as a man was really a man's skin stuffed tight
with prepared meat, as the skin of a Bologna sausage" (286). One
recalls the previous references to the dead—"the beastly Lazarus
of our idealism," which Lilly calls "dead as carrion," and Aaron's
apprehension that "he would be carrion" in a communion ritual.
In the human effigy, Aaron sees both his own dead, automated self
and that of his entire society—just as the location, a mine, recalls
his own previous Midlands job and suggests, besides, the entire
postwar industrial world. The death-committed society thus eats
the effigy of its own lack of essence—a materialistic cannibalism
that somewhat suggests St. Paul's description of one who, receiving the sacrament without proper belief, chews only its carnal
elements and "eateth and drinketh damnation to himself" (1 Corinthians 11:29). As the Judeo-Christian continuum of Aaron's time
is shown to lack vitality, its sterile perpetuation of old conventions
merely compounds its self-damnation. It was while Lawrence was
working on *Aaron's Rod,* in 1919, that he stated, in one of the
Symbolic Meaning essays, that people no longer know the "profound,
passional *experience*" of the Eucharist to mediaeval peasants (*SM*
222). It is this passional loss with which he most taxes the modern ritual.26

25. Ruderman, *D. H. Lawrence and the Devouring Mother.*
26. Many of Lawrence's uses of the eucharistic motif suggest Jung's

Aaron's cannibalistic dream, like the opening Christmas milieu, evokes a parodic Nativity scene. Wandering through a vast nursery, Aaron sees a host of children who—though cherubically flower-wreathed and dressed in white gowns (286)—represent the continuation of their elders' underground tradition and not a new dispensation. Lilly and Aaron have agreed earlier about modern children: "we know well enough what sort of millions and billions of people they'll grow up into" (99), for they will only swell "the mass" (perhaps a true pun), which is rigidly unaware of the deathliness within itself. A letter Lawrence wrote to a friend in 1916 throws further light on this subject. Many wartime women, he states, have only "a new crop of death in their wombs," for there must be "a new *flower* in us before there can be a new seed of a child" (2:636). The trouble in *Aaron's Rod* is the failure of the responsible generation to "flower" into newness of life.

The "grey" miners in the dream are the same colorless figures seen in *The Rainbow* and *Women in Love* as dehumanized automata at industrial centers like Wiggiston Colliery and the Crich mines. They are like the inhabitants of the hideous city at the end of *The Rainbow*—those in whom Ursula still hopefully foresaw the emergence of an organic "rainbow" even though she had earlier found them "like spectres" in a deathly setting (*R* 320). It is disquieting that Aaron, who, metaphorically, should bear the flowering rod of renewal, sees even less hope of regeneration for them now. Ironically, despite Italy's many benefits to him, *Aaron's Rod* records that "Italy becomes as idea-bound and as automatic as England" (152), and he may have to renounce Europe altogether.

As he proceeds in his dream to a voyage away from the deadly ritual, Aaron's "invisible" self watches as his visible self is repeatedly scourged by stakes (287-88). In Italy he has developed the "invisible presence" (164), the resurrecting man, which still seeks to free him completely from the blows of his victimage. The scene ingeniously combines the "old" and the "new" Aarons, the type and the antitype; at length, both seem to arrive at a new location— perhaps Mexico, where an Astarte idol holds eggs in her lap. The significance of this female deity is not clear, and possibly ominous, but the eggs seem likely symbols of a new start; they may suggest

discussion of the Mass: *Psychology and Religion*, in *Collected Works*, 11:203-96. See, for example, comparisons with pagan sacrificial rites, including Aztec and Mithraic (222-25), and "The Vision of Zosimos" (225-46).

"the egg of resurrection" that Lawrence finds in Etruscan wall paintings — a symbol in which he sees the soul in the tomb "before it breaks the shell and emerges again" (*EP* 45).

III

The novel counters its parody of the depleted modern Mass and the reign of the Christus with Aaron's revitalizing communion with natural and prehistoric forces. Transmuting the opening motif of the barren tree is his strategic encounter with Tuscan cypresses late in the novel. The cypress is important to Lawrence at this time in his canon, for he also introduces it in a key position in *Birds, Beasts and Flowers*. Writing of this poetic image, Gilbert finds in it a singular mythic significance: not only "the death tree," the cypress looms in its cosmology "as if it rose straight from the breast of hell";[27] and, in the novel's related description — written while Lawrence was planning the poem "Cypresses"[28] — it has a cosmic quality, as well. On one level, in fact, it is related to the tree of knowledge and the cross; yet it is not ultimately a deathly image. To Aaron, the cypresses seem to be "communicating," possessing "dark, *mindful* silence and inflection" (265; my emphasis). They are even seen "as it were walking," apparently echoing a biblical description of "men as trees, walking" (Mark 8:24). The biblical account is by a blind man regaining his sight, and Aaron, similarly, is retrieving a lost faculty.

The cypresses are not simply features of the mundane temporal setting but are the repositories of "lost races, lost language, lost human ways of feeling and of knowing." Standing like priests, "like so many high visitants from an old, lost, lost subtle world," they evoke an ancient religious order. Far from being trees of death, they are filled with "*life*-realities" (265; my emphasis); in fact, the word *life* recurs seven times in a nine-line passage on them. As the postlapsarian mental knowledge is metamorphosed back into the lost form of knowing, the cypresses offer something like a dark, sensuous parallel to the Christian "communion of saints," which unites the living and the dead during the celebra-

---

27. Gilbert, "D. H. Lawrence's Uncommon Prayers," 87.
28. See Rosalind Thornycroft Popham, in *D. H. Lawrence,* ed. Nehls, 2:49, telling how Lawrence wrote the poem at this time.

tion of the Mass; thus Aaron feels direct contact with the "lost
races." The trees in the poem "Cypresses," discussed further in
chapter 5 below, are related explicitly to the Etruscans, who communicate nonverbally through them. Such vital trees, with their
fiery pentecostal voices, are only parodied in *Aaron's Rod* in the
barren Christmas tree, with its false "tongues of flame" (33).
Earlier, in London, when Aaron had encountered trees like "some
wild dark grove" (69), he was unable to respond to the pagan past,
but he is now fitted to open himself to it, at least momentarily. The
interlude with the cypresses is crucial to the novel's typological
pattern, for in it the tree of death becomes once more the tree of
life. The "lost races" suggest not only Etruscan prehistory but also
the tribal time of Aaron, the prelapsarian world of Adam, and the
golden age of Pan, whose double flute Lawrence notes elsewhere
in Etruscan cave paintings (*EP* 39); all share in that dark and
intuitive awareness to which Aaron is exposed.

   This is not to say that he fully demonstrates the sensual fulfillment that Lawrence eventually associates with Etruscans; for the
novel's shrill misogynistic strain precludes the sexual balance
represented symbolically in the Etruscan tombs, which display
phallic stones, womb-like arks, and crosses of Aphrodite (*EP* 14-15,
65). Christopher Pollnitz suggests persuasively that the Etruscans
of "Cypresses" and *Aaron's Rod* should be associated not with
the heterosexual vitality that Lawrence later claimed for these
ancient people (*EP* 39-42) but with their reputed celebration of
men's solidarity and "maleness."[29] Hilary Simpson, too, finds
that *Aaron's Rod* is about "masculinist consciousness-raising."[30]
Ironically, even as Aaron progressively makes peace with himself
and the world, he is increasingly detached from others—especially,
of course, women. It remains for symbols, such as the egg in
Aaron's dream, to suggest the further dimension of Lawrentian
development.

   One of these symbols, the cypress—given its pentecostal imagery
—may suggest, in fact, the coming epoch of the Holy Spirit forecast by Joachim of Fiore in his extraordinary tree imagery. According to Marjorie Reeves and Beatrice Hirsch-Reich, Joachim's trees
may have been influenced by the Jesse tree but symbolize in their
branches not only Old and New Testament figures but also a
future beyond both, that of the Holy Spirit: "his trees of the

   29. Pollnitz, " 'Raptus Virginis,' " 124-26.
   30. Simpson, *D. H. Lawrence and Feminism*, 63.

generations mark a new departure, for . . . they grow on up into the new era and lift their heads to their final flowering at the end of history," which marks the beginning of the new age.[31] A tree image near the end of *Aaron's Rod* similarly suggests transformation within time. Lilly tells Aaron that one's "own Tree of Life" is the Holy Ghost that "puts forth new buds, and pushes past old limits, and shakes off a whole body of dying leaves"; although the change may seem unpleasant, it must come "if the tree-soul says so" (296). Using an almost Joachimite combination of the tree, the Holy Spirit, and temporal growth, the passage may recall the millennial context of Joachim's trees, changing it to refer not to a universal event but to a lone individual experience. It is the measure only of Aaron's personal growth.

Although his "male godhead" proves illusory, his "black rod of power," likened to "Jove's thunderbolt" (258), relates him obliquely to Lawrence's "dark gods." Underlying these powerful figures, wherever they appear in his canon, are assumptions about theocratic powers of the ancient world — ideas that are not far from the surface in the last chapters of *Aaron's Rod*. Lawrence's works on Etruria help to clarify this stratum of the novel. Etruscans had known, he believed, that "the centre of all power was at the depths of the earth" and had been aware of "the quick powers that run up the roots of plants and establish the great body of . . . the tree of life" (*EP* 107). (One is reminded of the novel's description of Florence Cathedral as a plant with its roots in "black-fierce earth.") This earthy "blood-consciousness" of the Etruscans bound them communally to the cosmos, to each other, and even to other cultures. This is why the poem "Cypresses" refers not only to the Etruscans but also (puzzlingly, at first glance), to Montezuma. *Etruscan Places* later brackets together Etruria, Egypt, Babylonia, Assyria, and the Mayan and Aztec "lordships of America," claiming that they had all shared in the universal religion of Atlantis and adhered to a strict system of hierarchy in which the Etruscan *Lucumones*, for example, were "religious seers" and "god-kings" (*EP* 31, 74), as was Montezuma himself in his own location.

In the background of *Aaron's Rod*, such lordly individuals are

31. Reeves and Hirsch-Reich, *Figurae of Joachim of Fiore*, 28. It is most unlikely that Lawrence could have seen the graphic designs since they were little known in his time; but Joachim's images, like the lily symbol mentioned above, had been transmitted in various forms by others, making it possible that Lawrence was unknowingly (as well as knowingly) influenced by the abbot.

apparently joined by ancient Africans, whom Lilly, reading a book
by Leo Frobenius, associates with Atlantis and "the world before
the flood" (110). According to Daniel J. Schneider, Frobenius's
appeal to Lawrence (and presumably to Lilly), lies in his focus
on the power of the *Adjes,* or priests, and the *Oro,* or social
structure featuring men, in the ancient Yoruban culture, which
Frobenius associates with Etruscans, New World Indians, and
the inhabitants of the lost Atlantis.[32] These claims, which Lawrence evidently read in 1918, must have confirmed him in his
earlier reading of Madame Blavatsky's arguments for a universal
secret doctrine. At any rate, Frobenius may help explain why,
in *Birds, Beasts and Flowers,* "once God was all negroid" (*CP*
286); in *Quetzalcoatl,* Cipriano/Huitzilopochtli is dark, almost
"like a negro" (345); and, in *The Boy in the Bush,* Jack Grant's
"Lord" is black: with "his dark face . . . , and his dark eyes,
that are so dark you can't see them, and his dark hair that is
blacker than the night on his forehead, and the dark feelings he
has" (285).[33]

To form the "dark gods," the leaders of remote civilizations,
like the *Adjes* and the *Lucumones,* combine in Lawrence's works
with mythological and Old Testament figures. A comprehensive
vision, eclectically combining several such strains, is an unspoken
element of the "leadership" theme in *Aaron's Rod,* for the silent
communal fellowship of the "lost races" (like that of the Bandinelli
figures in the Piazza della Signoria and the builders of early
Florence) stands in implied contrast to the anarchy of the novel's
present. While the vision infuses the main character with some
self-sufficiency (forming a calming antidote to his affair with the
marchesa), it does not quite move him to submit to the self-
proclaimed leader, Lilly. And the experience with the cypresses
makes this conclusion inevitable, leaving Aaron as his companion's
equal and, in some ways, his superior. Although Lilly has read a
book about Africa and although he resembles "a Byzantine eikon"
at the novel's end (299), it is, after all, Aaron who has communed
with the Etruscans.

Related to these quasi-historical power figures in the cypress
trees is another unseen presence: Pan, associated like Aaron and

32. See Schneider, "'Strange Wisdom,'" 184–87, who also mentions a
Nigerian leader named Lilli. For another African source, see Heywood,
"*Birds, Beasts and Flowers,*" 87–105.
33. This passage is in a part of the coauthored novel attributed to Lawrence,
according to Paul Eggert (*BB* xliv–liii).

Moses with a shepherd's rod[34] and like Aaron Sisson with a musical instrument. I have already noted that Lawrence's "dark heroes" and "dark gods" have been associated with Pan and Dionysus (especially Nietzsche's Dionysus).[35] With the double incitement of a Christ-Pan conflict in literature and Nietzsche's iconoclastic hero, notoriously "opposed to 'the Crucified,' "[36] it is no wonder that the conflict between the Lawrentian "dark gods" and Christianity is often intense. In "The Last Laugh" (1925), for example, Pan joyously despoils a church to the accompaniment of trills from panpipes (*CSS* 3:640). In *Aaron's Rod,* however, the Dionysian quality is assimilated to the Old Testament types (as in the essay description of Christ touching hands with Dionysus in the statue *David*).

One of Aaron's last locations is almost literally pastoral, in the countryside outside a church; neglected by critics, it is a significant setting for a Lawrence character.[37] He and Lilly lie under trees near a square little belfry as the bells ring for "one of the most precious hours: the hour of pause, noon, and the sun, and the quiet acceptance of the world"—a time at which "everything seems to fall into a true relationship" (292). This interlude beside the church may at first seem out of keeping with Aaron's experience of the pagan Etruscans; in fact, however, Lawrence later speculates in an ahistoric way that Christianity had origins in Etruscan Italy,[38] as had "that early, glad sort of Christian art, the free touch of Gothic within the classic" (*EP* 111).

The novel's church setting is precisely the kind the author celebrates in "A Propos of *Lady Chatterley's Lover*" for its perennial relevance to human life. Although this is a late essay, it deserves quotation here for its unexpected correspondences with this scene in *Aaron's Rod,* which it directly echoes. "The rhythm of life itself was preserved by the [old] Church," writes Lawrence in "A Propos": "We feel it, in the south, in the country, when we hear the jangle of the bells at dawn, at noon, at sunset, marking the hours with the sound of mass or prayers" (*PII* 503). Lawrence's interest is not in dogma but in a continuous relation between man

34. Merivale, *Pan the Goat-God,* 52, 162.
35. Ibid., 217. See also Pollnitz, " 'Raptus Virginis,' " 120, and Widmer, "Lawrence and the Nietzschean Matrix," 115–31.
36. Pollnitz, " 'Raptus Virginis,' " 121.
37. For more development of these aspects of Lawrence's settings, see my article "Architectural Monuments," 75–80.
38. See my introduction.

and the natural cosmos, for "the Christian peasants went on very much as the pagan peasants had gone, with . . . the three great daily moments of the sun" (*PII* 509). By placing Aaron in one of these privileged moments, Lawrence implies his recovery of ties with a pre-Christian continuum like that surviving in the essay's country people.

The broadening of Aaron's identity into a Pan-Christ antici-pates a combination often ascribed to the protagonist of *The Man Who Died*. [39] Still, the Old Testament types remain preeminent in *Aaron's Rod,* as the title suggests. As noted earlier, Lawrence's Pan and "old Adam" have much in common; for the author refers to "the oldest, old Adam, from whom God is not yet separated off" (*STH* 204-5) much as he does to "the oldest Pan" (*P* 26): "In the days before man got too much separated off from the universe, he *was* Pan" (*P* 24). Similarly, for the reborn figure of the essay "Resurrection," "the Man has disappeared into the God again" (*RDP* 233). The process Aaron undergoes is similar to the de-Christianizing of the "man who died," and Aaron's story even resembles that of this Christ figure in major respects: awakening from the old consciousness, wandering the earth, and maintaining an ultimate solitude. Sisson's resemblances to the later man should not be entirely unexpected since he is Aaron, the namesake of a major typological precursor of Christ.

Reading *Aaron's Rod* in the light of such typology reveals that it is neither simply a picaresque novel[40] nor the tale of an "anti-hero."[41] It is more centrally about Christianity's origins and decline than other approaches are able to reveal. The fact that the Christmas opening is matched by only a sketchy reference to Easter in the final pages shows how tenuous is Aaron's new birth. His continuing misanthropy promises no new world and extends the novel's ironic edge to the very end. However, if concluding imagery is indicative, he may be among the most fortunate individ-ual Lawrence characters in spite of it. While his rod has failed to signal a new beginning for an era, the image of the flowering branch is now internalized: the soul, says Lilly, can act "as a tree," the cells pushing "on into buds and boughs and flowers" (296).

---

39. Merivale, *Pan the Goat-God,* 215, finds that the Lawrentian conflict between Pan and Christ is resolved by making Christ "more Pan-like" in *The Man Who Died;* and Widmer, *The Art of Perversity,* goes further: in the late novella, he states, Lawrence turns "Christ into Pan" (200).

40. Barr, *"Aaron's Rod,"* 213-25.

41. Baker, "Profile of an Anti-Hero," 182-92.

But his wordy speech, despite giving voice to the inner change at the book's center, is termed a mere "harangue" by the author (296). Lawrence remarks in a letter on the lack of a "flowering end" for this novel (*Letters* 3:626), later reintroducing the burgeoning tree of life into broader contexts.

The Cosmology

The Cross and the Tree of Life
in *Birds, Beasts and Flowers*

5

In mid-career, D. H. Lawrence's tree images, so important already in *Aaron's Rod*, proliferate into an entire cosmology in which the tree of life and the cross are central. He adopts an archetypal world picture in which the globe has a cosmic pillar or tree at its core,[1] a cosmology associated not only with biblical typology (Schiller 2:108, 135-36) but also with diverse religious systems described by Blavatsky and others.[2] In this scheme, the central world pillar is itself timeless while nonetheless interacting with historic epochs. Lawrence even relates trees to "races" that "wander and are exiled" but may renew themselves in time (*CP* 304). In a

---

1. Near the end of his life, Lawrence was interested in receiving materials on the "Tree and Pillar cult," as he termed it, of the ancient Mediterranean, Chaldean, and Babylonian world: he wrote Charles Lahr on 1 October 1929 asking for books on this topic, as noted by Mara Kalnins in her introduction to the Cambridge Edition of *Apocalypse and the Writings on Revelation,* 12. Sir John Evans's *Tree and Pillar Cults,* mentioned in Carter's *Symbols of Revelation,* 40, may have been discussed by Carter and Lawrence when the two worked together earlier on a *Revelation* manuscript.

2. See, for example, Blavatsky (*Isis* 1:405-11), and Eliade, *Patterns in Comparative Religion,* 265-330, and *The Sacred and the Profane,* 33-38. See also Jung, *Archetypes and the Collective Unconscious,* in *Collected Works,* 9:355-90, proclaiming the mandala a true archetype and referring to the version that features the Four Evangelists (388).

body of work that may be called his "tree cluster," comparable in size to what Merivale has identified as his "Pan cluster,"[3] his images of the flourishing tree eventually tend to replace his earlier metaphors for cosmic well-being, such as the rainbow.[4]

His own illustrations for *Birds, Beasts and Flowers* offer graphic evidence of this increased interest. One previously unpublished sketch, produced in New Mexico in 1923 as a possible dust-jacket design for the English (Martin Secker) edition of the book (Fig. 11), features a Lawrentian tree of life—a central trunk with a snake on its lowest branch and a bird and a bat on higher branches.[5] It depicts four creatures at the corners, much as the emblems of the Evangelists Matthew, Mark, Luke, and John (man, lion, bull, and eagle) adorn the corners of many medieval illuminations, often flanking the venerated cross or the altar. While the animals Lawrence drew are by no means identical with these (except for the bull), it is likely that he had such figures in mind, for he would have encountered them in Jenner (Fig. 12); and later, while working on the poetry volume in 1921, he sought art examples of "the four beasts of the Evangelists," urging friends to look for them in old medieval missals and books of hours (*Letters* 4:124).[6] Holly Laird, in fact, suggests that *Birds, Beasts and*

3. Merivale, *Pan the Goat-God,* 215.

4. Although the pattern I suggest does not fully emerge until the middle 1920s, trees had always been important in Lawrence's works. Pollnitz, " 'Raptus Virginis,' " 131, traces the "dark god" back to a 1909 poem on sex and violence, "Discord in Childhood," with its prominent ash tree. In the *Sons and Lovers* manuscript fragments, Lawrence described woman as particularly close to nature, "the stuff of the Tree," but canceled the line, as shown in *Sons and Lovers,* ed. Mark Schorer, fragment 2, 32. In *Women in Love,* Birkin has a rebirth experience in which he communes with foliage at Breadalby. The trees of *Aaron's Rod* are vital to that novel's meaning and design. Even the final chapter of *The Rainbow* raises the possibility that Ursula's regenerative experience is symbolized by her climb up a version of the *axis mundi.* I have argued in chapter 2 that Ursula is peculiarly related to Christ. It is therefore significant that, as she escapes her climactic meeting with the apocalyptic horses, she climbs a tree in a way suggesting Dante's movements out of hell at the end of *The Inferno.* Whelan, *D. H. Lawrence,* 46, associates this tree with the oak of Zeus or of Thor.

5. This design is in the Harry Ransom Humanities Research Center, the University of Texas at Austin. It evidently became, in part, a model for the Secker dust jacket, a design composed of many tiny animals and plants but without the central tree Lawrence had proposed.

6. The letter, to Donald and Catherine Carswell, explains that Thomas Seltzer wanted some such design for the cover of a chapbook containing Lawrence's four poems on the Evangelists.

Fig. 11. Sketch by D. H. Lawrence, previously unpublished, intended for the book jacket of the English (Martin Secker) edition of *Birds, Beasts and Flowers* (1923).

Fig. 12. Evangelistic Beasts, detail of a ninth-century illustration in an English Bible (Book of Revelation), in the British Library (included in Jenner's *Christian Symbolism*).

Flowers was organized to suggest a book of hours.[7] Tablet-breaker as he was, Lawrence clearly welcomed such traditional patterns in order to turn them to his own uses.

The book jacket used for the English edition (Thomas Seltzer) of *Birds, Beasts and Flowers,* with a design fashioned by Lawrence (Fig. 13), shows a bird and serpent in the upper center; on the lower right side is Eve beneath a tree, perhaps that of knowledge since a fruit is visible (but untouched), and on the lower left side is the emblem of a fish, well known as a symbol of Christ because of the Greek acrostic IXOUS ($IX\Theta Y\Sigma$ in the printed versions of the poem "St. Matthew").[8] Beneath these figures, in the lower corners, are more heraldic animal designs, one apparently a dog (subject of one poem) and another the bull (St. Luke's emblem). Eve appears to stand on the bull, perhaps suggesting that she has her foundation on the animal nature that Lawrence wishes the modern Eve to regain (Fig. 14). While the bull sometimes correlates in Christian iconography with the Crucifixion (Schiller 2:120), and while sacrifice is an important theme of this volume of poetry, the pictured bull is hale and hearty, probably representing pagan sensuousness. Lawrence must have known that the pre-Christian sacred bull (associated with the Greek Dionysus and the Persian Mithras alike) was said to have been the substance from which all created things arose, what Gilbert Murray termed the source of *"mana,"* or animal life.[9] From her perch on the bull, Eve leaves the apple hanging on the tree, as if to reverse the fall from paradise. These right-hand figures, then, seemingly represent a new pagan era, beyond mere sacrifice and beyond the apple's curse. On the other side (and the left side) of Fig. 13, the fish may represent the Christian era, even though its sensual embodiment as a natural being seems to take precedence over this ideological meaning. The poems in the volume, besides similarly celebrating natural

7. Laird, *Self and Sequence,* 139–41.

8. On the acrostic IXOUS or $IX\Theta Y\Sigma$ for Christ, see, for example, Appleton and Bridges, *Symbolism in Liturgical Art,* 37. See also Jenner, *Christian Symbolism,* 33–34.

9. Murray, *Four Stages of Greek Religion,* 33. On the identification of the bull with Dionysus, see also Harrison, *Ancient Art and Ritual,* 83–91, and Frazer, *Spirits of the Corn,* in *The Golden Bough,* 7:16. Lawrence had read Murray's book by 1916, Harrison's in 1913, and Frazer's *Golden Bough* (at least some volumes) in 1915 and 1922. (I cite the edition of Frazer available in his time.) Jung, *Psychology and Religion,* in *Collected Works,* 11:224, gives a similar sense to the bull of Mithraism, calling it "a world bull."

forms, well justify the hints of typological motifs found in both
Lawrence drawings.

The fact that these designs have some features of missal art may
combine with the source of the volume's title—Sabine Baring-
Gould's tender "Evening Hymn" ("Birds and beasts and flowers /
Soon will be asleep")[10]—to raise false expectations about the
book's orthodoxy. It is radically heterodox, but I do not fully agree,
either, with Gilbert, who sees it as a subversive "Black Mass"
involving a "total reversal of Christian mythology."[11] The poems
are so rich in paradox as to give some warrant to both readings,
but neither can ultimately stand alone. If the biblical themes are
not entirely subversive, however, they do sometimes play with
ironic reversals; generally relinquishing the narrowly specific Judeo-
Christian types for broader archetypal forms, the book nonetheless
depends at key points upon its biblical typology in ways that are
not always negative. In its complexity, the volume is much like an
unpublished design Lawrence made for the "Trees" section.[12] At
the sides of this drawing are tall cypresses like those in *Aaron's
Rod* and the poem "Cypresses," each upright shape divided vertically
to form a light half and a dark half, suggesting the trees at once of
life and of death.[13]

I

If Lawrence was writing a "tree cluster," his work was itself part of
a larger such cluster, focusing on ancient religious rituals. W. B.
Yeats, for example, in his poem "Vacillation," creates a tree combining polarities somewhat as Lawrence's do: it is "half all glittering

10. Marshall, *The Psychic Mariner,* 117.

11. Gilbert, "D. H. Lawrence's Uncommon Prayers," 79.

12. Two such unpublished brush drawings, both intended for the "Trees"
section, are at the Harry Ransom Humanities Research Center, the University of Texas at Austin. Like the unpublished jacket design already described,
both of these drawings were created in 1923 in Taos.

13. Several of Vincent Van Gogh's paintings seem especially relevant to
Birds, Beasts and Flowers, and Lawrence may well have been familiar with
Almond-Tree Branch in Blossom (1890) and several studies of cypresses—
including *Road with Cypresses* (1890), *Cypresses with Two Figures* (1889),
and *Starry Night* (1889) with a cypress in it. Lawrence refers to the artist
with some frequency, as Stewart discusses: "Lawrence on Van Gogh," 1-24,
and "The Vital Art," 123-48.

Fig. 13. Book jacket by D. H. Lawrence, used for the American (Thomas Seltzer) edition of *Birds, Beasts and Flowers* (1923).

Fig. 14. Eve under a tree, by D. H. Lawrence (detail from the book jacket of the Seltzer *Birds, Beasts and Flowers*).

flame and half all green / Abounding foliage moistened with the dew," and "half and half consume what they renew."[14] On such a tree of opposites—life and death, good and evil—"Attis' image" is hung (like a sacrificial surrogate for the god) to facilitate rebirth in nature. A looming presence behind such imagery is, of course, Sir James G. Frazer, with his celebrated studies of ancient cult sacrifices.[15] T. S. Eliot, too, utilizing the tarot pack's image of a sacrificed man (often on a tree-cross), introduces the famous "Hanged Man," or "the Hanged God of Frazer," as he calls it, into *The Waste Land* (1922).[16] These poets had all been reading Frazer's voluminous *Golden Bough,* which, says Eliot, "influenced our generation profoundly."[17] All were particularly impressed with *Adonis, Attis, Osiris,* describing the rites of these dying and reviving gods, including Christ among them,[18] and all were aware of sacrificial trees mentioned in theosophy. Like Lawrence, Yeats and Eliot were seeking more than physical renewal for their civilizations, and Eliot even identifies his "Hanged God" with "the hooded figure" (apparently Christ) on the road to Emmaus in another part of his poem.[19] Despite such common sources and attitudes, however, Lawrence's work contains another element, owing as much to biblical typology as to Frazer; and this factor distinguishes him from the other poets.

For his "tree cluster," Lawrence's 1917 and 1922 readings of Frazer combine with his knowledge of Greek philosophers Heraclitus and Empedocles, theosophists Blavatsky and Pryse, astrologer Frederick Carter, and biblical typologists, among others.[20] He may have known cabbalistic models of the Garden of Eden featur-

14. Yeats, *Variorum Edition of the Poems,* 500. See also "the boughs of love and hate" in the early poem "To the Rose Upon the Rood of Time," 101, and "rich foliage that the starlight glittered through," holding "a beautiful seated boy" in "Parnell's Funeral," 541. Only the rose poem had appeared before Lawrence's death, but the other examples take Yeats's interest in the tree sacrifice into the 1930s.

15. In his *Essays and Introductions,* 176, Yeats gives an immediate source for this tree in a passage from *The Mabinogion.*

16. Eliot, *Complete Poems and Plays,* 51.

17. Ibid.

18. Frazer, *Adonis, Attis, Osiris,* in *The Golden Bough,* 5:302–10. (This is a volume of *The Golden Bough* that Lawrence evidently knew well.) See also Vickery, *Literary Impact of* The Golden Bough, 294–325.

19. Eliot, *Complete Poems and Plays,* 70.

20. See Kalnins, "Symbolic Seeing," 173–90, on the influence of Heraclitus, showing how Lawrence often conflates literal and symbolic levels from the Greek source.

ing a tree of life, shaped like a cross, bearing a personification of the mystic Sephiroth.[21] Madame Blavatsky herself sets Adam Kadmon at the cross-center of a Sephirothic diagram (*Isis* 2:263-71). Some of Lawrence's trees, as evidenced earlier, even suggest Joachim of Fiore's diagrams in their references to the Holy Ghost.[22] Despite all such influences, however, Lawrence's tree images are often oddly Christocentric—and more so than can be accounted for by Frazer's casual inclusion of Christ among dying and reviving gods.

It is no wonder that Lawrence's "dark god" often appears, in *Birds, Beasts and Flowers,* "among the uprights of trees," as Christopher Pollnitz notes.[23] These trees are neither simply haunts of Dionysus nor Frazerian groves. In a group of works overlapping with those of the tree cosmology, Lawrence explores his own variants of the Adam and Eve story, with its trees of Eden.[24] Even beyond establishing Edenic settings, however, he combines the trees of knowledge and life with the cross, presenting complex interconnections from biblical typology. *Birds, Beasts and Flowers* includes not only Adam and Eve but also two major iconographic stances of Jesus, the crucified Christ and the Bridegroom (as revealed in the description of a tree).

The Lawrentian cosmos, with its central tree or cross, follows a stylized pattern. In Christian iconography, as in certain other plans,[25] the tree-cross is in the center of a circular expanse,

21. Raine, in *Yeats, the Tarot and the Golden Dawn,* includes illustrations of such trees. Yeats, *Autobiographies,* 375, refers to a cabbalistic tree with a "green serpent winding through it" [showing the path of nature or instinct]. See also Waite, *Pictorial Key to the Tarot,* 116, who notes that "the tree of sacrifice [of the Hanged Man] is living wood, with leaves thereon." Some of Lawrence's work has been associated with tarot cards in terms of affinity (though not direct influence) by Heywood, "Reverberations: 'Snapdragon,'" 168-72.

22. Reeves and Hirsch-Reich, *Figurae of Joachim of Fiore,* 153-83. See also descriptions of the *Arbor bona* and *Arbor male,* trees of virtue and of vice associated with Ecclesia and Synagoga, the former flourishing but the latter withering (25).

23. Pollnitz, "'Raptus Virginis,'" 119.

24. See chapter 1 above. See also Ruderman, "The New Adam and Eve," 225-27.

25. For this scheme, Blavatsky is surely one source. Not only does she display diagrams of the universe, complete with heavens, underworld, and a central cross; she also refers to the tree of life and the tree of knowledge and discusses the point of intersection, the cross, formed in the universe by "the celestial perpendicular and the terrestrial horizontal base line" (*Isis* 2:270). Pryse, too, presents cosmological diagrams and refers to the cross and the tree of life: *The Apocalypse Unsealed,* 39, 68-69, 216. Another possible

surrounded by quaternian elements, winds, rivers, and the like
(Schiller 2:108), which — with their four arms — form the shape of
a cross. The centrality of the cross in such Christianized designs
signifies Christ's triumph over death and mastery of the cosmos
(Schiller 2:111, 119). In its most elaborate depiction, the tree of
Eden forms the cross of Christ (Schiller 2:136),[26] and the dead
Adam (the old Adam) lies underneath, while Christ (the new
Adam) is triumphant above, surrounded by the symbols of the
Four Evangelists and the four elements or four cardinal points
that they represent (Schiller 2:135-36). As I have demonstrated
earlier, Lawrence could have known graphic illustrations of these
relationships between Christ and Adam, as in the choir of Santa
Croce in Florence (where the medieval *Legend of the True Cross*
is painted) or on Strassburg Cathedral's central western tympanum (where Adam is depicted beneath the cross).[27] Certainly,
the 1923 *Quetzalcoatl* shows an exact knowledge of such lore.

   In *Quetzalcoatl,* it is true, the world's center will no longer be
the cross of sacrifice but the "rosy cross." For this ancient symbol,
which Lawrence had already discussed in "The Two Principles"
(1919),[28] he was doubtless influenced by Blavatsky and probably,
too, by Yeats, whose "To the Rood Upon the Rose of Time" he
surely knew, since in *Birds, Beasts and Flowers* he parodies some
of the lyrics collected under the title *The Rose* in Yeats's 1895
Poems. Apart from its Rosicrucian forms, however, a cross bearing flowers is also a significant typological image of Christ's

---

source lies in Yoruban African tradition, featuring a quaternian world plan,
as discussed by Schneider, " 'Strange Wisdom,' " 85-86. See also Jung,
Mysterium Coniunctionis, stating that Adam Kadmon and Mercurius may
both be symbolized by a tree (*Collected Works* 14:412, 440).

   26. See also Gettings, *The Occult in Art,* 152-53.

   27. See the *Legend of the True Cross,* discussed in my introduction and in
chapter 1.

   28. Although Lawrence once (in 1929) feigns bewilderment over the
meaning of the cross (*P* 567), his own essay "The Two Principles" explains
the "rosy cross," the Egyptian ankh, and Aphrodite's cross, among other cross
forms, as signs of creation and immortality (*SM* 177, 184). Earlier, too, he
produced his most extended description of freestanding crucifixes, one that
he cast in two separate versions — "Christs in the Tirol," an essay written in
1912, and "The Crucifix Across the Mountains," the first chapter of *Twilight
in Italy* — and a related crucifix appears in the poem "The Cross." (An even
more famous example of such a crucifix is the ominous image presiding over
the death of Gerald at the end of *Women in Love.*) The early accounts of
Martyrtafeln show that Lawrence's preoccupation with the Christian cross
was longstanding.

Resurrection,[29] and this is how Lawrence treats it, for his own revisionary purposes.

In 1920, at Christmastime, for example, he wrote the poem "Almond Blossom," showing the almond as the tree of crucifixion, transfigured:

> Oh, give me the tree of life in blossom
> And the Cross sprouting its superb and fearless flowers!
>
> (CP 305)

The almond is often identified with the trees of Eden[30] and also, of course, with Aaron's rod, which budded with these flowers. Both associations add importance to the poem's implied comparison between the flowering of an almond tree, with its iron-colored bark, and Christ's emergence from the tomb:

> So that the faith in his [the almond's] heart smiles
>   again
> And his blood ripples with that untellable delight of
>   once-more-vindicated faith,
> And the Gethsemane blood at the iron pores unfolds,
>   unfolds,
> Pearls itself into tenderness of bud
> And in a great and sacred forthcoming steps forth. . . .
>
> (306)

The blossoms that issue from "Gethsemane blood" are related to the stigmata of Christ: "Five times wide open, / Six times wide open / . . . And red at the core with the last sore-heartedness" (307).[31] However, this is an "epithalamion," and it is not the crucified Christ but a "bridegroom"—a sensual, "honey-bodied" form—that "steps forth"; thus the tree is transformed, by "supreme annunciation," from the death-tree to the tree of life, "the tree

29. In notes to my introduction, I deal with St. Bonaventura's influential flowering cross. While his tree symbolism has affinities with that of Joachim of Fiore, it is ultimately distinguished from it, centering on the traditional tree of redemption (cross and tree of life), not on a tree of historic progression (Reeves and Hirsch-Reich, *Figurae of Joachim of Fiore,* 306). Joachimist influence on Rosicrucianism in the early seventeenth century (Reeves and Hirsch-Reich, 299) is of interest in relation to the trees of theosophy.

30. Yarden, *The Tree of Light,* 40–42.

31. Sagar, *D. H. Lawrence: Life into Art,* 232, notes that the petals number "one more opening than the wounds of the crucified Christ."

being life-divine" (304-7). While this change comes from the roots, "from the dense under-earth" (304), the blossoms fan upward.

In the introductory epigraph to the "Flowers" section of *Birds, Beasts and Flowers,* the almond is a "symbol of resurrection" (303) on ancient seasonal grounds, and elsewhere, in "The Last Laugh," its scent accompanies Pan (*CSS* 3:646). It is clear, however, that Lawrence draws even more heavily upon the specific biblical typology that also informs *Aaron's Rod,* relating the budding almond rod to Christ. In the poem's imagery, the resurrected man, healed of his wounds, is delivered from the "iron age" (304), and the cross is replaced with the living tree of a new dispensation.

This "epithalamion" is particularly significant in light of Lawrence's frequent use elsewhere of the apocalyptic symbolism of Christ as the Bridegroom.[32] I believe that a change of eras is evoked as the number of the flower's petals, enumerated as stigmata, merges into the "six-fold" stages of ritual death and rebirth like that described later in *Apocalypse* (104). With the sixth seal ("six times wide open") comes "the divesting of the spirit from the last living quick" of the self; in the next, the "eternal self" emerges "at the very instant of extinction" as "a new whole cloven flame of a new-bodied man with golden thighs and a face of glory" (*A* 104, 105). Similarly, the new era may come at the death of the old just as the almond petal may open upon its "last sore-heartedness," new after winter death. The reborn Bridegroom of "Almond Blossom" contrasts in *Birds, Beasts and Flowers* with the crucified Christ in "St. Matthew," although I will show that the latter, containing a spectacular evocation of the Brazen Serpent, is far more complex than this contrast suggests.

In the year after the writing of "Almond Blossom," 1921, Lawrence combines Frazer's forest sacrifices and Heraclitus's opposites with Christian myth. Writing *Fantasia of the Unconscious* in the Black Forest, he describes a tree that reminds him at once of Eden and the cross of Christ. "I can so well understand tree-worship," he comments (82); confessing a realization of "the deepest motive" (sacrifice and death), he sees the duality of "the sacred tree, deep in the forest," embracing "the tree of life and death, tree of good and evil" (84) and "can understand that Jesus was crucified on a tree" (83). The tree is a cosmic creature: "He thrusts himself tremendously down to the middle earth, where dead men sink in darkness, in the damp, dense undersoil, and he

---

32. See examples in my introduction and in chapters 2, 3, 4, 6, and 7.

turns himself about in high air" (83). Like the typological tree of life, it encompasses three dimensions—the underworld, the "middle earth," and the heavens—resembling a cross described by Mircea Eliade as "a thoroughfare between heaven, earth and hell."[33] "He [the tree] turns two ways," Lawrence points out (83). This description is very much in keeping with his developing view, based in large part on John Burnet, of the Heraclitean tension between opposites—of vertical and horizontal, fire and water, and the like—as described, for example, in "The Two Principles" (*SM* 175-89). In fact, the introductory quotation heading the section "Trees" in *Birds, Beasts and Flowers* calls attention to just this kind of union in trees—to what Empedocles saw as "the symmetry of their mixture of fire and water" (*CP* 295).[34] The trees in Lawrence's collection are not "creatures of hell propelled upwards,"[35] but microcosms of the universe and symbols of death and immortality.

Eventually, Lawrence's tree imagery focuses on the earth's center, where "the axis," or cosmic pillar, is a locus of divinity, a "dark matrix" of creation (*MM* 5). Similarly, Blavatsky refers to a "spiritual bosom of mother nature" from which "proceed all the great saviours of the universe—the avatars of the invariable Deity" (*Isis* 2:270). In *The Plumed Serpent,* Lawrence describes this inner core; it is not, of course, the scientific axis of the world but another timeless dimension "inside the axis of our wheeling space": "And the axis of our worldly space, when you enter, is a vastness where even the trees come and go, and the soul is at home in its own dream" (*PS* 126). Richard O. Young has associated this particular passage with Lawrence's doctrine of "the fourth dimension," a supermundane reality beyond our usual perception.[36] Here, the saviors and their symbols come and go—and even come again—as do the trees or cosmic pillars, the sources of life and of new civilizations. The

33. Eliade, *Patterns in Comparative Religion,* 294. See his further description of the cross as a tree "whose roots are in hell, and whose summit at the throne of God, while its branches contain the whole world" (293-94).

34. For the epigraphs to the sections of *Birds, Beasts and Flowers,* Lawrence used Burnet, *Early Greek Philosophy* (1908), a major influence on his thinking.

35. Mandell, *The Phoenix Paradox,* 110.

36. Young, " 'Where Even the Trees,' " 30-44. I see in Lawrence's meaning, too, the Heraclitean view that all things are composed of the substances of former beings that will, in turn, feed future forms—all things "living each other's death and dying each other's life" or, in the words of Kalnins, "the living and the dead . . . continually changing places" ("Symbolic Seeing," 179-80).

drama fragment *Noah's Flood,* for instance, makes the world's center a tree inhabited by divinity. A character refers to this deity (called the Great White Bird) "at the centre of the tree" in the world's core "beyond our seeing"; the tree penetrates all space, for "the stars are the small white birds . . . among the outer leaves" (*P* 813). In other versions of such cosmology, the center is sometimes inhabited by a serpent rather than a bird (Blavatsky, *Isis* 1:297-98; 2:293)[37] and sometimes by both. Despite the focus on the animate center, such designs are often integral with the shape of a cross, the bird embodying the four cardinal points and the serpent clinging to the axial pole, as to a tree. Lawrence shows some humor in his projection of the serpentine center, once painting it prominently on an outhouse at his ranch near Taos, according to the outraged Mabel Dodge Luhan: "In the center, coil on coil, and swaying upwards, was a great, green snake wrapped around the stem of a sunflower."[38] In a more serious mood, "St. Matthew" explicitly links the cross of Christ to the famous Old Testament type, the Brazen Serpent.

By 1923, Lawrence avows that the world's pillar was once the Christian cross (a version of the tree of life) but insists that it must be displaced, being dead — the cross without promise of rebirth, a symbol of the depleted Christian era. In the essay "On Being Religious," written in this year, he explains, probably influenced by Frederick Carter's astrology,[39] that the cross "has shifted" in the heavenly zodiac, leaving the world with "only the Gap, and images, and hollow words" (*RDP* 190). Also in 1923, in *Quetzalcoatl,* however, he refers to the moving of the cross more positively: after Ramón claims to be the "Redeemed Adam," "the foot of the cross is in the House of Life, not in the grave" (*Q* 331). The essay "Resurrection," written while Lawrence was finishing *The Plumed Serpent,* states that "Christ has rejoined the Father at the axis" (*RDP* 234).

Looking forward to the new age beyond modern Christendom,

37. See, for example, in *Women in Love,* the image of the "serpent" in Gudrun's inner tree of life (451), as discussed in chapter 3 above. Although this particular entity is internalized, Lawrence's system of correspondences allows also for the cosmic version of this imagery. See also Yeats's reference to the tree and the serpent, as quoted above.

38. Luhan, *Lorenzo in Taos,* 173.

39. Lawrence had read a manuscript by Carter in 1923, encouraged him to publish in the *Adelphi* in 1924, and corresponded with him between late 1922 and 1924 and again in 1929-30. On the exchange of letters, see Woodman, " 'The Big Old Pagan Vision,' " 39-51.

this essay prophesies the reinstitution of the tree of life in place of
the Christian cross: "The world and the cosmos stagger to the new
axis" (where the cross has been displaced) as "the pillar of flame"
ascends again "from the nadir to the zenith." The cosmic center
seems altogether threatened: "The Tree shivers, and sheds its
leaves" and "the new fire spurts at its roots, the boughs writhe, the
twigs crackle from within, and the old leaves fall thick and red to
the ground," all showing "how a new day enters the Tree of Life"
(*RDP* 234). Remarkably, this change occurs entirely in terms of
Christian imagery: "The Cross has taken root again, and is putting
forth buds. Slim branches sprout out where the nails went in,
there is a tuft of sprouts like tongues of flame at the top, where the
inscription was. Even *Consummatum est* is dissolved in a rising
sap" (*RDP* 234). If this is one of Lawrence's most Joachimist
trees, dealing with the "third age" and the Holy Ghost (the
pentecostal flames), it is also explicitly the tree of redemption.

In *Birds, Beasts and Flowers,* Lawrence gives multiple meanings to the cross. On the one hand, it is the symbol of the deathly
asceticism of modern Christianity, causing him to inveigh against
the continuing emphasis on crucifixion. On the other hand, it is
the configuration at the heart of creation, as he had described it in
"The Two Principles": "Central within the fourfold division [of the
four alchemical elements and the directions] is the creative reality
itself, like the body of a four-winged bird" (*SM* 177). Thus "the
Cross, the epitome of all this fourfold division, still stirs us to the
depths with unaccountable emotions, emotions which go much
deeper than personality and the Christ drama" (*SM* 184). In the
poetry volume, this cross exists in the greatest cosmological
context — in the universe at large — and also appears as a physical
sign of inner reality on various creatures, like the tortoise and the
ass, which bear cross marks on their bodies. A system of correspondences exists, therefore, by which microcosm and macrocosm reflect each other, both being infused with the cross. In the
essay "On Being a Man," as mentioned earlier, Lawrence points to
the cross in the human condition: in the division into sex and into
individual being, man is forever on the cross (*RDP* 216), and this
is a source of both pain and ecstasy.[40] All of these cruciform
shapes — the one in the cosmos and the deep, immanental one, the

40. In the poem "The Cross," he adds social meaning, stating that a
"horizontal division" into hierarchies is as eternal as an "upright division"
into sex; that it "can never be wiped out" (*CP* 636–37).

ascetic cross of sacrifice and the sensual one of flesh — are variants of his tree of life.

II

The cross-centered cosmos is the setting for *Birds, Beasts and Flowers*. This poetry collection does not have a linear organization but, rather, a spherical one suggesting this cosmology; its model is the wheel focused, at its mathematical center (somewhat roughly, the middle twelve hundred lines), upon images of the cross. Much has been said about the order in which Lawrence arranged the contents for publication[41] and the way in which this collection fits into a scheme for *Collected Poems* of 1928.[42] It remains to be shown, however, that the two relatively autonomous sections, both written in the same month in 1920 — *Tortoises* (published as a unit in 1921) and "The Evangelistic Beasts" — are carefully centered in *Birds, Beasts and Flowers* so as to emphasize crosses. Mandell, too, finds *Tortoises* central to a larger context, for here "the central mystery of *Collected Poems*, the necessity of both separation and connection, is codified."[43] Not only do "Evangelistic Beasts" and *Tortoises* share the focus upon the cross but also several poems separating them — including "Snake," "Fish," "Bat," and "Man and Bat" — are linked in imagery to "St. Matthew," with its extended description of Christ crucified. Taken together, all these poems reveal both the old Christian center that cannot hold and a vaster cosmic center that can.

When Gilbert finds in *Birds, Beasts and Flowers* a hellish cosmology with a "supernatural" aura,[44] she is responding to the volume's strong evocation of an archetypal and in part otherworldly setting. While Lawrence does not limit the location to the underworld, he does undoubtedly sketch in a cosmos that is more than mundane. It is particularly fitting, therefore, that he places "The Evangelistic Beasts" in a central position, for these beasts once represented the cosmos (Schiller 1:18), as well as the very formulation of cosmos from chaos. He would have known these

41. See Gilbert, "D. H. Lawrence's Uncommon Prayers," 73–93; Mandell, *The Phoenix Paradox*, 103–4; and Trail, "West by East," 241–55.
42. See Mandell, *The Phoenix Paradox*, 96–119.
43. Ibid., 115.
44. Gilbert, "D. H. Lawrence's Uncommon Prayers," 78, 82.

meanings from Jenner,[45] and he refers to them in detail in "The Two Principles," finding "the four Evangels, with their symbols of man, eagle, lion, and bull, symbols parallel to the Four Elements" (*SM* 184). This cosmic symbolism is far removed, he notes later, from the modern evangelists' signs, which have degenerated to serve a sickly asceticism (*A* 83). The difference between the two is, in some ways, that between the restrictive biblical type, grown threadbare in the modern world, and the universal archetype. But this contrast is falsely simple, for the poem depends for its meaning and for some of its power upon its typological pattern.

"St. Matthew" is the one poem of its sequence to establish a majestic cosmology, ranging from the heavens—where Christ is the "Uplifted" (322)—to "the dark zenith of Thine antipodes" (322), leading "a strange way down the bottomless pit / To the great depths of its reversèd zenith" (322). The poem depicts Matthew, the only Evangelist whose symbol is not a beast but man, in a monologue to Christ on a cross. The upright of the cross forms the vertical axis of the poem's universe in a scheme that is more traditional than critics have recognized. Like the tree in *Fantasia* —and like the tree of life in both Christian and other versions—its expanse includes heaven, earth, and hell. In fact, the scene is generally Dantesque, not excluding the earthly and paradisal along with the infernal.[46] Matthew, the representative man, rises to the heavenly Christ with "wings of the spirit" but "must be put down" (321) because of his earthy side that has "dredged down to the zenith's reversal" (323). The suggestion of a vast cross in the heavens—the "Uplifted," the "Glorified"—is unmistakable; its upward-looming stem balances the earthly "horizontal" (321) so that the poem reproduces the image of a universal cross, one beyond that of crucifixion.

The most surprisingly neglected point about "St. Matthew" is that Lawrence deliberately evokes not only an image of sacrifice but also one of resurrection—that of the Brazen Serpent—in a quotation of Christ: "And I, if I be lifted up [from the earth], will

45. Jenner, *Christian Symbolism*, 103.

46. Sagar, *D. H. Lawrence: Life into Art*, 154, points out that, by 1915, "the structure and imagery [from Dante] provided [Lawrence] . . . with a way of looking at the world." The conventionalized universe of Fra Angelico's *Last Judgment*, prominent in *The Rainbow*, also provides another ready source for Lawrence's cosmos in "St. Matthew," for the painting shows "the huddled earth on either side, the seemly heaven arranged above, the singing progress to paradise on the one hand, the stuttering descent to hell on the other" (*R* 259).

draw all men unto me" (echoing John 12:32).[47] This passage, comprising the poem's fourth line, refers in part to the Crucifixion, for Jesus spoke, "signifying what death he would die" (John 12:33). The narrator also uses the words "lifted up" to describe the spiritual elevation of the Christ figure from the earth. But Lawrence knew the fuller meaning of the biblical text, which refers back to Christ's earlier statement, "And as Moses lifted up the serpent in the wilderness, even so must the Son of man be lifted up" (John 3:14).[48] This is a direct reference to the Brazen Serpent (Numbers 21:6-9), the typological prefiguration of Christ on the cross and a symbol of salvation.[49] I have shown earlier that *Quetzalcoatl* evokes the Brazen Serpent openly, the drama *David* includes it less overtly, and *Apocalypse* gives an account of its meaning. But this usage in "St. Matthew" is earlier than all of these examples and is in some ways more striking. It presents a compelling image of the saving serpent on the cross-pole of the universe.

Besides rendering the Brazen Serpent as a resurrection motif, "St. Matthew" contains other factors at variance with the prevailing view that its Christ is simply the tortured figure of the crucifix. He is associated not only with the serpent but with the fish (by means of a Greek acrostic) when Matthew, likening himself to "a fish seeking the bottom," addresses "Jesus/$IX\Theta YE$" (321). Lawrence set great store by these initials designating Christ; when writing to Harriet Monroe about the poem's original publication in *Poetry,* he voiced his concern to have them printed properly (*Letters* 4:404). Since the fish in the poem is related to Matthew's underworld journey, "down between the steep slopes of darkness . . . of the waters under the sea" and "into the . . . bottomless pit" (321–22), it is tempting to find it simply an infernal image. But Pollnitz, analyzing the related fish/Christ image in the poem "Fish," shows that it recalls Christ of the creation, a figure acquainted with "primal chaos," with attributes that predate creation and that "will carry life through the Apocalypse."[50] In "Fish," too, Lawrence associates the fish with "the waters under the earth" (*CP* 335), asking rhetorically "what moves" there. "The answer," states Pollnitz, "is Christ-Dagon-Vishnu, the Fish."[51]

47. See also John 8:28.
48. This biblical text was a favorite of Evangelicals and comparatists alike. Frazer refers to the Brazen Serpent, for example, in *The Golden Bough,* 8:281, as does Blavatsky (*SD* 2:208, 364, 387, and elsewhere).
49. See my introduction and chapter 1.
50. Pollnitz, " 'I Didn't Know His God,' " 43.
51. Ibid.

Indications that "St. Matthew" harbors an all but subliminal image of an underworld Christ also lie in Matthew's ambiguous statements following the fish imagery:

> To Thee I rose like a rocket ending in mid-heaven.
> But even thou, Son of Man, canst not quaff out the
>   dregs of terrestrial manhood!
> They fall back from Thee.
>
> They fall back, and like a dripping of quicksilver
>   taking the downward track,
> Break into drops, burn into drops of blood, and
>   dropping, dropping take wing
> Membraned, blood-veined wings,
> On fans of unsuspected tissue, like bats
> They thread and thrill and flicker ever downward
> To the dark zenith of Thine antipodes
> Jesus Uplifted.
>
> (322)

Although the "terrestrial manhood" seems most obviously that of Matthew, the term "Son of Man" for Christ blurs the distinction. The human "dregs," becoming "drops of blood," presumably Matthew's, may also suggest Christ's own blood, especially when associated with quicksilver, or mercury, meaningful in alchemy. The fact that they lead to "the dark zenith" indicates the attraction of the underworld to the human Matthew but may also have a model in Christ's harrowing of hell before the Resurrection. The possessive term "*Thine* antipodes" (my emphasis) presents yet another ambiguity, as if the opposites may belong to the "Son of Man" as well as to Matthew.

At any rate, the drops of "manhood" (whether altogether Matthew's or not), "like a dripping of quicksilver," undoubtedly carry alchemical associations such as Pollnitz notices here and in "Fish."[52] The alchemical meaning can be taken further. Is the line an oblique reference to Mercurius as *nous*, sometimes equated with the Uroboros, or snake with its tail in its mouth, a symbol of eternity?[53] This possibility recalls the Brazen Serpent. Blavatsky reports a belief that the creative spirit of God moving on chaos assumed the shape of the serpent with its tail in its mouth (*SD*

52. Ibid., 39–40.
53. Jung, *Psychology and Religion,* in *Collected Works,* 11:278.

2:505). Is the reference to Mercurius as Hermes, the underworld guide who has sometimes been related to Christ in the descent into Hades (*SD* 2:542)?[54] In keeping with this possibility, the poem deals with mediation between the spirit and the flesh and between this world and the next: as the drops of mercury fall, they reach the underworld, implicitly suggesting the sulphur that, united with mercury, forms an alchemical balance. One metaphor in alchemy parallels the slow transformation of matter, of *prima materia,* with the entombment of Christ; by this line of thinking, Christ in his emergence from the tomb corresponds with the perfect alchemical creation.[55] In the poem, the image of death is similarly transformed by its propinquity to images of dynamic life.

Like a shape beneath the poem's more obvious surface — and at odds with the limited, ascetic Christ of that surface — a cosmic figure takes shadowy substance, such a figure as Lawrence describes later in *Apocalypse:* "It is the Jesus that the early Church ... prominently believed in.... It is a vast Cosmic lord standing among ... the archaic planets" (*A* 74). The same late work explicitly discusses Christ as "Lord of the Underworld," a Hermes who "looks two ways" (*A* 75) like the tree of *Fantasia* and like the later mediator Ramón/Quetzalcoatl, "lord of the two ways" and "master of up and down" in *The Plumed Serpent* (179, 227, 341). "St. Matthew," then, makes the Christ figure a far more complex one than previous studies indicate. Like Ursula's evocation of a paganized Christ in *The Rainbow,* it shows Lawrence already, long before *The Man Who Died* and *Apocalypse,* casting Jesus in a heterodox mold with some features of the dark risen lord of later works.

If such cosmic touches characterize "St. Matthew," however, it is perhaps because it is simply a greater, more allusively effective poem than others in "The Evangelistic Beasts." The world of this sequence, like that of *Birds, Beasts and Flowers* as a whole, is Christendom at its end. In "St. Mark," for example, the cosmic

54. See also Pryse, *The Apocalypse Unsealed,* 110, identifying Hermes, "God of Occult Wisdom," as an "aspect of the Logos." Hermes is often seen as a god spanning the universe, cognate with the cosmic man, Adam Kadmon, of cabbalistic tradition — and both these and Christ (and others) "are all one," says Blavatsky (*Isis* 2:454). The poem shows Lawrence at his most allusive, yet it is not the "Platonic" Adam Kadmon but the sensual man that he ultimately exalts.

55. On the *lapis*-Christ connection, see Jung, *Psychology and Religion,* in *Collected Works,* 11:94, 99, 454. See also his *Psychology and Alchemy* (1953), in *Collected Works,* 12:332–411.

pillar is a mere caricature as the lion, like a cartoon figure, languishes in his long enchantment with "a lamb on a pinnacle, balancing a flag on its paw" (CP 324). The device on the flag is the cross, for the lamb is the *Agnus Dei,* symbol of Christ's rebirth (Schiller 1:12). I have discussed earlier how Will Brangwen, in *The Rainbow,* explains its typological significance when he and Anna argue about the lamb in a church window. This lamb, holding up "a little flag with a red cross," has behind it "the power of the tradition" (R 148, 149). While Anna sees the creature only naturalistically, Will declares, "It means the triumph of the Resurrection" (R 150). In "St. Mark," the secularized lamb has degenerated, even beyond Anna's expectation, into a ludicrous toy. "St. Luke" notes the emasculation of the bull after "the Lamb bewitched him with that red-struck flag," and now "the bull of the proletariat" must charge that very flag because of the "madness of his blood" after long repression (CP 327). Such mob actions in the modern world are the further steps in the process of desacralization anatomized in *The Rainbow* and dramatized in works, like *Aaron's Rod,* in which anarchy is rampant. St. John's eagle, with a parody of cosmic vision — a "bird's-eye view / Even of Calvary and Resurrection" — must be brought back to earth: "Shoo it down out of the empyrean" (CP 328-29). Without its earthiness, it lacks its ancient power. Elsewhere in *Birds, Beasts and Flowers,* Europe is a tree that withers ("The Evening Land," CP. 291), while the "white Christus" is now fallen from its cross (at least in a metaphor in "The Red Wolf," CP 403). Not only have the evangelistic beasts lost their ancient place as signs of creation; they seem devoid of sacred significance altogether. Lawrence is intentionally showing biblical typology in its most static and pointless form.

The major exception to this statement lies, of course, in "St. Matthew," providing a more provocative context for surrounding poems. As I have said, it is the one poem of its group that sketches in a comprehensive worldview, but several other poems in *Birds, Beasts and Flowers* share aspects of its ambitious expanse. Thus "Snake," presenting the underworld lord in nature, may be meaningfully placed near a poem that relates Christ to a serpent (through its biblical quotation) and that hints at Christ, too, as an underworld lord. This idea is at odds with the general view that the poems of "Creatures" and "Reptiles" are in complete opposition to "The Evangelistic Beasts," immediately preceding them. Without pondering the prominence in "St. Matthew" of the reference to the Brazen Serpent, one would indeed expect the natural, sensuous snake to contrast with the Christ in the earlier work. In fact, however, when Lawrence arranged the poems for publication in 1923, he furthered the identification between Christ and the serpent by placing the poems in their present relative proximity.

Lawrence had considerable warrant in theosophy, even if nowhere else, for making this connection. Madame Blavatsky herself had associated Christ with the "True and Perfect Serpent," a theosophical version of typology, in a volume that Lawrence had known for half a dozen years (*SD* 1:410).[56] He later states explicitly that the Logos came as a "white dragon" (serpent), initiating our era, but declined into a grey one with time (*A* 127). It is even quite possible that a reference to the Brazen Serpent in Frederick Carter's *Dragon of the Alchemists* was *written or inspired* by Lawrence in 1923-24 when he worked on the original *Dragon* manuscript with Carter. This point is worth emphasis because the opposite train of influence, from Carter to Lawrence, is claimed. According to the Carter passage, the serpent "is not only the image of the Tempter in Eden, but is again that of the Deliverer from the evil serpents."[57] Lawrence clearly had this meaning in mind when writing "St. Matthew," six years before receiving the Carter manuscript.[58]

"Bat" and "Man and Bat," both in the "Creatures" section followed by "Snake," share in the vertical pole of the cosmology established in "St. Matthew." The representative man of "Evangelistic Beasts" finds himself suspended between "the wings of the morning" and

56. See also Jung's reference to "those far from uncommon medieval pictures . . . in which a serpent is shown hanging on the Cross in place of Christ" (*Psychology and Religion,* in *Collected Works,* 11:229). In this context, he draws attention to the Brazen Serpent.

57. Carter, *The Dragon of the Alchemists,* 48.

58. Lawrence has been cast at times as a follower of Carter, at least partly because Carter claimed that Lawrence's *Apocalypse* did not properly acknowledge him. Lawrence received the original of Carter's manuscript in June 1923, four months after having arranged *Birds, Beasts and Flowers,* and he met with Carter 3-5 January 1924 to discuss the latter's work. In *D. H. Lawrence and the Body Mystical,* Carter tells how Lawrence put his stamp upon many passages and later became a collaborator on *The Dragon of Revelation,* based on material related to the previous manuscript (25, 42-43). The original *Dragon* manuscript no longer exists (and did not even in 1929, when Lawrence inquired about it), so it cannot be compared with *The Dragon of the Alchemists,* a revision of the original work, published in 1926; Mara Kalnins, in her introduction to Lawrence's *Apocalypse and the Writings on Revelation,* 11, calls this Carter publication "a much reduced and revised version."

"the bat-wings" of the "fathom-flickering spirit of darkness" (*CP* 323). The latter image may suggest the wings of Lucifer at the end of Dante's *Inferno* and certainly brings to mind creatures of the dark underworld. Curiously enough, however, Lawrence's sketch for the cover of the Secker *Birds, Beasts and Flowers* places the bat high on the tree of life (Fig. 11), affording us the useful reminder that the creatures in the poems are not simply symbols but also representations of highly evolved beings in their own right. This idea is, in fact, a main claim of the poem. In "Man and Bat," the speaker considers the bat "unclean," "obscene," and "impure," and at last exults, "*I escaped him*" (346–47). Despite his lack of affinities with bats, though, he recognizes their reality. He cannot imagine their deity (or that of fish in the poem "Fish"), but these poems, like "Snake," seek to include the polar habitats, and all their "gods," as features of the poem's universe.

In *Birds, Beasts and Flowers,* the crucified Christ has foils not only in the Bridegroom of "Almond Blossom" but also in the tortoises, creatures bearing natural stigmata, in the series of six poems published earlier as *Tortoises.* With this group in place near "The Evangelistic Beasts," the center section of the volume is complete. As I have shown, the universe of "St. Matthew," with its symmetry of up and down, creates a cross even larger and more balanced than that of the instrument of crucifixion. This is the cosmic counterpart of the inner and immanental cross of *Tortoises.* [59] "Tortoise Shell" states that "The Cross, the Cross / Goes deeper in than we know, / Deeper into life" (*CP* 354), stresses the five points of the shell reminiscent of the wounds of Christ, and notes that "the Lord" wrote this sign down visibly on the shell to suggest "the plan within" (356). A link exists between this idea and Lilly's speech to Aaron Sisson about the inner tree of life.[60] But the poem's thesis is far from being an expression of romantic self-absorption, for the immanental cross or tree (inside the tortoises) balances not only with their external stigmas but also with the cross in the universe at large.

Tortoises presents an evocative combination of cruciform shapes and Edenic setting in ways suggesting Adam as the typological precursor of Christ. The tortoise is "Adam" in "Tortoise Family Connections" (*CP* 358), and its connection with the "new Adam"

59. Similarly, the cabbalistic tree of life exists in both microcosm and macrocosm. See, for example, Halevy, *Tree of Life,* 35–71.
60. See chapter 4 above.

of biblical typology, Christ, is explicit in the later poems of the
sequence. "Tortoise Shell" suggests that crucifixion is a universal
experience—a sure potentiality of the baby tortoise, as emblematized
in the "outward and visible" sign on his shell (*CP* 356). "Lui et
Elle" more explicitly links the male tortoise to Christ, as well as
the torn god Osiris: "crucified into sex," he has "the spear . . .
through the side of his isolation" (*CP* 361). "Tortoise Shout"
further depicts a male tortoise as "Giving up the ghost, / Or
screaming in Pentecost" (*CP* 365) on "the cross, / The wheel on
which our silence first is broken, / Sex" (366). But crucifixion is
seldom the end for a Lawrence character, not even a tortoise—and
this poem presents no exception to the rule. As the tortoise gives
"the same cry . . . as from Christ, the Osiris-cry of abandonment,"
a paradox occurs: because of the separation from the female other
and from all other things, the creature can know ecstasy as the
torn part finds "its whole again throughout the universe" (367).
The ultimate parallel between the tortoise and Christ, then, is not
hellish parody[61] but lies in the theme of regeneration and renewal
of wholeness, a sensual version of the "fortunate fall." Lawrence's
use of typology in these works is again dynamic, experimental,
and effective.

III

Outside this "core" of poems in *Birds, Beasts and Flowers,* the
European setting is depicted in its degeneration, lacking its tree of
life because of the long reign of the crucifix. Despite this ironic
design, the volume's typological preoccupations often convey
Lawrence's hope for a new dispensation that might return the
Edenic condition and metaphorically reinstate the tree of life in
place of the tree of knowledge or the cross. In *Apocalypse,* he
refers to "the Golden Age, before the eating of the Fruit of
Knowledge" (135), contrasting it with the Iron Age or Age of Steel
(129, 135)—a state reproduced in his own mechanized, technological society, built up out of excess knowledge. He explains the
consequences for Adam: when "he ate of the Tree of Knowledge
instead of the Tree of Life," he "knew himself *apart* and separate"
(131). The poem "Figs" deals with the fall of Eve in the same

61. Gilbert, "D. H. Lawrence's Uncommon Prayers," 88.

terms. She "quickly sewed fig-leaves" when she became conscious
of her nakedness: "She'd been naked all her days before, / But
till . . . that apple of knowledge, she hadn't had the fact on her
mind" (CP 284).

In much of *Birds, Beasts and Flowers*, the garden setting and
the central tree are less present than suggested by contrast, for
Eden is long lost. In "Bare Fig-Trees," for instance, the tree of life
is not immediately obvious but emerges only with the reader's
recognition of the poem's iconographic imagery. Lawrence refers
repeatedly to the fig tree's "many-branching candelabrum," the
spires "flourishing from the rock" (CP 299). While he contrasts
the living plant to the "seven-branched, tallow-stinking candlestick"
(299), he works ironically and allusively with the fact that this
device, the menorah, is a symbol of the tree of life (Schiller 1:21)
and depicts a world picture with the central *axis mundi,* or world
tree, in the center of Eden, and with the heavens and the underworld at its vertical poles.[62] To Lawrence's Scripture-conscious
ear, the poem's wording must have evoked, if ironically, the "living
rock" (the fig "lives upon this rock"), which is a frequent term for
Christ.

Despite the assault on the "tallow righteousness" of this candlestick, the poem nonetheless fully indulges in the rich imagery of
the candelabrum. This treatment is typical of the poet's method
throughout *Birds, Beasts and Flowers,* as in many of his prose
fictions. A given motif has double permutations (as in the example of the cross, previously discussed) — one side that is exalted,
another that is denigrated. We see continually how preoccupied
Lawrence was with processes of rebirth, for it is as if even the
motifs themselves undergo the discarding of an old identity to
allow the affirmation of the new. In this poem, the bare trees
remind the speaker of the degeneration of the Judeo-Christian
civilization, now seen without a concept of order or natural
hierarchy. The evocation of the lost tree of life makes the modern
disaster the more unfortunate, setting up a contrast between a
virtual "golden age" of the past and the present age of dissolution.

"Cypresses," written just months earlier than "Almond Blossom"
and "Bare Fig-Trees," also explores the relation between the death-
tree and the tree of life. This poem extends the assault on modernity to the Romans, who suppressed the ancient Etruscans, and
draws a parallel between the Romans and "mechanical America"

62. Yarden, *The Tree of Light,* 35.

that resists Aztec antiquity. The cypresses are dark repositories of pagan faculties, oddly invoked in an oblique reference to the Christian Nativity, which Lawrence turns to his own uses: a rebirth must come from "the deeps / That churn the frankincense and ooze the myrrh" (*CP* 298). The context makes these Nativity gifts reminders not only of birth but also of death and rebirth. As embalming agents, they act in the grave and signify immortality — in this case, the ongoing "marrow-thought" of Etruria (297), enduring despite the apparent defeat of the Etruscans. I have argued that the cypress has cosmic importance in *Aaron's Rod,* even beyond that suggested by Gilbert, who finds that, in "Cypresses," it dominates its cosmos as if rising from the "breast of hell."[63] Fittingly, the tree reaches to the underworld, but this is by no means the sum of it, and it eventually stands forth in the sky as a tree of life. The cypresses are "pillars of dark flame" (297), Lawrence's adaptation of the biblical pillar of fire (Exodus 13:21-22). Related by orthodox typology to the coming of Christ (Schiller 1:29) and by Lawrence to the trees of Eden (*RDP* 234), the pillar of fire is here a symbol of resurrection for the Etruscans — with whom, of course, Lawrence elsewhere explicitly associates an esoteric "science . . . of *life*" (*F* 54; my emphasis). The poet urges these ancients to restore to the world their "meaning," now "wrapt inviolable in soft cypress-trees" (297-98). Just as the related passage in *Aaron's Rod* describes cypresses by seven repetitions of the word "life" and presents a pagan communion between the living Aaron and dead "lost races," the poem contains nine repetitions of "dark" or "darkness," referring not only to the grave but, far more importantly, to "dark thought / For which the language is lost" — to sentient, nonverbal communication such as the departed races can restore (296). Although their "tongues are dead," a vaguely pentecostal flame seems to move through the trees that are "dark, like cypress-trees in a wind" (296, 297), somewhat recalling Van Gogh's shimmering cypresses but also suggesting the wind that accompanied the biblical Pentecost.

A related idea of ongoing human life appears in the tree imagery in "Hibiscus and Salvia Flowers," written a little more than a year after "Cypresses." Lawrence sees Sunday strollers on the Corso "bloom . . . on the living, perambulating bush" (*CP* 313). The passage suggests Moses' burning bush, one of Lawrence's favorite

---

63. Gilbert, "D. H. Lawrence's Uncommon Prayers," 87. The poem was planned while Lawrence was writing the novel. See chapter 4 above.

biblical references. Like the pillar of fire, it is sometimes associated typologically with Christ's birth (Schiller 1:71), and Lawrence mentions it with Eden's trees (*RDP* 234). In the essay "Democracy" (written in 1919), he refers to "the bush where he [God] sings," and this is in individual creatures (*RDP* 73). In this poem, however, the allusion to the burning bush is an ironic one, for the socialists wearing the flowers—and thus seeming to "bloom"—represent a late and wrongheaded application of the Christian ideal of human equality; they therefore misuse the royal blossoms.

One major factor making the cross and the tree of life central to the volume *Birds, Beasts and Flowers* has not yet been explored: eucharistic imagery. In "Medlars and Sorb-Apples," the poet suggests "a sip of Marsala" with the fruits (*CP* 281), prescribing a dark wine, for "Grapes" reveals an attempt to regain an age "when . . . Gods were dark-skinned" (*CP* 286). It is a time like the one Aaron Sisson senses in his communion with Etruscan (and possibly African) spirits in the cypress trees of *Aaron's Rod*. [64] The sacrament in these poems is plainly not to be the Christian one, for Dionysus himself appears in "Medlars and Sorb-Apples." Celebrating the vine, "Grapes" satirizes the "rose of all roses, rose of all the world" (*CP* 285), no doubt recalling Yeats's poems "Rose of the World" and "Rose of Battle" (with this opening line). Lawrence may have been thinking of another poem in the same collection, "To the Rose Upon the Rood of Time," choosing to see Christian imagery in the *Rose* poems generally.[65] The rose is now to give place to the "swart" grape, the "dark gods," and a newly dark consciousness, for "dusky are the avenues of wine" (286, 287). The volume's emphasis on darkness is not because the sequence takes place exclusively in hell but because Lawrence wants to reverse the sharp, conscious vision associated with the Fall in Eden—to return to the age "before eyes saw too much" (285). This meaning borrows directly from Genesis 3:7, in which the *eyes* of Adam and Eve open to their nakedness and division. The same theme of changed eyesight is similarly associated with sacrament in the early story "The Thorn in the Flesh" ("Vin Ordinaire"). "Grapes" suggests that, "as we sip the wine," we may regain the "naked communion" not possible to people of our "clothed vision" (286).

64. See chapter 4 above.
65. See Yeats, *Variorum Edition of the Poems*, 100–101, 111–12, 113–15. Although these poems seem far from being "Christian," Lawrence may have identified their dreamy, ethereal quality with the modern spirituality he was opposing.

Birds, Beasts and Flowers moves far beyond the suggestions of sacrament in its "Fruits" poems to deal with more complex eucharistic motifs. Typologically, the crucifixion imagery at the poem's center correlates with that of sacrifice in "St. Luke," the third poem in "The Evangelistic Beasts." Lawrence has made it clear that the beast in this case is not simply a calf, as in some representations of St. Luke's symbol, but a sacrificial bull:

Is his breast a wall?

. . . .

But now it is a burning hearthstone only,
Massive old altar of his own burnt offering.

It was always an altar of burnt offering
His own black blood poured out like a sheet of flame
    over his fecundating herd
As he gave himself forth.

(CP 326)

The bull of sacrifice is sometimes present in iconography of the Crucifixion (Schiller 2:128), and Lawrence's bull is evidently an embodiment of Christian self-sacrifice, no longer having, like Moses, "golden horns of power" (326)[66] but being "over-full of offering, a vast, vast offer of himself" (327). Unlike the calm animal supporting Eve on the dust jacket of Seltzer's edition of the volume (Fig. 14), the bull in the poem is "over-charged" and, being identified with the proletariat of latter-day Christendom, is ready to fight, presumably adding to the anarchy in the world rather than performing a cleansing destruction.

The Old Testament sacrifice, the typological forerunner not only of the Crucifixion but also of the Mass, appears even in apparently minor metaphors in *Birds, Beasts and Flowers.* For instance, in "Hibiscus and Salvia Flowers," the poet asks of the flower-adorned socialists, "Who smeared their doors with blood?" (*CP* 313). Who, that is, allowed them to appropriate the mark of salvation (from animal blood) that, in the Old Testament, spared the followers of Moses and Aaron from the final plague in Egypt? The biblical reference has recently caused the poet and critic Tom Paulin to identify these socialists with the Israelites' related delivery from

66. Lawrence evidently accepts an incorrect translation of the Bible, attributing to Moses horns instead of rays of light. (See, for example, Merivale, *Pan the Goat-God,* 41).

Egypt and journey to the Promised Land,[67] but I find the poem more ironic than this. In the Bible story, Moses and Aaron were instructed by God how the children of Israel should mark their doors with blood from their Passover lamb so that God would "pass over" them when smiting the firstborn of Egypt (Exodus 12:5–30). The protective blood, reputedly marked in the form of the tau cross (the shape associated with the Brazen Serpent),[68] was interpreted in biblical exegesis as a prefiguration of Christ's protection of the redeemed through his own ultimate sacrifice (Schiller 2:125, 124). The allusion greatly deepens the meaning of the poem, for it suggests that the world is being visited with plagues and needs the marks of salvation. The poem's restive bands of socialists and Bolshevists may feel this threat and this need; but they are aimless "louts" instead of pilgrims, and the flowers, in their "native royalty" and "molten gold," are incongruous decorations for those who have, in fact, "pulled down" the flowers to "their disgusting level" (314–15, 317). Since the strollers are ideologically opposed to the leadership principle by which the Old Testament leaders decreed the sign of the blood sacrifice to God, the poem's questions about the modern wanderers are particularly apt: "Who said they might assume these blossoms? / What god did they consult?" (313).

The final poem in *Birds, Beasts and Flowers*, "The American Eagle," presents a New World version of the sacrifice theme. Although hatched by "the dove of Liberty" (*CP* 413) and posing "with an olive-sprig in his mouth" (413), the American bird is indeed a fierce eagle, not a humble Christian dove. He is, however, "trying to look like a pelican, / And plucking out of his plumage a few loose feathers" (413) that turn out to be golden in the materialistic sense. But this proffer of the "golden egg" is "just a stone to anyone asking for meat" (414). These images have great complexity that turns upon motifs of the eucharistic sacrifice, for Christ is often symbolized by the pelican (Schiller 136–37), feeding its young from its heart's blood as Christ feeds the church through his own blood. Instead of offering its blood with its breast feathers, however, the American eagle gives the materialistic substitute for sacrament—a substitute condemned by the poem's allusion to Christ's question, from the Sermon on

67. Paulin, " 'Hibiscus and Salvia Flowers,' " 184–85.

68. Appleton and Bridges, *Symbolism in Liturgical Art*, 21. See also Jenner, *Christian Symbolism*, 49, and Blavatsky (*SD* 2:551; *Isis* 2:454).

the Mount, "Or what man . . . if his son ask bread, will he give him a stone?" (Matthew 7:9) The American eagle, by giving the "golden egg," withholds the true bread of life. To Lawrence, neither the materialistic golden egg nor the ascetic Eucharist is the nourishment needed.

The speaker, lamenting the loss of all things sacred and royal, hopes that these will yet be restored by the eagle, which may cease to identify itself with the humble and, instead, fly in the face of "the sheep-faced ewe / Who is losing her lamb"—an evident reference to the church. In this case, the bird may offer a new kind of sacrifice, "Lifting the rabbit-blood of the myriads up into something splendid" and "drinking a little blood, and loosing another royalty unto the world" (414). This final poem echoes the reference to "red blood-sacrifices" of Aztecs (*CP* 371) in an earlier poem, "Turkey-Cock," and even more closely recalls "Eagle in New Mexico": "When you [the eagle] pick the red smoky heart from a rabbit or a light-blooded bird / Do you lift it to the sun, as the Aztec priests used to lift red hearts of men?" (*CP* 374) In "Eagle in New Mexico," however, the poet/narrator rejects the eagle "priest": "I don't yield to you," he states, "And you . . . / Can be put out of office as sacrifice bringer" by "the life in the hearts of men" (374). In the final poem, too, the eagle's offering stands for "power of life," fitting well with the quotation introducing the "Flowers" section of *Birds, Beasts and Flowers:* "But blood is red, and blood is life. Red was the colour of kings. Kings, far-off kings, painted their faces vermilion, and were almost gods" (*CP* 303).

Lawrence is looking back beyond modern self-sacrifice to "the old idea of sacrifice" that he celebrates elsewhere in a poem of the same name: "O when the old world sacrificed a ram / it was to the gods who make us splendid" in order to attain "the further splendour of being men" (*CP* 679). In a related poem, "Shedding of Blood," he urges the sacrifice "not of your firstling lamb, without spot or blemish" but of "the scabbed and ugly lamb, that spreads contagion" (*CP* 678). Evidently alluding to the instructions to Moses and Aaron to sacrifice "a lamb without blemish, a male of the first year" (Exodus 12:5), the poet reverses the Passover law but calls for some therapeutic form of sacrifice, nonetheless.

The idea of renewal of life out of death is central to *Birds, Beasts and Flowers* —as it is central to the typology of the Eucharist that some of the poems contain for Lawrence's own purposes. The "naked communion" of "Grapes," with its return to Eden, proves no easy achievement, and the poet, dispensing in other

poems with the rather innocuous play of words on "communion,"
places a more austere, indeed chilling, emphasis on blood sacrifice.
In "The Revolutionary," Samson must pull down the pillars of the
modern world, the very "high and super-gothic heavens" of the
era, to allow for rebirth. As discussed in chapter 1, his destruction
of the Philistine temple and victory over his enemies correlate in
the typological pattern with Christ's rending of the tomb and
triumph over death and hell. Lawrence's Samson may also experience such triumph, but ironically: his resurrection will be that of
the old Samson, rising above the dead Christendom. A similarly
inverted typology informs much of *The Plumed Serpent.* Even
more remarkable, however, is this novel's development of an entirely
"new" cast of typological characters — those of the New World,
already suggested by the "Aztec priests" of "Eagle in New Mexico."

The New World Schema

New Eve and the Aztec Patriarchs in *Quetzalcoatl* and *The Plumed Serpent*

6

According to Frank Kermode, Lawrence's works "headed danger-ously toward a typological predominance, and paid the price," for "preordained types" can suppress the "randomness" important to a novel's sense of life.[1] Something of this problem does beset *The Plumed Serpent,* which has been faulted for "static vitalism"[2] and likened to works of stasis in the graphic arts, both admiringly and otherwise.[3] This effect of arrested motion is largely owing to its sustained concentration on culmination: apocalypse and paradise restored (though not, of course, in Milton's sense). Although this completion is cast as part of a cyclic pattern, the cycle itself seems rather mechanical.[4] And even *Women in Love,*

1. Kermode, "Lawrence and the Apocalyptic Types," 25.
2. Spilka, *Love Ethic of D. H. Lawrence,* 110.
3. Rossman, in "D. H. Lawrence and Mexico," 198, compares the novel, in its assault on society, to some propagandistic frescoes it satirizes; while he makes no point of the graphic art, the fresco parallel is interesting for this aesthetic aspect. For William York Tindall's well-known comparison of the novel with Gauguin's paintings, an admiring one, see his introduction to *The Plumed Serpent,* v.
4. Humma, "Imagery of *The Plumed Serpent,*" 207, believes that the cycle will bring Quetzalcoatl's end again: "The implication is that Quetzalcoatl's present emergent triumph is subject to the same cyclical sinking as his former dominion had been subject to."

with its emphatic sense of terminus, never incurs the problem of what to do with the achieved goal.

Although it is inadequate to see *The Rainbow, Women in Love,* and *The Plumed Serpent* as the representatives of the Old Testament, the New, and the apocalyptic new era, they do suggest a sequence of this general kind; thus the last work in the line eventually loses the haptic quest aspect most typical of Lawrence's typological design. He prefers the unfinished pattern to its ultimate fulfillment. Even in the making of souls, likened to the weaving of blankets, his character Cipriano advocates continual open-endedness: "It is very nice while all the wools are rolling their different threads and different colours, and the pattern is being made," but, "finished," it "has no interest any more" (*PS* 234). England's pattern, he claims, is finished, while "Mexico hasn't started to weave the pattern of her soul" (234). The novel means, therefore, to deal with a developing, incomplete new movement, but instead it has the slow-motion of excessive stylization.

Another difficulty occurs when Lawrence changes the cast of characters in his scheme of typological recurrence. Instead of the biblical patriarchs, often the inheritors of his "third age," the unfamiliar Aztec gods Quetzalcoatl and Huitzilopochtli institute a pagan version of the millennium. Lawrence made this change with great deliberation, striving to adopt a mythic framework fitted to the New World rather than the Old. A comparison of the 1923 *Quetzalcoatl* with the final *Plumed Serpent* reveals that, while both include the Aztec gods, the second is more indebted to Aztec lore. Because the exotic nature of the new "patriarchs" can distract one significantly from the underlying typological scheme of the novel, it is instructive to glance first at another work of the same general period that still incorporates the biblical patriarchs in a forward-looking vision: *The Boy in the Bush.*

Lawrence's interest in the Bible, especially the Old Testament and the Book of Revelation, was never greater than in the middle and late 1920s. To 1925 belongs his one Biblical drama, *David.* Slightly earlier, in 1923, his concern with apocalyptic themes, already present in earlier works like *Women in Love,* intensified when he read a manuscript by the astrologer Frederick Carter, interpreting Revelation.[5] Eschatology and a return to Old Testa-

5. Lawrence had seen a Carter manuscript in 1923, but it cannot be reconstructed because it had already been changed and scattered when he asked for it in 1929. (See footnote 58 to chapter 5.) Lawrence's *Apocalypse*

ment patriarchy go hand in hand in the hero's mind in *The Boy in the Bush,* largely written in 1923 between the first and second versions of *The Plumed Serpent.* Although Lawrence coauthored the Australian novel with Mollie Skinner, Lawrence "had made the novel his own," according to Paul Eggert, and the concluding chapters, especially, are clearly Lawrentian (*BB* liii, xlvi).[6] Several of their ideas and motifs link them to *Quetzalcoatl* of a scant few months earlier. All four of these creations—the Australian novel, both versions of the Mexican novel, and *David*—deal with an ending world and a shifting of eras: *David* moves from an epoch of ancient tribal power toward the Christian epoch, already foreshadowed by David, but the three other works reverse this direction.

It is tantalizing to consider whether the final *Plumed Serpent* might have continued Lawrence's interest in the biblical patriarchs more openly if he had written it immediately after *Quetzalcoatl,* a version so different from the final work that it has been termed a separate creative effort.[7] Instead, he turned to *The Boy in the Bush,* rewriting from a manuscript sent him by Skinner and adding to it a focus upon the aristocratic "kingdom of death" and the "Lords of Death" (*BB* 307, 284), suggesting the "Masters of Death" in the Mexican novel (*PS* 378).

The "boy" of the title, Jack Grant, is, like a number of Lawrence characters, an émigré from a depleted civilization. Having come from England, he eventually fits far better into his new, wild surroundings, where he dreams of establishing a new world of his own in the bush, a theocracy. Although "the Bible was perhaps the foundation of his consciousness," he has "no use for Christianity proper" (141). A worshiper not of Jesus (a "side issue") but of "Almighty God, Maker of Heaven and Earth," he identifies himself

---

grew out of his agreement to write an introduction for Carter's later *The Dragon of Revelation,* as recounted by Carter, *D. H. Lawrence and the Body Mystical,* 25, 42-43.

6. Because Skinner's original manuscript (which Lawrence revised in the New World) is lost, it is impossible to be certain at all times which sections of *The Boy in the Bush* are Lawrence's; but, according to a copy of the published book containing Skinner's holograph comments, the last chapters are entirely his. Besides Paul Eggert, see Rossman, *"The Boy in the Bush,"* 187-88.

7. L. D. Clark states that " 'Quetzalcoatl' differs from *The Plumed Serpent* much as the three versions of *Lady Chatterley's Lover* differ" (*PS* xxv). Louis Martz, in his introduction to *Quetzalcoatl,* finds it a less finished work.

early with such Old Testament figures as Abraham, Isaiah, Jacob, Moses, and Joshua (141). If the original manuscript included biblical names, such as Jacob and Esau (for whom the villain Easu is named), Lawrence clearly turned them to his own purposes. Jack's appreciation of these men owes much to their bold and often amorous adventures, and especially to their multiple wives. Beyond feeling these attractions, however, he genuinely sees his life in terms of their destined wilderness journeys toward the Promised Land—the same motif we have seen in *The Rainbow* and elsewhere in Lawrence's works.

Jack's story, a form of "thriller," never suffers from stasis. His special regard for Abraham rests on the patriarch's role in a rising movement, not a finished one: "at the beginning of time," Abraham parallels Jack "at another, later beginning" (*BB* 337). Thus Jack has dreamed of going "like Abraham under the wild sky, speaking to a fierce wild Lord, and having angels stand in his doorway" (333). This passage draws upon several biblical events, beginning when Abraham follows God's bidding to leave his homeland (Genesis 12) and continuing through his meeting with three divine messengers as "he sat in the tent door" (Genesis 18:1)—the "three strange angels" of a 1914 Lawrence poem, "Song of a Man Who Has Come Through" (*CP* 250), and of a *Rainbow* allusion (271). Jack sees himself similarly attended by God, the recipient of extraordinary promises and visitants, while his enemies fall around him. The biblical reference is not only to Genesis but also to Hebrews, in which Abraham is cast as the exemplary émigré: "by faith" he "went out, not knowing whither he went," being one of the holy "strangers and pilgrims on earth" (Hebrews 11:8, 13). Such wanderers, like Lawrence's refugees, turn their backs on the country behind them in their search for a new land. This passage may serve as a general gloss on his questers:

> And truly, if they [strangers and pilgrims] had been mindful of the country from whence they came out, they might have had opportunity to have returned.

> But now they desire a better country, that is, an heavenly: wherefore God is not ashamed to be called their God: for he hath prepared for them a city.
>
> (Hebrews 11:15-16)

In keeping with this biblical emphasis not only on the Promised Land but on that which it foreshadows—the "city . . . whose builder and maker is God" (Hebrews 11:10)—Jack's expectations are supermundane, as are those of the new religious movement in the Mexican novel.[8]

Not, of course, that he quite expects, or desires, the New Jerusalem—quite the opposite. But he does expect, like so many other Lawrence protagonists, a new condition on the face of the earth. The attitude of seeking beyond the merely mortal is deeply ingrained in him, apparently from the typological patterns that fill his mind.[9] He considers himself his Lord's anointed one, "with the dark unction between his brows" (292), for a near-death experience gives him a sense of mastery over the afterlife, like that of Count Dionys Psanek in *The Ladybird*. But his "kingdom" would be worldly—and hierarchical—as well as obscurely otherworldly. Directly from his "Lord," he would have "earth-royalty" like Abraham's or Saul's (*BB* 337-38). He will not play "the mild Saint Joseph" but will emulate "the old fathers of red earth" (*BB* 331, 330), and we know precisely who these fathers are. The new code would be dependent on the Old Testament again instead of the New: "Let there be another, deeper, fiercer, untamed sort of goodness, like in the days of Abraham and Samson and Saul" because "the Christian goodness had gone bad" (*BB* 319).[10] His projected life-style has much in common with that of Ramón's Mexico, for both feature hierarchy under vaguely supernatural sanctions. In Jack's case, however, while the values of an old patriarchy are invoked to replace those of his modern world, his new dispensation is largely an object of quest and vision, not fulfillment. He even grows disillusioned with it momentarily in the penultimate chapter.

Quetzalcoatl, too, which refers more openly to the Bible than does *The Plumed Serpent*, contains elements of the wilderness

8. Doherty, "White Mythologies," 485, might well have included *The Boy in the Bush* when referring to the supernaturalism and "unchecked sublimations" found "notoriously in the leadership novels." Jack expects to be "a lord in death, and sway the destinies of the life to come" (*BB* 338).

9. Lawrence's characters are, to some extent, representative in this preoccupation. In my introduction and its notes, I touch upon the effect of the Apocalypse on the thought of the Western world. See also Clark, "The Apocalypse of Lorenzo," 141-59.

10. Along with Abraham, Lawrence refers to "David even" (*BB* 130), showing by this expression his mature reservations about the king, as discussed in chapter 1 above. As I have pointed out, Samson and Saul are heroes exalted elsewhere in Lawrence's works. Jack imagines himself as a literal patriarch with children "like a new race" (*BB* 337).

theme from Genesis and Exodus as Kate Burns (Kate Leslie in the later novel) observes her surroundings in Mexico, seeing a virtually biblical scene: "The strange groups of animals trailing down the irregular, dirty beach to the water somehow reminded Kate of her old visions of Israelites in deserts, and Abraham seeking water: remote pictures having an inward Jewish dreariness, which remained to her from the Old Testament" (Q 152½). Even a group of pigs seems biblical to her (possibly because of the Gadarene swine), and she sees, again, "a dry, unreal land of unliving mountains, that reminded her of the awful dry abstraction and ugliness of Mount Sinai" (Q 153). Despite Kate's sense that such scenes are ugly, the allusions point appropriately to locations and events of another Holy Land. Paralleling Abraham's search for water, the Mexican religious movement, too, awaits the rains and gropes toward its own forms of revelation and sacrament. Mount Sinai recalls Moses, coming down the mountain with the Tables of the Law, much as the inspired Mexican prophet, Ramón, issues "written hymns" and instructions for his people. Lawrence's usage is probably ironic, since Ramón will replace the Judeo-Christian heritage altogether, but both he and his creator have difficulty dispensing with its images. At one point, the Mexican movement even seems to have borrowed some liturgical raimant from Judaism, for its new ceremonial clothing reminds Kate of "synagogue robes" (Q 235). Such references are reminders that Lawrence's biblical drama, *David,* only two years in the future. While Ramón, even in the later *Plumed Serpent,* reminds Kate of "the old, old Europe" (203) and "feels European" (237), she might have said, too, that he "feels" somewhat biblical in spite of his elaborate neo-Aztec trappings—though less so than in *Quetzalcoatl.*

I

Although *The Plumed Serpent* shows a great transformation of Lawrence's material, often supplanting the biblical in order to showcase native Indian lore, it does not rid itself of its typological pattern. In keeping with L. D. Clark's observation of the "paradox" posed by the apocalyptist's literal and symbolic meanings,[11] the novel's actions are twofold, affecting actual political life and

11. Clark, "The Apocalypse of Lorenzo," 158.

deep inner being. While Lawrence saw history itself in an apocalyptic light, he also believed that the Book of Revelation contained an ancient initiation rite, depicting the mystic death and
rebirth "of Adam: of any man": "The old Adam is going to be . . .
re-born as the new Adam" (A 101). *The Plumed Serpent* depicts
both an "end of the world" and a series of initiations in which
characters are fitted to respond and contribute to the new Eden.
Kate, a forty-year-old Irishwoman from a sterile English civilization, is the chief initiate, while Ramón is her most obvious savior;
but all the characters go through initiatory rites and all save
each other at different times. As I have pointed out in my
introduction, Ramón is explicitly identified, in the novel's 1923
version, with the "Redeemed Adam" (Q 332) — a term often denoting Christ.[12] As if this were not enough, however, Ramón, in both
versions, is also the avatar of the Aztec god Quetzalcoatl. Indeed,
the Christian and pagan gods have changed places: Christ has
earlier replaced Quetzalcoatl as vicar of Mexico and now Quetzalcoatl reappears, while Christ goes, in his turn, to "the bath"
of oblivion and renewal (PS 125).[13] Thus Ramón, despite his
numerous resemblances to Christ, *cannot* embody the Christian
deity. Topping off all of these complexities, Ramón's general
and friend (eventually Kate's husband in *The Plumed Serpent*),
Cipriano, is both Huitzilopochtli, a warlike Aztec god, and the
representative of Pan. He is also Kate's dark savior. Of course,
Lawrence elsewhere speaks quite similarly of the "old Adam" and
the "oldest Pan," symbolizing in both the primal sacred vision
before man felt detached from God.[14] It is even understandable
why Cipriano is further identified with the snake in the novel's

12. Carter, in *D. H. Lawrence and the Body Mystical*, refers, also, to the
"regenerate Adam," by which he means the cosmic man he evidently discussed
with Lawrence (14, 90–91). Although Carter is sometimes credited with
introducing such lore to Lawrence, the two had evidently developed similar
interests independently before they shared them with each other, for Lawrence
would have known of Adam Kadmon from Blavatsky. Carter's influence did
serve, however, to recall Lawrence to some of his earlier preoccupations and
to teach him about astrology, as Lawrence states (*Letters* 4:460–61). See also
my introduction.

13. Clark's appendix I shows that Aztec mythology posited a cycle in
which gods alternated with each other in successive epochs — usually Quetzalcoatl and Tezcatlipoca (PS 553). Lawrence has adapted this system to his own
purposes, thus altering — but only somewhat — his characteristic expectation
of a return of paganism after Christendom.

14. See my discussion of Aaron Sisson as Adam, Pan, and risen man in
chapter 5.

Edenic paradigm, for the underworld consciousness is a significant part of that primal Pan vision. Besides, he turns out, amazingly,
to be associated with the Brazen Serpent. But *The Plumed Serpent*
almost topples at times under the burden of these complications.
Although multiple mythologies are characteristic of Lawrence's
eclectic and syncretic style — and his best work is the richer for
them — they do not always cohere in this instance.

Yet much goes right in this well-crafted novel, the first since
Women in Love to undergo such exhaustive rewriting and revision. Stock figures from the Book of Revelation — such as the
four horsemen of the Apocalypse (6:1-8) — develop progressively
from mere tropes to dynamic embodiments.[15] For example, a
horse motif, beginning in an ironic reference to "four Spanish
horsemen of the Apocalypse" and appearing again to designate
spirit and blood as "the rider on the white horse" and "the
rider on the red," culminates in a look at Cipriano and his red
horse as creatures of "one birth" (15, 418, 424).[16] In addition,
the apocalyptic "woman clothed with the sun" (Revelation 12:1) —
the figure Lawrence admired despite its traditional reference to
Mary (Schiller 4,2:174-77) — unfolds progressively in Kate, with
an important twist that I shall examine later. Associated early
with madonna dolls and cast as a Mother of Sorrows still grieving
at times over the death of her second husband, Kate comes to
embody deep womanly godhead as the wife of Cipriano.[17] The
hellish drought of early chapters contrasts with the later flowering
of the land as Kate and Cipriano, representing cosmogonic polarities (fire and water), as well as opposite races, develop their life
together (405).[18] Thus individual lives are invested with cosmic
significance, and individuals seemingly affect cosmic conditions.
Never elsewhere, with the exception of the earliest pages of

15. Bonds, *Language and the Self,*" 56-62, 77-91, deals with similar
"literalization" elsewhere in Lawrence.

16. "Oh four Spanish horsemen of the Apocalypse!" is apparently an
allusion to a novel by the Spanish writer Vicente Blasco Ibáñez (Clark, *PS*
448), but the immediate target of irony is a bullfight, in which the horses and
bulls alike are brutally misused.

17. See Urang, *Kindled in the Flame,* 88, who notes that Kate is "intended"
to be "the woman clothed with the sun," in the Book of Revelation; but Urang
holds that this identification never succeeds.

18. The flourishing of the desert is often associated with the millennium,
an idea involving a typological reading of Isaiah 51:3: "For the Lord shall
comfort Zion . . . and will make her wilderness like Eden, and her desert like
the garden of the Lord."

The Rainbow, do Lawrence characters have such sustained reciprocity with their universe. The Mexican experiment is eventually seen as a virtual extension of Atlantis, being related to "the world before the Flood, before the mental-spiritual world came into being" (415).[19]

The novel's highly developed cosmology is in some ways an adaptation of the Eden-centered one discussed in chapter 5. Lake Sayula, where all the major characters live, is to be "the centre of a new world" (325). While this setting is literally — and memorably — one in Mexico, it has a symbolic relationship with the *axis mundi*. From the matrix of creation, "the heart of the world," the various saviors of mankind cycle forth: in this "infinite room," where "even the trees come and go," Christ and Quetzalcoatl pass each other in their cycling (128, 126).[20] According to the "written hymns" of the new religion, this is the dwelling of the ultimate deity of many names — the "Master-Sun," the "dark sun," and the "Unknown God" (124, 341).[21] Quetzalcoatl is also said to come out of the lake, but, since the "infinite room" cannot be specifically described, this need represent no contradiction.[22] The saviors are depicted climbing up and down a "long slope, / Past the mount of the sun," a cosmic center that apparently coincides with the volcano where Quetzalcoatl, according to legend, immolated himself (119, 123, 223).

A number of these details are consonant with Aztec myths about a paradise in the west, at the earth's navel, the source of the four directions and the four winds (itself the fifth).[23] But the location also has some features of the universal sacred center, with its quaternian elements, as adapted in Christian iconography (Schiller 2:108, 111); and aspects of the "new heaven and new earth" of the Book of Revelation (21:1) are distinguishable in both

19. For one more possible source of this use of Atlantis, see Ballin, "Lewis Spence and the Myth," 63–78. See also my introduction.

20. See Young, " 'Where Even the Trees,' " 39–44. See also my chapter 5.

21. Until late revisions, the novel referred to "the Wonder-dragon at the centre of the cosmos," and Kate was brought to understand "that the great First Cause was like a dragon coiled at the very centre of all the cosmos, and peeping out, like her snake" (*PS* 542). The effect of excising such passages is, at least in part, to leave the reader with a stronger sense of the "dark sun" introduced earlier in the novel. For information on a mystic tradition of the dark sun, see Iida, "On a Topos Called," 271–90.

22. Ballin, "Lewis Spence and the Myth," 36, finds that the first version is more explicit than the final novel about the gods' lake dwelling.

23. See Clark's appendix I on Aztec mythology (*PS* 553).

literal and symbolic settings.[24] In the "written hymns," the "water
of life" is in Quetzalcoatl's hand, and a "Fountain" in the after-
world (123, 385); both echo the biblical "fountain of the water of
life" (Revelation 21:6). In a passage discarded from the final novel,
Ramón states that "the Cross is a Tree again" and that people "may
eat the fruit if they can reach the branches" (547).[25] In Revelation, the faithful may "eat of the tree of life, which is in the midst
of the paradise of God" (2:7). Ramón's line, referring to the restored
tree of life after the terrors of the Apocalypse (Revelation 22:2),
recalls a lengthy explanation in *Quetzalcoatl* that "the Cross is
accomplished" and "the rose is exalted around" it (Q 332).[26] As
elsewhere in Lawrence's works, the return of the tree signifies
paradise regained, and this "rosy cross" represents the Lawrentian
millennium, a sensuous pagan dispensation after the asceticism
of Christendom. In *The Plumed Serpent,* too, the earth's center
proves, symbolically, to contain a tree, for "men are still part
of the Tree of Life, and the roots go down to the centre of the
earth" (80)—one of a cluster of references to this tree.[27] While
Christ is, of course, identified with the cross, Quetzalcoatl likens
himself to a cosmic flowering plant, if not a rosy cross: one with
its "stem . . . in the air" and "roots . . . in all the dark" (226). Thus
the final novel, while dispensing with the more obvious statement
that "the Cross is a Tree again," does depict this change in more

24. "New Heaven and Earth," from one of Lawrence's favorite Bible quota-
tions, is the title of a poem he wrote in 1915 (*CP* 256–61).

25. The passage is part of a lengthy excision, including the further
statements that "the serpent has flung his fold round the Cross again" and
that "the pole of the earth has shifted" (*PS* 547, 548). The lines suggest
Carter's description of an astrological change, in which the constellation
Draco will be "transfixed on the pole itself" (*Symbols of Revelation,* 83).
Recalling his 1923 reading of a Carter manuscript, Lawrence wrote to the
astrologer in 1929: "I liked so much in the old Dragon—which I saw some
years ago," including "the foot of the cross moving into Pisces and now
moving out, the gradual shifting of the Pole" (holograph letter, 3, one of
twenty-nine Lawrence letters to Carter located at the Harry Ransom Humanities Research Center, the University of Texas at Austin). As I have shown,
this shifting pole appears not only in *Quetzalcoatl* and in the passages
excised from *The Plumed Serpent* (quoted above) but also in the imagery of
the 1925 essay "Resurrection."

26. On the "rosy cross," see my chapter 5. The "scentless rose-trees" and
the "white roses" of paradise, mentioned in one of the neo-Aztec movement's
myths about Christ (*PS* 124), seem more associated with Christianity than
with the pagan "rosy cross."

27. See Humma, "Imagery of *The Plumed Serpent,* " 200, 211, remarking
on the novel's tree imagery.

subtle terms. Quetzalcoatl, metaphorically the blossoming tree, with "the cup of [his] flowering unfolded" (226), replaces Christ and the cross.

The most obvious removal of the cross from the literal world-center occurs when the images of crucifixion are taken out of the Sayula church, to be replaced by statues of Quetzalcoatl and Huitzilopochtli. Not only crucifixes but also other ascetic images of Christ, saints, and the Virgin Mary are transported to an island in the lake and committed to fire. In *Quetzalcoatl*, during his long sermon to Kate, Ramón remarks (rather obviously) that the age of the Logos has ended (Q 333).[28] It is on this same occasion that he calls himself Adam.

The sermon attempts, in part, to show Kate that she should allow the Mexican setting to be her new Eden. The attempt fails in this early version of the novel, but Ramón's argument (which has no counterpart in *The Plumed Serpent*) is well worth describing here. It includes a Neoplatonic account—only partly atypical, I think, for Lawrence—of the soul's descent from "the great moveless, changeless lake of bright souls, which was god" (Q 336) through the seven spheres, each adding cosmic embodiment as the soul passes. For example, it was "clothed in the Sun" and "clothed in the moon of blood" and at last reached full "incarnation into flesh" on the earth (Q 334). At each sphere, the two opposites, soul and matter, were "bride" and "bridegroom," moving through "wedding after wedding" until, on earth, the female soul joins her "husband": "This," says Ramón, "was the perfect Adam, and the perfect Eve" (Q 334-35). Oblivious of the origin behind them, and therefore perfect in their happiness, the couple provoked the envy of one imperfect creature, the serpent, which, not having developed properly in the journey through the spheres, still recollected the spiritual past. By tempting Adam and Eve to eat from "the Tree of Memory, the Tree of the Knowledge of Return" (Q 335), he initiated in humanity its "reverse" journey—supposedly the way of the cross, of ascetic sacrifice of the flesh in the attempt to return to disembodied spirit, here figured forth in the guise of a malign New Jerusalem (Q 337). "You have triumphed, you Galileans," says Ramón, adding that the spiritual white people "unclothe" themselves of the sun, while the dark races are now being clothed with it (Q 338).[29]

28. For a further account of Ramón's sermon, conducted over a sacramental wine cup in imitation of the Mass, see my introduction.

29. The allusion to A. C. Swinburne's "Hymn to Proserpine" occurs

Hence the necessity for Kate, representing this "spiritual" movement, to become again the woman "clothed with the sun." I have shown earlier that this cosmic being, with the moon under her feet and stars on her head, is to Lawrence a "great woman goddess" who really belongs to ancient paganism rather than to Christianity (*A* 120). Kate needs to reverse her Marian identity and restore her cosmic and sensual being, her relation to sun, moon, stars, and earth. Significantly, Cipriano, appearing "red as fire" in the lake at sunrise, is explicitly "clothed with the sun" in the novel's first form (*Q* 345). In *The Plumed Serpent*, this imagery is reversed for Kate, whose saving desire is to be "covered with deep and living darkness" (351)—clothed, no doubt, with the Dark Sun, the ultimate deity in the neo-Aztec mythology. The annunciation of this dark power comes from Cipriano, a Mexican Indian who represents "the old, twilit Pan power" (311).[30] When he describes the wife of Huitzilopochtli as having "on [her] head the new moon of flowers" (323), he subtly alters the image of the Madonna with the crescent moon under her feet and adds flower imagery characteristic of some Aztec goddesses.[31]

In Ramón's Neoplatonic myth, the "perfect" Eve must have experienced the "wedding" of soul and flesh at each stage of incarnation. Thus "the seven heavens were substantiated" in her (*Q* 334). In many of Lawrence's works, the introjection of the seven heavens comes through the seven body centers, or *chakras*, of Yoga—which are further associated with the seven seals of

---

elsewhere in Lawrence, as in *Lady Chatterley's Lover*, 94, when Connie, before her sexual awakening to Mellors, finds that "the world has grown pale with thy breath" (associating the slightly misquoted line with Persephone instead of Christ).

30. The focus on darkness is not absent in *Quetzalcoatl*, in which Cipriano is dark, almost "like a negro," as noted in chapter 4 above. Nor is this focus confined to Cipriano. Ramón calls Kate "poor Persephone" and adds, "You can be queen in hell, with us" (*Q* 333). This passage can be read as a reference to an initiation rite, like the one Lawrence divines beneath the surface of the Book of Revelation. To him, the "sixth seal" represents the mystic death of the initiate, whose soul keeps its "final flame-point of life, down in Hades" before emerging new (*A* 105). On the other hand, the Mexican experiment, especially in the final form of the novel, is sometimes clearly in the grips of less innocuous powers of darkness than those of initiation.

31. On the Aztec flower imagery incorporated into the novel, see Clark (*PS* 473-74).

initiation that he divines in the Apocalypse.[32] In his own idiosyncratic version of this system, he emphasizes the three lower centers; and in Kate, he "substantiates" the heavens, or at least the elements related to them, by three initiatory stages, all parts of her union with Cipriano.[33]

Except for the idea that soul precedes flesh (which Lawrence generally denies),[34] some such myth as Ramón narrates in *Quetzalcoatl* underlies all Lawrentian quests for redemption in the flesh; certainly it helps to explain the connection elsewhere between man, woman, and cosmos. In "A Propos of *Lady Chatterley's Lover*," for instance, Lawrence states that true marriage is invariably "linked up with the sun and the earth, the moon and the fixed stars and the planets" (*PII* 505). Indeed, "almost every initiation" figures forth "the supreme achievement of the mystic marriage," and "all the religions know" the significance of the joining of male and female: "this Communion, this touching on one another of the two rivers, Euphrates and Tigris—to use old jargon—and the enclosing of the land of Mesopotamia, where Paradise was, or the Park of Eden" (*PII* 506).[35] Once again, as in *Quetzalcoatl*, the

32. In the *chakra* system, the life force (*kundalini*, or the serpent in the flesh) moves upward toward the head; Lawrence reverses the flow to emphasize the lower centers. While Ramón and Cipriano do Yoga exercises to channel *kundalini* and achieve a mesmerized darkness, perhaps the most famous fictional use of this system is in the first seven love encounters between Connie and Mellors in *Lady Chatterley's Lover*. According to Doherty, "Connie and the Chakras," 86, 89–92, the emphasis on the lower centers features contact with sun (fire), moon (water), and earth, and the lovemaking scenes feature "cosmogonic imagery" relating Connie's orgasms to the creation of the world by the combining of the elements. See also Kermode, *D. H. Lawrence*, 138–42, relating Connie's first seven love scenes to the seven seals of the Book of Revelation. See also footnote 26 to chapter 3 above.

33. Kessler, "Descent into Darkness," 239–61, also deals with Kate's initiation in *The Plumed Serpent*, finding her plunged into "the soul's underworld," a "Mexican Sheol" (248, 255). See also Vickery, "*The Plumed Serpent*," 505–32, tracing, like Kessler, the "monomyth" of separation, initiation, and return. Clark, *Dark Night of the Body*, 66, relates the marriage to "the union of Above and Below," and Cowan, *D. H. Lawrence and the Trembling Balance*, 201–3, traces its alchemical dimension.

34. On Lawrence's usual rejection of Neoplatonic allegory of the soul's descent into flesh, see, for instance, Marcus, "Lawrence, Yeats, and 'the Resurrection,'" 233. See also, however, Ballin, "Lewis Spence and the Myth," 69, 74, who identifies Ramón as a "gnostic teacher" using "Hermetic symbolism." See also footnote 9 to chapter 1, dealing with Platonism.

35. In a canceled portion of "A Propos of *Lady Chatterley's Lover*," extant in a holograph (Roberts, *A Bibliography of D. H. Lawrence*, E1.5c), Lawrence

"old jargon" turns out to be biblical, a "jargon" strangely shared by the avatars of the Aztec gods.

Marriage has at least as much significance in *The Plumed Serpent* as it has in *The Rainbow* and *Women in Love.* Its central-ity is fitting in a work focused on the Apocalypse itself, in which the Bride (as the New Jerusalem) joins the Bridegroom at the end of the world; and, while it is difficult to think of Kate and Cipriano in this way, the mystic meaning is never entirely absent in Lawrence's description of their marriage. The two even have their counterpart of the "Cathedral" chapter in *The Rainbow,* reversing its removal of the sanctuary from married life. While Birkin and Ursula have no temple beyond themselves, Kate and Cipriano have a whole church to themselves as they make love. In light of the symbolic importance of the altar in *The Rainbow,* it is significant in the later novel that a ceremonial sex act is at the altar of the new Mexican church. If marriage is not the New Jerusalem in the Mexican novel, it is at least something like the "Canaan" to which Cipriano urges Kate in the earlier version (Q 342).

Imagery surrounding their wedding in *The Plumed Serpent* emphasizes its symbolic character even more fully than critics have already recognized. Shortly before deciding to marry, Kate feels that her soul and spirit have "departed into the middle of some desert" (306), and she next passes with Cipriano through landscapes that symbolize both her "desert" ordeal and her trium-phant renewal. First they visit a "sun-decayed" plaza, "the waste space of the centre of life" (319). Oddly enough, this desolate location is the setting for their first lovemaking, an event seem-ingly linked, albeit obscurely, to Christ's entry into Jerusalem. L. D. Clark notes that the soon-to-be-lovers "make a ritual of entering the town" of Jaramay.[36] In fact, Kate's journey has the particu-larly auspicious prototype of Christ's to Jerusalem among palm

---

imagines "the park of dawn" — no doubt the Park of Eden — in which God is "a great laughing naked man" (29). The association between Eden and dawn bears upon the meaning of "the sons of the morning," a term frequently used for the members of the new era in *The Plumed Serpent.* It means not only that they are "sons" of the Morning Star (associated with Quetzalcoatl) but also that they are as if newly created. For further discussion of this use of the Morning Star, see note 39. For the detail of the laughing man, Carter may have been an influence, for he states in *Symbols of Revelation,* 44, that "seven thunderous laughs were the means of creation," according to "The Eighth Book of Moses." Although Carter's book appeared in print some years later, Lawrence had read a related manuscript in 1923.

36. Clark, *Dark Night of the Body,* 66.

fronds: she rides a donkey near palm trees (319), and one is reminded that Tom Brangwen's wedding night was explicitly his Gethsemane and Triumphal Entry (*R* 56). I see the sex act at Jaramay as one comparable to Lady Chatterley's fifth-seal encounter with Mellors, which is linked to fire imagery and the sun.[37] Kate, in a darkened room with the blazing sun outside, is "gone as the burning bush was gone" (320)—that is, not "gone" at all but eternal, suffused with God. Significantly, though, the couple's sexuality, here as elsewhere, is associated with darkness.

The two go next to their nuptials in a garden at Ramón's estate. Here Kate receives the white raimant of an initiate (as well as bride), for she must wear "no thread . . . that can touch [her] from the past" (328). She receives her new name, Malintzi, a feature of initiation that possibly recalls the new name given to the faithful in the Book of Revelation (2:17). Rain falls, reversing the earlier desert imagery and suggesting baptism. Although this is not a sexual scene, it has a great deal in common with the sixth lovemaking between Connie and Mellors—when the two frolic in the rain and Connie's sexuality is likened to water and flood.[38] For Kate, it is not a wedding *day* but "the new twilight," the time of the Evening Star, which can combine the day and the night (328).[39]

37. Doherty, "Connie and the Chakras," 89.
38. Ibid., 90.
39. Quetzalcoatl is the Evening and the Morning Star (Venus). Biblical sources for the attempts to associate him with the Morning Star are exceedingly complex, far more so than is usually recognized. Isaiah 14:12 refers to "Lucifer, son of the morning," and Milton alludes to this passage frequently in *Paradise Lost,* as, for example, when he terms Lucifer's hosts "Sons of Morn" (in *Complete Poems and Major Prose,* 319 [Book 5, line 716]). However, in Revelation 22:16, Christ is "the bright and morning star," and Lawrence was writing the novel while strongly stimulated by Carter to think about the Book of Revelation. A statement in Lawrence's later *Apocalypse* throws light on his usage in *The Plumed Serpent:* "The morning-star was always a god, from the time when gods began. But when the cult of dying and re-born gods started all over the old world, about 600 B.C., he became symbolic of the new god, because he rules in the twilight, between day and night, and for the same reason he is supposed to be lord of both, and to stand gleaming with one foot on the flood of night and one foot on the world of day, one foot on sea and one on shore" (132). Similarly, Quetzalcoatl is "lord of the two ways" (*PS* 179, 227). The reference to the "dying and re-born gods" may suggest a source in Frazer, who finds that the Morning Star was associated with the festival of Adonis (*Adonis, Attis, Osiris,* in *The Golden Bough,* 5:258). See also Frazer, *Folk-Lore in the Old Testament,* 3:226, stating that the Morning Star was important in religions and mythologies of Mexican as well as other North American Indian tribes. Carter, *The Dragon of the Alchemists,* 21, also emphasizes the star.

If she is not to be "clothed with the sun," at least she forms the light complement to Cipriano's darkness; and their vows, like the twilight hour, signify the meeting of opposite sensibilities.

While the new husband kisses Kate's brow and breasts (upper centers), she kisses his feet and heels (lower centers). Somewhat like Kate, Daphne in *The Ladybird* lies at the feet of Count Dionys in a posture that Joost Daalder relates to the ministrations of the woman who bathed Christ's feet with her tears (Luke 7:36–50); Daalder therefore identifies the count with a greatly revised Osiris-like Christ and the woman's position with worship (119-20).[40] While it is difficult to relate Cipriano similarly to Christ (even harder than it is to see Count Psanek this way), he is undoubtedly cast in some of Christ's roles. Kate's homage may, depressingly, reflect the place of women in the new church of Quetzalcoatl— they kneel while men stand—but I suggest that it also has symbolic resonance within the novel's Edenic design. It curiously reverses the biblical dictum that the seed of Eve shall bruise the serpent's head while he shall bruise her heel. The two lovers seem to shift roles, for each will receive of the other's opposite nature, Cipriano gaining intellect and emotion while Kate secures serpent power, connecting her with the earth. She has been "clothed" with fire and water and is yet to be "clothed" with the earth, when she can be reconciled with the serpent in a later chapter.[41]

In the Edenic paradigm, it is obvious who Kate is, for she longs to be delivered from her lesser self, the "curse of Eve" (184), whose consciousness since the Fall, and particularly in the modern period, is too sharply cerebral.[42] At the end of *Quetzalcoatl,* Ramón still refers to Kate as "insatiable Eve" (Q 341), but her very marriage to Cipriano in the later novel shows that she is becoming again the "perfect" Eve from before the Fall. Although Kate is Eve, her husband is clearly, on a variety of levels, not Adam but the

40. Daalder, "Background and Significance," 119-20.

41. In the chapter "Kate Is a Wife," not long before her unwonted equanimity at viewing the serpent, "she had sunk to the deep bed of pure rest" (*PS* 421). This line is echoed in Connie's seventh "seal," when, in the famous night of "Italian" sensuality with Mellors, she reaches the "real bedrock of her nature" (*LCL* 280).

42. See Clarke, "The Eye and the Soul," 289–301, who shows that Kate must develop her bodily, or "dark," eyesight to reverse the "opened" eyes of Adam and Eve in Genesis 3:7.

snake.[43] In *Quetzalcoatl,* a local legend has it that Cipriano's bite contains serpent poison (Q 41, 236), and he is compared to a dangerous snake, like the unfulfilled one in Ramón's myth of Eden. Vestiges of this treatment remain in *The Plumed Serpent,* as when Kate, before her sensual awakening, finds Cipriano "limited as a snake or a lizard is limited" (310). She senses in him the very "dragon of Mexico" (67). Cipriano even sees himself as a snake, once wishing "to be a serpent, and be big enough to wrap one's folds round the globe of the world, and crush it," egg-like (192). Beyond all these associations with the snake—and *The Plumed Serpent* undoubtedly has a superfluity of them—Cipriano also represents the dragon that pursues the "woman clothed with the sun" in the Apocalypse. Identical biblically with the evil serpent of Genesis, it is "wroth with the woman," who must hide in the wilderness "from the face of the serpent" (Revelation 12:14, 17). During the *Quetzalcoatl* sermon over the wine cup, Kate feels Cipriano is like a snake wrapping itself around her, but he completely revalues the biblical context, telling her the dragon is desire—and desire is Moses' "Serpent in the Wilderness" (Q 343, 342).

This image of the Brazen Serpent, the typological symbol of salvation, recurs, albeit obliquely, in *The Plumed Serpent.* Cipriano, rather than being either the hostile dragon or the "poisonous" viper, is eventually identified with the "Serpent in the Wilderness." Shortly before the decisive encounter at Jaramay, he arouses Kate's desire—at the same time that he appears as the Brazen Serpent: "from his body of blood could rise up that pillar of cloud . . . like a *rearing serpent*" (310; my emphasis).[44] In combination with the other motif from Moses' wilderness trek, the pillar of cloud, the "rearing serpent" strongly suggests the brass image that he raised to save his people from a plague of poisonous snakes. The image almost made it into *The Plumed Serpent* in a more obvious form, for Ramón, in one of the late excisions, tells

43. Ruderman, *D. H. Lawrence and the Devouring Mother,* 76, points out that Lawrence's Eve is commonly paired with Satan.

44. There may also be an allusion to Milton's serpent in the garden in *Paradise Lost,* for it "tow'r'd" and stood "erect" (*Complete Poems and Major Prose,* 390 [Book 9, lines 494–503]). The serpent image appears in *The Plumed Serpent* at every level, from the microcosmic *kundalini* in the individual body to the macrocosmic dragon of the epoch. Of course, half of Quetzalcoatl's symbol is the serpent, but Ramón is far less associated with the serpent imagery than is Cipriano.

Kate to inform the Europeans that "the serpent is desire, and they must put up his image in gold" (548).[45] These high claims for desire are not simply frivolous, for this quality is shown to be what Kate needs to embrace a new life. It is Cipriano himself who embodies "the living Wish" (391) and who keeps Kate from leaving Mexico by saying, "*Te quiero mucho . . .* I like [desire] you very much!" (444) It is no coincidence that the church "of the Black Saviour" is one of the centers for the neo-Aztec movement (419),[46] and it is Cipriano, not Ramón, who best fits this description of the dark Christ. An Aztec ritual, recorded in the sixteenth century, gives Huitzilopochtli a role similar to Christ's in the Mass,[47] but it is unclear whether Lawrence knew of this parallel.

Cipriano is clearly one of Lawrence's famous "dark gods," but it is a vexed question what that means. Gilbert relates even the creature of Lawrence's famous "Snake" to Lucifer because it is an underworld king.[48] Is Cipriano more like Lucifer or like a "Saviour"? At almost the same time that he is related to the Brazen Serpent, he is also revealed as the "god-demon Pan" (312). The text abounds in complications of this sort, showing the broadest possible union of opposites. Lawrence finally refuses to categorize, a refusal implemented by his use of extremely mixed types (biblical, classical, and archetypal). As I have already suggested, Cipriano has at least two potentialities, a fact that will appear increasingly certain as I later examine the pledge ceremonies in *Quetzalcoatl.* Says Lawrence in *Apocalypse,* "When Moses set up the brazen serpent in the wilderness . . . he was substituting the potency of the good dragon for the sting of the bad dragon, or serpents. That is, man can have the serpent with him or against him" (124). The author goes on to discuss the benign and malign aspects of dragons,

45. I take this description of the golden serpent to owe something to alchemy. After marrying Kate and Cipriano, Ramón gives them necklace talismans incorporating this image: Cipriano puts the gold serpent (balanced with a jet bird) around Kate's neck, and she puts the silver serpent (with a turquoise bird) around his (*PS* 331). On the alchemical import of this jewelry, see also Cowan, *D. H. Lawrence and the Trembling Balance,* 201.

46. See Clark (*PS* 478) for an exploration of possible real-life models for this church.

47. Bernardino de Sahagún's account is cited by Jung, in *Psychology and Religion,* in *Collected Works,* 11:223–24.

48. Gilbert, "D. H. Lawrence's Uncommon Prayers," 79. See also Cipriano's "dark pinions" (*PS* 362): in *Dark Night of the Body,* 96, Clark refers rightly to his "Luciferlike shoulders."

the *agathodaimon* and the *kakodaimon* (125).[49] The benign dragon is a "Kosmosdynamos," representing a new era, while the malign dragon represents the entrenched era, like the Logos in modern times, once great but now "the evil snake" (126). Kate is actually the victim of the old dragon in a situation Lawrence explains in *Apocalypse:* "no-one is coiled more bitterly in the folds of the old Logos than woman" (126). Not only is Cipriano at last like the new dragon; he is in some ways the rescuer of the woman from the old dragon—though Ramón claims this honor for himself in a passage excised late from *The Plumed Serpent:* "Quetzalcoatl is delivering the maiden from the dragon" (548). Of course, Ramón, who functions much like God in the Edenic paradigm, combines within himself both bird and serpent (the "plumed serpent"), which Kate and Cipriano must try the harder to unite because they incarnate them separately.

Because of Cipriano, the real snake is not dangerous or repugnant to Kate when she encounters it in *The Plumed Serpent.* (In the earlier novel's scene with the snake, she still regards it as "poisonous" and limited.) Like the speaker in the poem "Snake," she has needed to learn acceptance of "one of the lords / Of life" (*CP* 351). For his part, Cipriano's desire saves him from the stubborn failure to develop that has so frequently, according to Kate and Ramón, plagued his people. Thus he is the better fitted to be a powerful leader, like the snake of the poem: "a king in exile, uncrowned in the underworld, / Now due to be crowned again" (*CP* 351). As Kate hesitates over whether to return to England near the end of *The Plumed Serpent,* she is deterred, in part, by thinking what separation from Cipriano would mean to both of them: she imagines him "turned into a sort of serpent, that reared and looked at her with glittering eyes, then slid away into the void, leaving her blank, the sense of power gone out of her" (438).

49. Mara Kalnins names Jung's *Psychoanalysis and the Unconscious* as Lawrence's source for the dual roles of the dragon (*A* 225), but Blavatsky could also be an influence (*SD* 1:410, 412; *Isis* 1:133). For a fuller discussion of the snake scenes in both *Quetzalcoatl* and *The Plumed Serpent,* see my introduction.

II

With only the paradisal theme of *The Plumed Serpent* in mind, it is easy to understand why the work has been described as somewhat static. Quite beyond the relative calm of paradise regained, however, the novel's realistic level includes the terrors of revolution and the continual potential for atavistic bloodshed that may be encouraged by the neo-Aztec movement. Kermode's view that typology can be a "rigid, flux-denying *schema*"[50] holds especially true when the types are foreknown and apocalyptic. A further problem in this novel is that its violent events grate strangely against its highly wrought ritualism, for they are not always grappled with on the realistic level where they arise but often only on the ritualistic level. The reader is not fully mindful of the plot because of a method that produces mythic depth but uncomfortable politics.

In one key chapter, assassins attack Ramón at his home while Kate is visiting there. Despite the use of knives and guns, the scene is in some ways parallel to the Crucifixion. Clark points out that Ramón undergoes "ritual death and resurrection," with Kate cast as one of the women at Christ's tomb.[51] In fact, Kate holds his head in her arms very much in the posture of a *Pietà* (300). As his "bloody body" lies as if dead, she realizes "the terrible absence of the living soul of it" and the mystery of its return (300). She has killed a man, herself, and is numbed by the experience. But the ritualization of these events, partly by religious iconography and partly by typological underpinnings, tends to obscure them as action scenes.[52] Events fit into a somewhat predictable pattern, complete with a Judas, and the reader may be less aware of the revolution than of Ramón's rather ironic similarity to Christ (less startling, no doubt, than Cipriano's).[53]

50. Kermode, "Lawrence and the Apocalyptic Types," 25.
51. Clark, *Dark Night of the Body,* 86.
52. In *Quetzalcoatl,* the ritualization is in some ways much clumsier: Kate is urged to offer up the blood of the man she has killed as a "sacrament" (Q 219).
53. Curiously, Ramón, in *Quetzalcoatl,* even calls himself "a fragment of the Virgin Mother," in that each race is like the Virgin, who "bears divine sons and divine daughters to the Most High," and he wears blue, a color traditional to Mary (196). When regretting that the Mexicans have had no Christ or Muhammad of their own, he muses that Christ had prevented the Old World's destruction long ago by his "ultimate heroism" (Q 134), and Ramón clearly sees himself as such a hero for Mexico. In this early version of

Ramón's near-death is well timed, for he has just been invested as Quetzalcoatl. He may fall to his would-be assassin as Ramón, but he rises with his godhead fully upon him. The attack follows another dangerous situation, illustrating the pattern of alternating gods: Ramón's opening of the new church, emptied of its Christian images. (Fittingly, they perish just before his own apotheosis.) His wife, Carlota, representing the hollow old institution, now falls into convulsions and dies, supplanted by the new movement. Despite her Mexican background, she is bound to habits and viewpoints of European civilization, and she no doubt represents Ecclesia in a malign form. Kate, who attends her, is, symbolically, a potential victim, too; as the other representative of the old way of life, she has even agreed with Carlota on occasion. While criticism has faulted Kate for her detachment from the dying woman,[54] it is symbolically important to her role as survivor. Not for nothing is she "frightened" (350). While Carlota dies, the Mexican Indians, having "rolled the stone of their heaviness away," sing—and "a new world had begun" (350). Their song reports that a cock crows, perhaps recalling Peter's betrayal of Christ but also proclaiming the dawning age. It is the very moment of Apocalypse, and Kate, the refugee, is torn between two worlds. Significantly, she reaches out tangibly, with her hand, to her husband, "her soul appealing" to him for soothing darkness. As he holds her hand throughout the ordeal, his silence "satisfie[s] where all speech had failed" (351).

Clark has called attention to the similarity between the dying Carlota and the destroyed Christian images of the church;[55] her death is a delayed extension of the auto-da-fé. Kate, too, has been shown earlier as the Mother of Sorrows, reminding her own servants and Cipriano of dolls of the Madonna. Even in the past, he has divined, through her Marian widow's grief, the universal goddess that will arise in her: "The wonder, the mystery, the

---

the novel, he believes that even the Spanish padres had been "beautiful heroes" in Mexico for an "interval" (Q 135). While holding that Christ could not give the Mexicans the "complete sacrament"—could "never put the final bread of Indian manhood between Indian lips"—he asserts that it is not Christ himself who will destroy them: "Christ would never destroy them. But the anti-Christ of industrialism, commerce, mechanisation, and fathomless greed, this would destroy them" (Q 134). In *The Plumed Serpent,* while Ramón still meets with the bishop and attempts to make peace with the church, his antagonism is more complete.

54. See Clark, *Dark Night of the Body,* 67.
55. Ibid.

magic that used to flood over him as a boy and a youth, when he kneeled before the babyish figure of the Santa Maria de la Soledad, flooded him again. He was in the presence of the goddess, white-handed, mysterious, gleaming with a moon-like power and the intense potency of grief" (71). Now, at Carlota's deathbed, it is fortunate for Kate that she does not belong entirely to the old dispensation, that she is already the wife of Huitzilopochtli. As the ancient types—here, the Aztec gods—"return," they displace the antitypes.

Cipriano's angry confrontation with the dying Carlota is in part gratuitous—and Lawrence shortened it in late revision.[56] But it is important to the chapter's symbolic content that he is forcefully explaining the efficacy of sacraments to her just before she is to receive the Roman Catholic viaticum: "The priest is coming. — But you can take no sacrament, unless you give it. . . . The oil and the wine and the bread! They are not for the priest to give. If you pour neither oil nor wine into the mixing-bowl [of human relation-ships], from the mixing-bowl you cannot drink. So you have no sacrament" (347). In an excised passage, Cipriano accused her of having given her "unnourishing body as a wafer, the oil and the wine held back" (529). The old Mass has been displaced, and it is meaningful that Kate explicitly desires the new "sacrament" of "star-oil" (351).

In this scene, as in the account of the attack on Jamiltepec, the dangers and horrors of the realistic setting are absorbed into ritual, somewhat nullifying the effect of action. This technique is never at a greater peak than in the strange chapter "Huitzilopochtli's Night," in which Cipriano must preside over the executions of Ramón's would-be assassins. After execution, the bodies of the dead are placed in the church at the feet of the statue of Huitzilo-pochtli, and blood is sprinkled into the fire on the altar. The latter detail may be borrowed from the Old Testament, in which Moses sprinkles blood into the fire when initiating the sacrifice of oxen as ordained by God (Exodus 24:6), but Lawrence leaves no doubt of the intended parallel with Aztec human sacrifice. Cipriano is elaborately decked out in war paint and performs three of the killings himself. If the stylized ritual of this scene suppresses a sense of action, its hypnotic effect makes it the more nightmarish. The deliberate celebration of a deity like Huitzilopochtli, even in a

56. In the same excised passage, Cipriano even identifies Carlota with the thieves crucified with Christ (*PS* 529).

new and partly benign guise, can have done nothing to mitigate the disquiet of those who divined barbarism, male dominance, and even fascism in this novel.[57]

III

The main characters are all aware that a return to past modes could bring about regressive atrocities. But Ramón intends this movement to be selective, as he explains in *Quetzalcoatl*: the "return" is to be part of "the spiral of evolution," in which "we must make a great swerve, and gather up the past, before we can have any future" (Q 144). Even Ramón, however, has momentarily imagined how he could emulate his ancestors by striking out hearts to "hold them smoking to the sun" (Q 132), an act that would bring revenge upon the enemies of his people. Even more dangerous is Cipriano, who, besides acknowledging similar atavistic desires, thinks pragmatically of setting himself up as a dictator (Q 136). In *The Plumed Serpent*, too, both men obviously have their violent potential, as does the general populace. One night when an intruder enters Kate's house, she feels true "Panic" until she can articulate a defensive creed: "I don't believe the old Pan can wrench us back into the old, evil forms of consciousness, unless we wish it. I do believe there is a greater power, which will give us the greater strength, while we keep the faith in it, and the spark of contact" (137).[58] It is clear that Cipriano's Pan power is, in fact, somewhat channeled by his relationship with Kate. And this relationship takes its place in a natural hierarchy to which much of the novel is devoted — one intended to allow a chain of command from that "higher power."

Both versions of the novel agree that only this system will prevent regressive calamities while also saving Mexico from the various evils of the modern world — Communism, exploitation by foreign capitalists, unbridled militarism, and misplaced Christian charity. But *Quetzalcoatl* is particularly detailed on the means to achieve this solution. Nowhere else in his writing is Lawrence's "leadership" scheme so thoroughly explained as in this work, in

57. On Lawrence and fascism, see my introduction and its note 82.

58. Merivale, in *Pan the Goat-God*, 218, points out that Lawrence, preeminently among moderns, represents "the Pan of sex and terror," as well as other forms of this deity.

which hierarchy has full metaphysical underpinnings that ultimately connect it with typological meaning. Ramón's Mexico is to
be "at the base, patriarchal" (Q 273)—naturally enough, if he is
Adam. It will feature an aristocracy "of the soul," and its members
must be "chosen" in the "religious spirit" (Q 271).

In a fairly early chapter, "Conversion," which has no counterpart in *The Plumed Serpent,* Lawrence provides an elaborate
example of such choosing in the "religious spirit." As in the later
novel, Ramón has come to see that what Mexicans need most is
the achievement of their own "manhood"—by which he means, in
part, their national identity but, in greater part, their souls or
inner sense of self-identity and connection with God and man.
This quality of "manliness" has always eluded them because of the
lack of a true indigenous hero to guide them (one like Christ or
Muhammad). Knowing himself to be such a leader, Ramón longs
to "call one man" to himself, into a discipleship out of which can
flow the further fellowship and development of his entire people.
In response, Cipriano offers his "fealty" to Ramón in no uncertain
terms: while Ramón contacts a higher source, Cipriano (himself
in a trance) presses Ramón's uplifted hand over his eyes and
intones, "I will obey you" (Q 140). Further, he states, "I shall
know the Unknown God and the gods through you" (Q 143). Yet
he agrees not only to obey but to "judge" his leader, a liberalizing
change from the absolute and unquestioned aristocracy expounded
by Count Dionys Psanek in *The Ladybird,* written in 1921, two
years earlier than *Quetzalcoatl.*[59] Lawrence is working with a
dilemma he poses in his textbook, *Movements in European History,*
when projecting a great world leader: "He must be chosen [by
people], but at the same time responsible to God alone. Here is a
problem of which a stormy future will have to evolve the solution"
(306). When Cipriano asks for a "blessing," apparently to seal his
pledge, Ramón places his hand over the other man's eyes and the
Mexican general kneels and kisses his leader's feet (Q 144). This
mode of homage, echoed in Kate's wedding ceremony when she
kisses Cipriano's feet, suggests the chain of authority.

Although Ramón has struggled to decide whether to accept the
responsibility of the other man's service, it is clearly his duty
within the natural hierarchy. In this section of his manuscript,

59. Count Psanek explains how his own scheme would work: "If you
choose me, you give up forever your right to judge me. . . . Henceforth you
can only obey" (*CSN* 255).

Lawrence had even written (but canceled) the telling term noblesse oblige.[60] The entire scene somewhat resembles Samuel's anointment of David in Lawrence's biblical drama, where it is more expected (and without the ritual foot-kissing). Of course, the relationship between Ramón and Cipriano, somewhat suggesting that between David and Jonathan in that drama, also recalls earlier pairs of men in Lawrence's works: at last, Ramón has from Cipriano the pledge that Birkin wanted from Gerald, Lilly from Aaron, and Kangaroo from Somers.[61] Cornelia Nixon, echoing a long-standing claim about the "leadership" novels, finds in them the political "sublimation" of homoerotic urges.[62] Despite this well-recognized fact, the pledge between the two Mexican leaders is ostensibly religious.

The relationship is explicitly intended to promote "good" instead of evil — and this is Ramón's word. Seeming to lapse nearly out of consciousness in search of an alternative to the revenge that appeals to both men, he perceives a choice "between the demon in us, and — the good —"; and his voice is "not his own voice" (Q 140). Cipriano soon tells him, "You have sworn me over to the good" (Q 142). Earlier, the general has been tempted to give way to random violent urges. Now, however, he finds, "My demons are gods" (Q 145), allowing him to use them (his underlying energies) for the "good."[63] It is true that his particular god is the warlike Huitzilopochtli, but Ramón reminds him that this should not be the evil god but "the resurrected Huitzilopochtli," who "has learned a great deal in his four centuries of oblivion" (Q 145). Apparently, both men consider the later sacrificial executions to lie within the bounds of this education. Cipriano, much involved in the politics and intrigues of a changing world, is intermittently tempted to forget his godhead, but Yoga with Ramón keeps him true to the source. We see, then, by what machinery the new aristocracy of Mexico arises from a religious base.

While this new system sometimes seems a particularly indige-

60. The term occurs in the manuscript of the first version of the novel (E313a in Roberts, *A Bibliography of D. H. Lawrence*), located at the Harry Ransom Humanities Research Center, the University of Texas at Austin.

61. The relationship somewhat recalls, too, less political situations in the earlier novels like the bathing scene between George and Cyril in *The White Peacock* and the meetings between Paul and Baxter Dawes in *Sons and Lovers*.

62. Nixon, *Lawrence's Leadership Politics*, 191.

63. See Blavatsky for an obvious source: "Why did you make of your god a devil . . . ?" (SD 2:228)

nous one, resembling "the old Indian village system" (Q 239),[64] it elsewhere resembles historic feudalism on the European model. Cipriano, when denying Ramón's interest in Communism, describes the new system to the Mexican landowners in terms of a supposedly genteel and chivalric Mexican past: "No, he [Ramón] wants to get back more to the old-fashioned hacienda system, much more patriarchal. A humane, religious system. . . . His chief idea is the sacredness of authority" (Q 273). Indeed, the land should be managed in the manner of "the decent haciendadoes . . . in the old days, with unquestioned authority, but like fathers, fond of their people, and looking after them well" (Q 273). While one must make allowance for Cipriano's propagandistic wish to convince the landowners that Ramón's new dispensation is no threat, other sections of the novel clearly portray this kind of paternalism in action. Kate observes that people are "overjoyed to salute their superior, and to give service," rendering to Ramón "a beautiful easy fealty" because "he was the Chief, he had something godly in him" (Q 326).

This is not a new idea in Lawrence's works. Even in *Twilight in Italy* and "The Thorn in the Flesh," characters have a need to worship the "higher being." The curiously significant contact between Paolo and the *signore,* between Emilie and her employer (and, later, her husband) — relationships mentioned in chapter 1 above — are early examples of the Lawrentian mystique of aristocracy, and I have shown that issues of hierarchy pervade major novels, including *The Rainbow* and *Women in Love* as well as the first "leadership" novel, *Aaron's Rod.* As in these examples, authority in *Quetzalcoatl* and *The Plumed Serpent* does not come simply by inheritance. Kate finds that she can no longer rely on her "good family" or "fine blood" to secure reverence (Q 325). It comes only by intrinsic worth — which, in its most extreme form, equates with godhood. To gain (or understand) such worth, as Ramón has taught Cipriano, one must connect with "the place" from which "manhood" flows — the "God source."

The fact that Ramón so often refers to "manhood" as a synonym for the achieved soul raises issues of male dominance to complicate the other forms of leadership in *Quetzalcoatl.* Although the new society must have a "chieftainess" in the pantheon along with

64. See Clark (*PS* 464), stating that both novels uphold something like the *ejido* system, dating to pre-Conquest Mexico, in which a clan or village held a portion of land, or *ejido,* for hereditary *use* but not ownership.

a war chief and a peace chief (Q 239), Ramón's system is "at the base, patriarchal." While Kate seems to evoke in the people a recognition that she is "a higher being," one "tinged with divinity" (Q 325), it remains unresolved in the early version of the novel whether she needs intimate contact with a man in order to realize this dimension of her self.

Ramón and Cipriano muster the support of their entire metaphysical system to prove that she should join them and marry Cipriano. It is as Huitzilopochtli, preeminently, that he needs a wife, he says—and that wife must be Kate as the goddess Malintzi. He even believes that Kate is fated to him because "the gods make it so" and informs her, "Apart from my life, you have no life" (Q 283). She is also tutored in a woman's role by Ramón's second wife, Teresa. In some of the most awkward dialogue in all Lawrence— happily, a speech he discarded for the final version of his novel— Teresa exemplifies how her husband "takes charge of" her soul (Q 316): "If thou sayst thou art a god, then it is true. . . . If thou art not a god, there are no gods. And if thou wishest me to be a goddess, I will be it. Always at your service" (Q 317). Earlier works contain ideas that border upon these pronouncements, but never are they expressed so blatantly as here. In *The Rainbow,* Tom Brangwen notes that man and woman together make one angel, that the unmarried soul cannot make an angel; and the idea of achieving immortality through relationship, particularly through marriage, is central to that novel. In *The Plumed Serpent,* Ramón states the same philosophy: "It takes a man and a woman together to make a soul" (389). But a further dimension of relationship is especially obvious in the earlier Mexican novel (and implicit in the final version): as Cipriano has a direct, even physical bond with Ramón—through whom he can "know the Unknown God and the gods"—so Kate presumably needs such a tie to secure her in the hierarchy. In *Women in Love,* the same cosmic seriousness underlies Birkin's desire for something other than love from Ursula—his desire that they should meet beyond personality, where they do not know their "own existence" (*WL* 148). Insisting that love "gives out in the last issues," Birkin requires a "mystic" bond, "the ultimate unison between people" (*WL* 145, 152).

Kate recognizes, in *Quetzalcoatl,* that something of this kind is offered by Cipriano: he wants her not for love but for something larger, and this, she thinks, is perhaps "better than being loved" (Q 282). In this early version, however, Kate never manages to want the connection, and her rejection of it leaves the reader unconvinced of its meaning. Some of her own speeches are more persuasive than those of her Mexican friends, as when she asserts, "I think I am myself, and perhaps a good deal more myself, and more of a woman, when I am alone, than when I am submitting to some man" (Q 315). Even here, however, Teresa gets a last word, attempting to explain that the proper relationship may look like submission but is really something different. Not surprisingly, language proves inadequate to unfold such Lawrentian subtleties, and the impasse carries forward into *The Plumed Serpent.* When correcting proofs for the final novel, Lawrence changed its concluding line, causing Kate to stay in Mexico as the wife of Cipriano because, as she says to him, "You won't let me go!" (444).[65] The line is resonant, harking back in part to Cipriano's knowledge that he can prevent her from leaving if he chooses to exercise his authority. (In *Quetzalcoatl,* he even plans for a time to hold her against her will.) More importantly, the line recalls the natural hierarchy by which the characters hold each other in blood unison. Cipriano has once asserted that he is happy because he cannot "escape" from the bond with Ramón and that, similarly, Kate would be "happy" if she "could not escape from Mexico" or "even from such a man, as me" (204).

It is important to see Kate in the line of Lawrentian émigrés who must not look back but who are salvaged from their depleted civilizations only because they are grafted onto a more dynamic culture. In *The Rainbow,* for example, Lydia is a refugee from a tragic Polish situation, a transplant who only precariously makes the initial bond to the new man and the new country. Kate jokingly refers to "Lot's wife," but this biblical character's fate—looking back on the doomed Sodom and turning into a "pillar of salt" (Genesis 19:15–26)—suggests the serious threat posed to Kate by her own past.

Almost everything in her life has "let her down" or "let her go" in the end. "Men like my first husband . . . let you down horribly, somewhere," she says early in the book, adding that her second husband feared he had "let [her] down" (70, 71). Worldly-wise Kate tells Ramón wearily that people will "let [him] down" (313). In contrast to this rather bitter expectation, though, a telling line ends the chapter in which Cipriano holds Kate's hand during Carlota's death and the shifting of the epochs: "Nor did he let go her hand" (351). Elsewhere in the novel, Cipriano "would not let

65. See Clark (*PS* xl, 549).

her [Kate] go" (389), a line meaning that he will try to keep not only his wife but what she stands for in his life, the complement to himself that allows him to develop as a person.

Above all, the novel's last line points to Lawrence's mystique of the tangible soul as it binds together the natural hierarchy. Teresa has explained how she and Ramón hold each other together in a bond of blood, man and woman each keeping the other's soul in the "womb" (409–12). This word was specifically chosen for the man as well as the woman, for in *Quetzalcoatl* Ramón holds his wife's soul in his heart (Q 316). But Lawrence wants to avoid any merely metaphorical reading of this idea, for he emphasizes a virtually physical, tactile bond of unity. In "A Propos of *Lady Chatterley's Lover*" he states, "The blood is the substance of the soul, and of the deepest consciousness" — and it has known no Fall in Eden: "In the blood, knowing and being, or feeling, are one and undivided: no serpent and no apple has caused a split" (*PII* 505). This, he adds, is realized best through marriage, in which "the great river of male blood touches... the great river of female blood" (*PII* 505). Similarly, in *The Plumed Serpent,* man is "a column of blood" and woman "a valley of blood" (412); the concept of womb-contact highlights this meaning, even while referring to the soul. Thus, when Ramón is away from Teresa, her soul "goes with him" and "does not let him go alone" (410), so veritably tangible is the bond. The novel even suggests that, if Kate had given this kind of blood contact to her beloved second husband, he would not have died (412), and Teresa almost appears to give transfusions of life to the exhausted Ramón. This mode of intimate mutual renovation is reminiscent of the early Will Brangwen's desire to give his blood to Anna. The lack of such replenishment explains the tragedies of figures like Gerald, partly illuminating Birkin's stubborn belief, at the end of *Women in Love,* that Gerald died because he had not pledged himself properly to his friend. For these blood ties are not exclusively between the opposite sexes but clearly cement others as well, like Ramón and Cipriano.

The idea in the poem once entitled "Eve's Mass" — that the sex act is an exchange of blood metaphorically comparable to the Mass — is related to the meaning of the blood doctrine in late pages of *The Plumed Serpent,* as in *The Rainbow.* [66] But *The Plumed Serpent* goes far beyond this meaning alone to embrace issues of the combining of racial bloodstreams. Kate is tortured, but instructed,

66. See my introduction and chapter 2.

by the fact that her own blood and that of the Mexican Indians is "one blood" (417), allowing and even necessitating that she merge with Cipriano. Something like a cosmic Eucharist is implied by the Mexican experiment: "The blood of the individual is given back to the great blood-being, the god, the nation, the tribe" (417). The social tie is no longer an abstract or mechanical one but "the renewal of the old, terrible bond of the blood-unison of man," reflected in the "soft, quaking, deep communion of blood-oneness" between Cipriano and his men and Ramón and his men (417). The natural hierarchy is in place not only between the leaders of the theocracy but among the followers. Perhaps most curious — and characteristic — is the way Lawrence relates this unison continually to marriage, which remains his metaphor for wholeness. The unity of blood is the opposite of spiritual oneness, but the novel does not contemplate one without the other. "The marriage which is the only step to the new world of man" (416) is that between the light and the dark, the spirit and the blood; its exemplar is, of course, the marriage between Kate and Cipriano. When no such combination holds, "when the spirit and the blood . . . begin to go asunder," there is "the great death" (418).

IV

I have quoted at some length to show the extent of Lawrence's concern with the blood in this novel. It is no random chance that, in *Quetzalcoatl*, Ramón and Cipriano offer Kate the new Eucharist — red wine that Cipriano describes as transubstantiating into her own and his own blood (Q 342-43). Nor is it a random anomaly that Ramón, on the same occasion, states that he will accept the Easter Mass from the Catholic Church — "the great mass of the Sacrifice" and "the sacrament of the Crucified Redeemer" — but that his act will be the ritual of "the Redeemed Adam" (Q 331). Something of this thinking, de-Christianized, underlies *The Plumed Serpent*, in which Ramón means to restore to life its sacramental sense. Lawrence may have known of the Aztec ritual in which Huitzilopochtli is the host in a rite of *teoqualo* ("god-eating"), as mentioned above. Whether or not he was conscious of this source, however, the novelist creates this context in order to contrast the death sacrifice with ongoing life. In *The Plumed Serpent*, of course, Cipriano shares body and blood with Kate in their ceremonial sexuality.

According to Ramón's sermon in *Quetzalcoatl,* mankind is now to be unified "beyond even the Tau" (Q 332). He refers to the Hebrew cross mark that, according to Christian tradition, pre-figured the redemption through Christ (Schiller 2:124-25). I have already noted above the biblical context of this mark, used so effectively as an allusion in the poem "Hibiscus and Salvia Flowers."[67] When the Israelites were in bondage and God was visiting plagues upon the Egyptians, the mark of blood on the Jewish doors exempted them from wrath; presumably, Aaron the priest had marked there the sign of the tau cross in the blood from animal sacrifice. In traditional exegesis, this mark looked forward to Christ's sacrifice but also to his triumph over death. The new mark that Ramón intends as a replacement for the tau is no doubt the symbol of Quetzalcoatl, the cross-like bird enclosed by the Uroboros (serpent with its tail in its mouth). But Lawrence omit-ted his statement from the final novel, perhaps out of fondness for the tau, with its traditional relation to the Brazen Serpent—a link so strong and ancient that early forms of the crozier, the crooked pastoral staff of a bishop, had at the top a tau cross with arms made to depict snakes.[68]

While meditating on the "oneness" of blood near the end of *The Plumed Serpent,* Kate remarks upon "the old, terrible bond of the blood-unison of man, which made blood sacrifice so potent a factor of life" (417). Such sacrifice is eventually the living offering by which full-blooded beings give themselves to the cosmos and to each other. This idea is the culmination of a motif of sacrifice running throughout the novel. At one time, when Cipriano accom-panies her into the church long before their marriage, Kate wonders, "Was she a sacrifice?" (336). Since the two first make love after a ritual obscurely recalling the Entry into Jerusalem, it is worth recollecting that Christ's entrance there, while ultimately trium-phant, was to sacrifice; in fact, one iconographic pattern corre-lates the Entry with leading the Old Testament lamb to sacrifice (Schiller 2:125). Thoughts about such subjects had preoccupied Lawrence for many years. In the poem "New Year's Night," writ-ten in 1913, he likens his loved one to a dove sacrificed up "to the ancient, inexorable God" (CP 238). His later character Somers, sharing Lawrence's own wartime experiences of 1916-17 in Cornwall, recalls the "mystery of blood-sacrifice" he has felt in

---

67. See chapters 4 and 5 above.
68. Appleton and Bridges, *Symbolism in Liturgical Art,* 21, 27-28.

that ancient Celtic land (*K* 242). *Birds, Beasts and Flowers* takes
sacrifice for a major theme. But *The Plumed Serpent* gives Lawrence
his fullest opportunity to deal with it, often far beneath the surface
of the plot.

The earlier version is especially filled with exotic sacrifice
imagery. *Quetzalcoatl*, like *The Plumed Serpent*, begins with the
sacrifice in one of its shoddiest modern forms — the commercial-
ized bullfight. In counterpoint to this beginning, Ramón's sermon
attempts to resacralize the bull, expounding upon the value of
drinking from the neck of Taurus, as, he says, the Catholic church
does not allow. Besides referring to some deficiency he sees in the
Mass (even though offering later to take it), he probably means to
aggrandize the bull of Mithraism, whose ritual Lawrence describes
in *Apocalypse:* the blood of the sacred Mithraic bull covers the
initiate from "the cut throat of the bull" (the neck, mentioned
above), making "a new man" (99).[69] It is the "new man," of
course, that is most significant, revealing the initiation pattern
common to both religions.

Ramón's observation about the bull also refers to the sign of
Taurus in the zodiac. Lawrence's acquaintance Frederick Carter,
in an article of the following year, discusses the human significance of the zodiacal animals, and he and Lawrence had evidently
discussed these ideas earlier. Carter, like Pryse before him, refers
to a cosmic man, asserting his astrological identity in a way that
Lawrence had not previously understood.[70] Carter identifies Aries,
the Ram (now the Lamb) with the head but the Bull with the
neck.[71] In *Quetzalcoatl*, Ramón calls for a renewal of the bull and
the ram, both suggesting an earlier epoch of power but also relating to the human body, much as in *chakra* patterns. To Lawrence,
the beasts mean sensual life, an idea best illuminated by a letter he
wrote to Carter in 1929: "the great effort of pre-spiritual man was
to get to himself the *powers* — the *honours and powers and might*

69. In *Apocalypse,* Lawrence muses about singers of a line from a hymn,
"Wash me in the blood of the Lamb"; he adds, "How surprised they [the
singers] would be if you told them it might as well have been a bull" (*A* 99).
In fact, however, this information would be no surprise to some Christian iconographers. The Old Testament rituals involving bulls are sometimes coordinated, in Christian art, with the Crucifixion, so that even
St. Luke's bull symbol, discussed above in chapter 5, suggests it (Schiller
2:120, 128).
70. Carter, *D. H. Lawrence and the Body Mystical,* 17.
71. Carter, "The Ancient Science of Astrology," 1001.

—the Mana—of the vivid beasts."[72] This is the attempt not only of the main characters in both versions of the Mexican novel but also of those in most other Lawrence works.

It helps explain, for instance, the ultimate Lawrentian joke about the "old Adam" in *The Boy in the Bush,* also written when Carter was preparing his article. In the last chapter, added to the collaborated novel in 1924, it is Jack Grant's horse that is really named Adam (339–41)—and it is the horse that seems destined to found a new race.[73] The fiery red stallion's mating with Hilda Blessington's blue-gray mare is described in apocalyptic terms as the union of the sun with the moon. The idea of the horse as patriarch is present, too, in *St. Mawr* (1924), in which one character reportedly wants the stallion St. Mawr for "Father Abraham" (father of nations) on a ranch in Arizona (*CSN* 382). As in *Quetzalcoatl* and *The Plumed Serpent,* such accounts of the vibrant beasts serve as reminders that people must regain the dynamic animal qualities. These faculties are lost in the modern white world, Ramón explains in *Quetzalcoatl,* stating that man has "killed the passion of the body and the bowels and the heart, and ruled all this with the mind"; thus man killed "Taurus of the neck where the bull's blood is at its most perfect" (*Q* 337).

The novel does not, finally, champion animal sacrifice but animal life. Near the end of both versions, a majestic, vital bull joins a mate in a boat on Lake Chapala (Sayula in the later book). The black-and-white creature is "huge and silvery, dappled like the sky, with black snake-markings down his haunches" (*PS* 432)—like the living Quetzalcoatl of bulls, uniting the sky and serpent markings as Quetzalcoatl himself combines features of the bird and the serpent and as Kate and Cipriano between them combine the same polarities. Such a conclusion represents a triumph—perhaps a limited one—of the life force over the death urge in the Mexican experiment. Scenes like this are understandably the ones most critics praise, and in them Lawrence is never better. In recasting his first version, he perhaps sensed that the novel needed more

72. Lawrence seems to be echoing Murray's view of *"mana,"* explained in *Four Stages of Greek Religion,* 33, which the novelist had read. (See notes to chapter 5 above.) On Lawrence's correspondence with Carter, see Woodman, " 'The Big Old Pagan Vision,' " 39–51.

73. Similarly, Lawrence's own black horse at his Del Monte Ranch in New Mexico was named Aaron, according to his letter of 14 July 1925 to Emily King (*Letters* 5:278).

such living embodiment, less abstract explanation. In this respect, the final effort is a better book, although never a popular one (perhaps because its ritualism overwhelms its story line). But the earlier *Quetzalcoatl* provides invaluable insights into the author's thought and creative methods.

Conclusion:
The Central Theme

Resurrection in *The Man Who Died* and Related Works

Because of Lawrence's outspoken celebration of spontaneity in art, some readers who will approve this new interpretation of individual texts may yet find it hard to attribute to them the schematization of an underlying typology. But stylized, ritualistic elements are obvious in most of his writing and especially in his reworking of biblical patterns: in these, despite his creative revision, he does not wholly dispense with the Bible originals. His "quarrel with Christianity" turns out to be a strange "lover's quarrel," sometimes taking bitter and bizarre forms but often broaching reconciliation; thus his treatment of it includes paradox as well as irony. So pervasive is his use of biblical typology, not just Bible sources, that it affects his characterization, time schemes, settings, cosmology, and politics (sexual and otherwise). Tracing his use of Old Testament leaders like Adam, I have shown the origin and development of Lawrence's patriarchal ideal and belief in natural hierarchy; the "leadership" theme proves earlier and more deeply ingrained in his thinking and method than critics have generally supposed, for it is but one aspect of the typological pattern that informs even some of his early writing. In spite of this concentration on the patriarchs, however, his work often shows men and women as mutual saviors to each other. In *The Man Who Died*, his most obvious "Christ figure" is salvaged by a woman, revising both the iconography and the typology of the Crucifixion. I have traced Lawrence's biblical typology to a number of sources, including the medieval iconography in which it inheres, and my study of this novella (first published in its entirety as *The Escaped Cock* in 1929) further explores this influence.

I have argued in chapter 1 and elsewhere in this book that Lawrence's characters are often, at one level, embodiments of biblical types, like Adam and Eve, or the antitypes Christ and Mary; they are more than this, for the author endows some of them with the intensity and immediacy of life while intentionally leaving others static and hollow. Thus some are powerful "risen lords," including the famous "dark gods" descending in part from Adam and Samson, and others are inept, unappealing martyrs. When most successful, Lawrence's type-based characters serve to reveal the universal beyond the particular — are indeed individuals but are caught up in biblical and even archetypal contexts.

Chapter 1, dealing with a selection of short stories, as well as the drama *David* and other works, traces significant development in Lawrence's presentations of Adam, David, and Samson. Chapters on *The Rainbow* and *Women in Love* show how the novelist conjoins history with mythic time, positing the opposing poles of Old Law and New, medieval and modern, pagan and Christian. His concern with what he considered the lingering decline of Christendom is expressed in ironic eucharistic imagery and in the call for a new pagan sacrament that is implied in *Aaron's Rod* and made explicit in *Quetzalcoatl*, the first version of *The Plumed Serpent*. Even Lawrence's cosmology comes to reflect this shift, featuring a central world axis that may transform itself from the cross of sacrifice to the renewed tree of life, a shift repudiating the tree of knowledge and its modern descendants, industrialism and sensual deprivation. In part of *Birds, Beasts and Flowers* and in *Quetzalcoatl* and *The Plumed Serpent*, the arena of this transformation is the New World, but the hope for it still lives faintly in the England of *Lady Chatterley's Lover*, while the even later *Man Who Died* places this typological reversal, most appropriately, in the Holy Land.

It remains for this study to answer a question posed earlier: why does a modernist like Lawrence employ biblical typology when it comprises to most readers of this century a relatively arcane system? The long answers are diverse. For one thing, he delighted in esoterica gathered from theosophy, Yoga, alchemy, astrology, and other obscure lore; biblical typology is no rarer than any of these. Besides, he welcomed its metaphysical content even when he inverted it; it allowed him to direct particularly pointed irony at the modern church and society at the same time that it gave him a vocabulary of symbolism for his own religious impulses. Perhaps, too, he could not help himself, so imbued was his imagination with typological patterns; his unconscious creative force produced them whether or not he attempted to revise them out of his work. But the short answer about Lawrence's motives in reproducing such patterns is clearer and truer than any of these explanations: his central theme—one might say his only theme—is resurrection, and biblical typology is above all a drama of resurrection. He employed it in order to tap that theme, repeatedly reworking aspects of the "fortunate fall" that dominates *Adamtypologie,* in which the "old Adam" is redeemed by the "new." To Lawrence, as to orthodox typologists, the loss of paradise is meaningful only in relation to regaining it; the Crucifixion has its force because of the Resurrection.

A similar preoccupation shows in his use of iconography from ecclesiastical art. Clearly, he knew it almost as well as typology. Not only does he refer to specific scenes, such as the *Marriage at Cana* in *The Rainbow;* his texts also reveal the *Maria Victrix,* the *Salvator Mundi,* the *Christus Triumphans,* and many others. He was probably familiar with the distinctions between a *Lamentation,* or *Pietà,* and a *Resurrection,* standard iconographic poses, but it fitted his central design to use the former pose unconventionally—as the basis for a *Resurrection.* The best example of this alteration occurs in his own 1927 painting, *Resurrection* (Fig. 15). Its iconography is that of the *Lamentation,* in which the dead Christ is touched or supported by the Virgin Mary, often assisted on the other side by Mary Magdalene (or St. John) after the descent from the cross.[1] Thematically, the *Lamentation* presents the opposite of resurrection, for the crucified figure is given over to physical death and the attendant or attendants grieve bitterly. A conventional *Resurrection* scene, on the contrary, features the living Christ, often carrying a white banner of triumph; Mary Magdalene, when she is present, is amazed at the miracle of rebirth. Lawrence's Christ, too, is awake, reversing the usual content of the *Lamentation.*

Just this kind of transformation occurs in *The Man Who Died,*

1. Read, in "Lawrence as a Painter," 56, notes that "the disposition of the three figures would conform to a 'Lamentation' rather than a 'Resurrection' and this suggests that Lawrence may have been looking at Giovanni da Milano's *Lamentation* in the Academy, Florence."

Fig. 15. *Resurrection,* oil painting by D. H. Lawrence (1927).

and its renewal of the Christ figure's earthly life should make this
tale the ultimate example of Lawrence's inverted typological scheme.
The antitype denies his own role, returning from the underworld
only in the natural sense (not really having died) and having no
interest in heaven or that New Jerusalem that Lawrence later, in
Apocalypse, calls a "jeweller's paradise" (122). Since no new era is
at hand, the man is not the cosmic Bridegroom of the Song of
Solomon and the Book of Revelation; rather, he is a literal bridegroom of sorts, entering into a sexual interlude with a priestess.

To some extent, he resumes Adam's role as a member of the archetypal marriage. Rather surprisingly, however, the protagonist of this novella, like the self-portrait in *Resurrection,* continues to resemble the "new Adam" (Christ) in many ways despite the author's usual valorization of the Old Testament types.

Critics have previously noticed Lawrence's literary use of the *Pietà* iconography, assuming too easily that it is totally antipathetic to him since it concentrates, like the crucifix, on the dead Christ. John J. Teunissen and Evelyn J. Hinz have even seriously bracketed his literary assault on this image with a 1970s vandalism of Michelangelo's *Pietà* in the Vatican.[2] They show convincingly that works like *Lady Chatterley's Lover* contain devastating parodies of this iconographic form (like a scene in which Mrs. Bolton weeps over Clifford), satirizing the pose itself and the modern man and woman who enter into the mother-and-son stance represented in it.[3] But Lawrence also shows the image's great attraction for him, filling his works with it time and again because its initial focus upon death allows the greatest possible contrast with life. A similar effect is gained in another way in *Lady Chatterley's Lover* when Connie, before her relationship with Mellors, first shivers at the sight of the graveyard (83–84) and later is drawn to the more vital forest and the gamekeeper; issues of life and death are in juxtaposition and interrelation. In *The Rainbow,* Will Brangwen argues that the *Pietà* does not simply display a body "with slits" (149) but signifies the Eucharist, with its hope of immortality. Seemingly related to the *Pietà* is a dead masculine figure Lawrence de-Christianizes and reinterprets in some of his earliest works and in some of his latest, from "Odour of Chrysanthemums" (1910, 1911, and 1914)[4] through *Last Poems* (published in 1932).

From the outset of his career, then, Lawrence works the lines of the *Pietà* organically into his fiction, placing characters in the attitudes of the tableau traditional to scenes of the Crucifixion. Perhaps the early poem "A Man Who Died" is related to the later novella *The Man Who Died* largely in title; but the author's early depictions of dead men generally share more than this with the

2. Teunissen and Hinz, "The Attack on the *Pietà,*" 43–50.

3. Ibid., 49. Teunissen and Hinz show Lawrence's conflation of the Pietà with the Madonna and Child.

4. Kalnins, "D. H. Lawrence's 'Odour of Chrysanthemums,'" 145–53, shows how Lawrence's development of the final scene through three versions helped him to achieve the related response of Lydia Brangwen to Tom's death in *The Rainbow.*

Christ figure of the late tale. Even the poem's female narrator, washing a dead man "with weeping water," contains a hint of the grieving Virgin Mary or of the woman who washed Christ's feet with her tears (Luke 7:37–50). In fact, Lawrence often implicitly compares or contrasts the *Lamentation* situation with the anointment of Christ's feet. In the poem, the washer chides the man, "Do you set your face against the daughter / Of life?" (*CP* 55) That is, she sees death-commitment in the man and life reserves in the woman — a pattern employed in *The Man Who Died* and elsewhere. In "Odour of Chrysanthemums," a mother, shedding "the fountains of her tears" (*CSS* 2:294), bends over her dead son in an attitude suggesting the mourning Virgin Mary, and the man's wife thinks of his death in biblical terms: "It was finished then" (2:301), echoing the words of Christ on the cross (John 19:30). But the play based on this story, *The Widowing of Mrs. Holroyd* (written in 1910), moves further in the direction of Christian myth. The family name suggests this heightened dimension, and now the dead Mr. Holroyd is "naked to the waist," with "marred hands and feet," the wife washing his feet while the mother again bends over him to liken him to a lily as well as a lamb (*Plays* 60), common terms for Christ.

The Man Who Died, though partly set at the tomb of a reviving man (never actually named Jesus), avoids the Lamentation at the cross altogether, but reminders of it and of the foot-washing scene from the Bible recur throughout the tale.[5] In the "carved hole" of the tomb, the Christ figure has a faint prescience of "chinks of light" just as a cockerel crows, as if heralding this event as well as the rising of the sun (EC 15–16). But the man is not thoroughly resurrected until he undergoes rituals of healing that resemble the activation of the body's *chakra* centers, the physical initiation that Lawrence characters often experience. In this case, the Yogic system is adapted to accommodate the five wounds of Christ, wounds that are transformed into centers of healing. This treatment somewhat recalls the imagery in "Almond Blossom," in which the enumeration of the petals, likened to the wounds of Christ, suggests stages of death and rebirth. The ritual in *The Man Who Died* functions on the level of initiation, not supernatural resurrection, since the man in the story has, of course, not liter-

5. *The Escaped Cock* was Lawrence's choice for the title. The first half was written in 1927 and published in 1928 in *Forum* before completion of the second half. See Gerald M. Lacy's scholarly edition of the full two-part text, *The Escaped Cock,* which I cite in this chapter.

ally died; the new life he must attain is a sensuous one in place of the old spiritual one.

The scene merges features of a *Lamentation* with those of a *Resurrection*. When a priestess of Isis, in the tale's second half, mistakes the man for Osiris, she knows she must restore him before they can know sexual fulfillment. Thus she takes him into her hands, filling her palms with oil and anointing his wounds. This scene occurs in a temple, before the statue of the goddess, somewhat recalling the ceremonial lovemaking between Kate and Cipriano at the church altar in *The Plumed Serpent*. As the priestess oils and chafes the man's hands, he remembers "the nails, the holes," but she intones as a true functionary of Isis, "What was torn becomes a new flesh..., this scar is the eye of the violet" (54). Next, she chafes his feet "with oil and tender healing" (54), an act paralleling but contrasting with the biblical bathing of Christ's feet; the man now regrets having accepted the self-sacrifice of a woman who once washed his feet with her tears. At last, in the paramount challenge to the death threat, the lady of Isis turns to the deep spear mark in the man's side, where "his blood had left him" (55); besides anointing it with oil, she girdles his body with healing warmth. The sealing of the five wounds, like five *chakra* points, is now complete.

But the ceremony, now following the lines of the initiation Lawrence describes in *Apocalypse,* is not over. His interpretation of the Book of Revelation, referring explicitly to the Mysteries of Isis (*A* 107), states that the sixth seal is the deepening experience of death ("the mystic death is fulfilled six-fold") and the seventh "is at once the last thunder of death and the first thundrous paean of new birth and tremendous joy" (*A* 104). In a recently published *Apocalypse* fragment, Lawrence also associates this climactic seal with "a marriage" (*A* 188). In the novella, the sixth stage occurs when the man's agony momentarily increases at the first touch of his wounds and he knows "the death in me," his pain arising partly from the realization of a mistaken old life (56). Next comes the seventh seal: "A new sun was coming up in him, in the perfect inner darkness of himself" (56), leading to the renovatory lovemaking between the man and woman. "I am risen!" exclaims the man (57), acknowledging his new masculine sun power and also equating a sexual triumph with Christ's victorious emergence from the tomb, somewhat in the sense that Tom Brangwen experiences his wedding night as his Gethsemane and Triumphal Entry (R 56).

This is obviously far removed from the Resurrection and the Ascent to heaven of the biblical Christ. It illustrates several aspects of Lawrence's usual replacement of the spiritual antitype with the physical type—but only in a very modest way; the character is not the powerful patriarch of Lawrence's pet theory. Still, he is newly interested in the flesh, and this is why Northrop Frye notes that, whereas "the main thrust" of New Testament typology is "into the future and into the eternal world," *The Man Who Died* contains "the reverse movement," fitting Jesus to the here and now and "to the revolving cycle of nature."[6] The gain in the natural is a loss in the transcendent, and this ultimate example of the antitype/type in Lawrence seems surprisingly mundane—more so than a number of "Gothic" heroes in the supernatural tales like "The Border Line," discussed above in chapter 1.

Yet the author had seemingly been preparing throughout his career to write this story—and to write it in this way. In *The Rainbow,* the voice of Christ (possibly projected by Ursula), cries out for wholeness of body: "Can I not, then, walk this earth in gladness, being risen from sorrow? Can I not . . . celebrate my marriage in the flesh with feastings . . . ?" (R 262). Resurrected people, according to the same passage, are those "living in the flesh, loving in the flesh, begetting children in the flesh, arrived at last to wholeness, perfect without scar or blemish" (R 262). In the essay "The Risen Lord," Lawrence states, "If Jesus rose in the full flesh, He rose to know the tenderness of a woman, and the great pleasure of her, and to have children by her" (PII 575). In *Lady Chatterley's Lover,* Connie recasts the Apostles' Creed, thinking, "I believe in the resurrection of the body" (LCL 94), meaning the sexual body like the one roused in her in seven-fold sexual/Yogic stages—not unlike those undergone by the "man who died." Like the Christ projected in *The Rainbow* and "The Risen Lord," the man knows "marriage," fathers a child, and wanders the earth on healed feet, finally letting a boat take him where it may; like Frazer's fertility deities and like the earth's perennial fruition, he will return seasonally, for he alters the concept of the Second Coming of Christ when he tells the lady of Isis, "I shall come again, sure as spring" (60). It is no wonder one recent critic feels "as if Christ had stepped from the New Testament into the world

6. Frye, *The Great Code,* 85, 96.

of *The Golden Bough.*"[7] Another sees the man as "an Etruscan," adjusted to the rhythms of the cosmos.[8]

Although the character's adaptation to the natural cycle accounts for the claims by Merivale and Widmer that he becomes Pan (or, at least, like Pan),[9] he is oddly dissociated from the sylvan deity. In this tale, Pan is a minor and vulgar god heeded only by the lusty peasants for whom the risen man has a rather philosophical contempt: "All-tolerant Pan should be their god for ever," he thinks (*MWD* 48).[10] As his reversal to the "old Adam" is incomplete, so is his embodiment of Pan as either the pagan type of Christ or his antagonist. But the assertion of the recurrent natural cycle does give the tale some of the stasis of a fulfilled typology — no longer "forward-looking" toward transcendent events but becalmed in the diurnal round. The story, like much of Lawrence, depends less on a haptic plot than on rituals and significant symbolism.

For the 1929 Black Sun edition of *The Escaped Cock*, Lawrence devised illustrations that illuminate three of its symbols. One of these shows the cock of the title,[11] evidently crowing, foregrounded against a red sky. The cocks of *The Plumed Serpent* both signal the betrayal of Christ (in the transformation of the Catholic church to the Church of Quetzalcoatl) and herald the "third era," something like a new pagan millennium. The cock in the later novella has some of the same function; as the biblical Peter's denial of his Lord is associated with the cock's crowing, the bird appropriately accompanies the novella's Christ figure as he denies his own former self, regretting that he has offered his followers the spiritual "corpse" of his love (55) and even regretting his public mission altogether, repudiating a leadership role. The bird may also have something in common with the mystic cocks, familiar to readers of W. B. Yeats, that crow as eras change.[12] But this function is more limited in *The Man Who Died* than in *The Plumed Serpent*,

7. Marcus, "Lawrence, Yeats, and 'the Resurrection,'" 229.

8. Sagar, *D. H. Lawrence: Life into Art*, 318, finds this the tale of "how Christ became an Etruscan."

9. Merivale, *Pan the Goat-God*, 215; Widmer, *The Art of Perversity*, 200.

10. Merivale, *Pan the Goat-God*, 216–17, also notes that Pan is, rather surprisingly, a minor deity in this novella.

11. Although Lawrence claimed to take his inspiration from a toy (a white rooster emerging from the egg) that he saw in Volterra with Earl Brewster in 1927 (*Letters* 6:50), he had already included symbolism of cocks in *The Plumed Serpent*, much of it added in the second version, written in 1924–25.

12. Wilson, *Yeats's Iconography*, 279–80, identifies one such image with a Hermetic solary bird. See also Jeffares, *A New Commentary*, 185, 298.

for no large public change is at hand. While responding to faraway cocks "out of limbo," sounding in the mornings (14), this bird is preeminently of this world, one of the phenomena confronting the "man who died": "a black-and-orange cock, or the green flame tongues out of the extremes of the fig-tree," both reveal to him the ongoing life force (21). Furthermore, the bird inspires him to take up "the destiny of life . . . more fierce and compulsive to him even than the destiny of death" (22). Its retorts to limbo are the affirmations of the living over the dead. Above all, its presence with the living man reverses one of the *Arma Christi,* the objects associated in iconography with the Crucifixion. These objects sometimes include a cock perched near the cross as an ongoing witness to the denial and sacrifice of Christ. In this tale, the bird, no longer in this context of death, is in the full flow of life; like the man, it is newly free, loosed from its bonds as he is loosed from his graveclothes.

Since the man becomes a wandering "healer" carrying the cock, Hinz and Teunissen are persuasive as they identify it with the cock of Asclepius, signifying the profession of a healer; since Asclepius was occasionally seen as a pagan type of Christ, the "man who died" is reverting from the antitype to the type in taking up the life of a "this-worldly" healer.[13] Hinz and Teunissen further suggest that the cock in this tale is a serious symbol in phallic worship, suggesting an icon in the Vatican that combines a phallus with a cock's head.[14] Isis's search for the torn parts of Osiris, underlying the action of the novella's second half, accords well with this idea, for the most urgent part of the goddess's quest is traditionally for the missing phallus. Thus the healing of the man's "slain penis" in the novella (56) has deep mythic significance. In a recently published fragment of *Apocalypse,* Lawrence more openly asserts the importance of such restoration for modern people: "The phallos is the point at which man is broken off from his context, and at which he can be re-joined" (*A* 181), a claim expanding upon the statement in "A Propos of *Lady Chatterley's Lover"* that the phallus is "the bridge to the future" (*PII* 508). This means that only genuine potency can unite the sexes and that from this union "all things human spring, children and beauty and well-made things" (*PII* 506). Significantly, the cock in *The Man Who Died* is said to rise "to the Father" through procreation

13. This argument is suggested by Hinz and Teunissen, "Savior and Cock," 283–84.
14. Ibid., 294–96.

(28) before the man does, underlining its role as a representative of ongoing earthly life.

Another important symbol, pictured in the frontispiece of the 1929 *Escaped Cock,* is the lady of Isis herself, for the illustration clearly casts her as the sun goddess whom Lawrence sees in the "woman clothed with the sun" from the Book of Revelation (Fig. 16).[15] This biblical figure—Mary or the church to the typologist— is now most appropriately reified in the de-Christianized pagan goddess Isis or at least her votary, a shift that accords with the man's reversal of the antitype. In the painting, the lady stands in front of a brilliant golden sun and the sickle shape of a huge white crescent moon that fill the entire background. Between the two figures is a brazier, its flames perhaps suggesting the fire of life corresponding to the solar rays.[16] Although Christ is himself often symbolized by the sun, the man in the novella basks in the "sunshine" of the lady of Isis: "Suns beyond suns had dipped her in mysterious fire," and her desire for him is "such sunshine" as he has never known before (52). This is a significant reversal, greatly increasing her importance as a savior to the man, a relationship reinforced by the lady's dominant stance in the Lawrence painting. Since the man is ironically deficient in the masculine sun force, he must secure it from her to achieve his physical wholeness. This focus on the sun recalls the myth of incarnation in *Quetzalcoatl,* in which the soul must be "clothed" with sun and moon and stars as it moves through the seven spheres to become at last fully embodied, "the perfect Adam, and the perfect Eve" (Q 335). Inverting the customary direction of biblical typology—the progression from physical to spiritual—the novella shows "the man who died" regaining his body.

15. See references to this figure in chapters 2, 3, and 6 above. See also Urang, *Kindled in the Flame,* 102, who also finds this goddess in *The Man Who Died,* although she does not base her identification on Lawrence's drawing.

16. The setting is puzzling in terms of the novella, for the pictured priestess seems to be performing healing ceremonies on the naked man outdoors near a brazier for cooking. The painting seems to conflate the novella's episode of healing (which occurs inside the temple) with an earlier outdoor scene, in which both characters are fully clothed. Picturing the outdoors allows Lawrence to show the sun and moon important to his symbolism. In addition, the brilliant green grass of the illustration may suggest Isis's aspect as a vegetation and fertility goddess comparable to Ceres, the aspect stressed by Frazer's "Isis" chapter in *Adonis, Attis, Osiris,* volume 5 in *The Golden Bough,* which Lacy has identified in his edition as a source for *The Escaped Cock* (125–26).

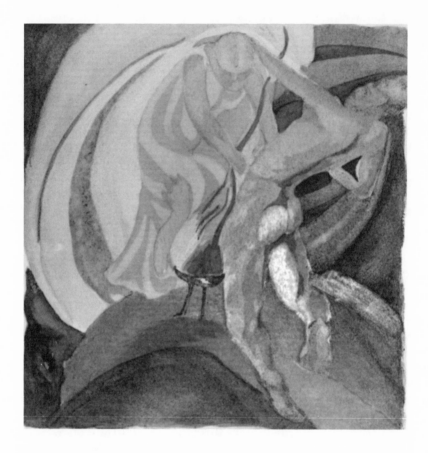

Fig. 16. The "man who died" and the Priestess of Isis, frontispiece by
D. H. Lawrence, used in the Black Sun edition of *The Escaped Cock*
(1929).

Lawrence's painting of the refulgent lady of Isis suggests that
she is a moon as well as a sun goddess, for the crescent moon
behind her is particularly prominent. This identity is especially
apt for a surrogate of Isis, long associated with the moon, as
Blavatsky points out on more than one occasion (*SD* 2:464; *Isis*
2:489). The priestess has features of the lunar deity addressed in

one of Lawrence's last poems, "Invocation to the Moon," which deals similarly with incarnation anew—if not reincarnation in Yeats's sense, yet the remaking of the body. Although the poem has a cosmic setting, partly beyond the earth, its plea is for the flesh. The speaker, seemingly the dying poet himself, tells the moon, the "lady of the last house," that he has moved through the spheres ("down the long, long street of the stars"): "six have given me gifts, and kissed me god-speed." He has known Venus and the Evening Star—"the far-off lingering lady who looks over the distant fence of the twilight"—and has received the "gift" of the sun, "one warm kind kiss of the lion with golden paws." Now he appeals for a bodily garment from the moon, "who will give me back my lost limbs / and my lost white fearless breast" to make "a healed, whole man" (*CP* 695-96). In *Apocalypse*, Lawrence explains that "the moon is mother of the watery body of men," giving "the cool water of the body's fountain of flesh," while "the blood belongs to the sun" (*A* 105). The priestess of *The Man Who Died* embodies both. In Lawrence's frontispiece—a distant relative of a *Pietà* in some of its lines—she seems to be lifting him up bodily, infusing him with her light and substance in a way that recalls how Teresa, in *The Plumed Serpent*, almost transfuses Ramón through their deep "blood contact." As a sun goddess, the priestess renews the blood; as a moon goddess, she restores the limbs to the Christ/Osiris figure.

In doing so, she reverses the theme *Noli me Tangere*, which runs through two-thirds of the novella. Based upon Christ's injunction to Mary Magdalene after the Resurrection—"Touch me not; for I am not yet ascended to my Father" (John 20:17)—the *Noli me Tangere* is a famous scene in art, rendered, for example, by Giotto and Fra Angelico. The iconography of the *Noli me Tangere* is often part of a *Resurrection* (Schiller 3:95-98). In Giotto's painting, the upright Christ bears the white banner of triumph over death while the soldiers at the tomb sleep and Mary Magdalene, kneeling, tries to touch her risen Lord.[17] Christ stands beyond her, his face

17. Numerous details in Lawrence's novella suggest those in Giotto's *Noli me Tangere*. The sleeping soldiers (not pictured in the detail of Giotto's painting in Fig. 17) look in the painting as Lawrence describes them in the tale, with their "inert, heap-like bodies" and "a slow squalor of limbs" (19). The setting of the meeting between Madeleine and the Christ figure—and some of their clothing—is similar: "And as he turned round the screen of laurels, near the rock-face, he saw a woman hovering by the tomb, a woman in blue and yellow. . . . And she wrung her hands and wept. And as she turned away, she saw the man in white, standing by the laurels, and she gave a cry" (53).

set toward the Ascension, clearly indicating, "Touch me not" (Fig. 17). Lawrence's writings allude with some frequency to this biblical scene, and *The Man Who Died* offers an extended example of its use somewhat comparable to that of *The Marriage at Cana* that dominates imagery and theme in one section of *The Rainbow.* In the novella, as in the traditional paintings, Madeleine (Magdalene) tries to renew her relation to the resurrected man. But he says, "Don't touch me," adding that he is "not yet healed and in touch with men" (23); he repeats, "Don't touch me, brother," to a peasant with whom he lodges briefly (28); and the same words occur to him again as he first realizes and shrinks from the destiny of love that awaits him with the priestess: "*Noli me tangere!* Touch me not! Oh, don't touch me!" (46)

This rejection of touch arises in part from his old abstract spiritual consciousness, and the Lawrentian metaphysic of blood and tactile contact must triumph over it and must dispel, too, the fearful aftershock of near death caused by the violent touch of crucifixion. While pain and annihilation have been dealt by the hands of others, healing and life are dispensed by those of the lady. She is likened to a living rock that is firm and tender to the touch—"the soft white rock of life" (57), altering the rock imagery relating traditionally to Christ. The man also revises Christ's biblical words—"upon this rock [traditionally, Peter] I will build my church" (Matthew 16:18)—when he says of the lady, "On this rock I built my life!" (57) Having joined with her, he knows "the peace and the delight of being in touch," which is "the great atonement" (58). The use of touch in this novella recalls a line based on the same biblical allusion in "Glad Ghosts" (written in 1925): "Ah, touch me, touch me *alive!*" (*CSS* 3:689). It also harks back to a Bible story in which a woman who touches Christ is healed (Luke 8:43-48),[18] a tale contributing to the title of the short story "You Touched Me." In *The Man Who Died,* of course, the roles of the woman and man are reversed.

A third drawing for *The Escaped Cock* presents the cross as a symbol not of death but of life; significantly, it is a form of the cross peculiarly related to the tree of life. The drawing shows the priestess of Isis in dynamic dance-like obeisance before a flower-like cosmic background, worshiping two Egyptian crosses, ankhs,

---

Giotto's woman wears some gold (though not blue), and his Christ wears white.

18. See also Matthew 9:20–22 and Mark 5:27–34.

Fig. 17. *Noli me Tangere* by Giotto di Bondone (c. 1310), Arena Chapel, Padua.

and holding a third in her hand. In "The Two Principles," this cross is to Lawrence "the symbol of life," signifying "the soul undivided resting upon division" (*SM* 184). Often called the "life-loop," its top is a circle, and its base the tau. According to Blavatsky, it represented in Egypt the union between female and male, Isis and Osiris (*SD* 2:216). In the novella, it undoubtedly replaces the cross of Christ's sacrifice, in keeping with the pattern already revealed in *Birds, Beasts and Flowers*, transforming the crucifix into a flowering cross of resurrection. Lawrence may well have known that the ankh was understood by Coptic Christians to represent the tree of life,[19] and he would have found the same correspondence between the cross and the tree in Blavatsky (*SD* 2:216-17). The drawing's red, flower-like background, hung with the ankhs, suggests a blossoming tree. During their lovemaking, the lady of Isis is flower-like to the "man who died"—and Isis is traditionally linked with the lotus (*SD* 1:366)—but the tale's flower imagery is even more expansive than this, gaining cosmic scale in the man's new view of the night sky after their union: "Now the world is one flower of many-petalled darknesses, and I am in its perfume as in a touch" (58). Flowering trees are prominent elsewhere in Lawrence's late imagery. In "A Propos of *Lady Chatterley's Lover*," for example, modern "counterfeit" love is "a grinning mockery, because, poor blossom, we plucked it from its stem on the tree of Life, and expected it to keep on blooming in our civilized vase on the table" (*PII* 504). In the same essay, the human race is "like a great uprooted tree" so that "we must plant ourselves again in the universe" (*PII* 510). The plant images in *The Man Who Died* suggest such replanting, and the renewal of the tree of life in place of the cross is equivalent to turning the *Pietà* into the *Resurrection*. Both express Lawrence's invariable theme, renewed life intensified by the nearness of death.

It is not surprising to find that *The Man Who Died* stimulates ongoing debate about how "Christian" or pagan is its Christ figure.[20] More startling, however, is a similar difference of opinion about his famous "dark gods." To reveal Lawrence's resurrection theme fully, it is necessary to look more closely at one of these figures, for they possess the supernaturalism lacking in the "man who died," whose rebirth is metaphorical. The "dark" heroes, too, descend in part from Christological patterns, for Christ's descent

19. Appleton and Bridges, *Symbolism in Liturgical Art,* 22.

20. Besides Hinz and Teunissen, "Savior and Cock," 279-96, see, for example, Cowan, "Allusions and Symbols," 174-88; LeDoux, "Christ and Isis," 132-48; Fiderer, "D. H. Lawrence's *The Man Who Died,*" 91-96; and Harris, "The Many Faces of Lazarus," 291-311, and *Short Fiction of D. H. Lawrence,* 237-50.

into hell and triumph over death influences characterizations like that of Samson, as discussed above in chapter 1.

One such "dark" protagonist is Count Dionys Psanek of *The Ladybird*, written in 1921 as an expansion of "The Thimble."[21] The count, despite having some similarity to Dracula,[22] has been seen not only as an underworld deity (whose name is an anagram for snake)[23] but also as a "re-created Lawrentian Christ," a forerunner of "the man who died" himself.[24] The story's doppelgänger format highlights both of these roles, for the two male characters are "Christ figures," one "light" and one "dark," like Philip and Alan in "The Border Line." Both men in *The Ladybird* have barely escaped death in the First World War, and one in particular illustrates Lawrence's belief, expressed later in "The Risen Lord," that such men are obsessed with Christ Crucified (*PII* 572). Lady Daphne likens her husband, Basil, to both Dionysus and the heavenly Bridegroom, expecting from the returning soldier "a new bridegroom — a new, superhuman wedding night" (*CSN* 240). The first appellation proves ironic, but the second is apt in Lawrence's terms, borne out by the character's almost entirely spiritual love for her. "White death" still sits upon him, seeming to say, "Touch me not" (243). Count Dionys, on the other hand, true to his given name, undergoes a Lawrentian resurrection in the flesh — and he is able to do this despite being assisted in the hospital, *Pietà*-like, by Daphne's mother, the "Mater Dolorosa" in person (206).

But there is more to the count than his sensuous consciousness. Intuiting that "the after-life belonged to him," he seriously tells Daphne he will be "king in Hades," where she will join him: "You will never leave me any more, in the after-death" (270, 274). His expectation is not greatly unlike that of Jack Grant, in *The Boy in the Bush*, that he will still be a lordly patriarch (something like Abraham) in the "halls of death" (*BB* 338). From the count's name and statements, one would naturally expect his mythic forebears to be Dionysus and Pluto, in conflict with Basil's Christian prototype.

---

21. On the reading and the massive revision that turned the short story, written in 1915, into *The Ladybird*, see Scott, "Thimble into *Ladybird*, 161–76.

22. Gilbert, "Potent Griselda," 145.

23. Ruderman, *D. H. Lawrence and the Devouring Mother*, 76, examines Psanek's snake-like ways, seeing the tale as "a rewriting and revising of the Book of Genesis."

24. Daalder, "Background and Significance," 120.

To one's surprise, however, Psanek, like Cipriano in *The Plumed Serpent,* has some of the roles of Christ. Daphne, who kneels down before him and leaves "his bare feet wet with her tears" (269), takes the part of the woman who washed Jesus' feet with her tears. In this case, however, seven years earlier than the account of the Bible story in *The Man Who Died,* this submission is evidently intended to be seen as an admirable trait.[25] In response to Psanek's masterly power mode, the usually restless Daphne is "meek" and "maidenly" (271). Such behavior recalls Lilly's pronouncement in *Aaron's Rod* that in a power epoch, unlike a love epoch, women submit to men. But the count's Christ-like features persist. He appears, like Basil, as the Bridegroom— not in daytime but in darkness—and Daphne is the Bride, "the night wife of the ladybird" (270). The ladybird itself, the heraldic emblem of his maternal family, is explicitly named for the Virgin Mary; while its Christian meaning is revised by exotic Egyptian lore and a gold snake paired with it, the original identification is never quite expunged. Joost Daalder sees a Christ-Osiris combination in Psanek and declares that *The Man Who Died* "has received undue attention" that is due to *The Ladybird* for showing "that Lawrence came to rewrite the Christian myth."[26]

These are not simply anomalous readings, for Lawrence, while he generally privileges dark over light, at other times conflates mythic embodiments of the two. Christopher Pollnitz, writing about *Birds, Beasts and Flowers,* lists Christ among the "dark gods" of that volume.[27] And chapters above reveal that the Christ in "St. Matthew" possesses chthonic qualities, while Cipriano in *The Plumed Serpent* is associated with the Brazen Serpent and Christ. The practice of such eclecticism greatly complicates a typological

25. Yet Lawrence has a mixed personal attitude toward this biblical scene. In 1917, he sees "subservience" in the foot-washing and believes that, without it, Christ and the woman (whom he wrongly supposes to be Mary Magdalene) understood each other well; in the same letter, he states, "It was not the ointment-pouring which was so devastating, but the discipleship of the twelve" (*Letters* 3:179–80). In 1922, still wrongly identifying the biblical woman, he satirically calls Mabel Dodge (later Luhan) "a Mary of Bethany at Jesus's feet"—apparently meaning to accuse her of feigned meekness (*Letters* 4:352).

26. Daalder, "Background and Significance," 120. This article also points out that, in keeping with the count's Osiris identity, Daphne is called Isis; thus the link with *The Man Who Died* is reinforced.

27. "Pollnitz, " 'Raptus Virginis,' " 119.

reading. When a writer inverts a "radical Christology"[28] comparable to Blake's, is the result the demonism that several writers have isolated in Lawrence's works?[29] I confess I once supposed this must be so, but the matter is by no means this simple. Lawrence is rich in paradox beyond parody and irony. And he is, on occasion, contradictory. In the same year in which he admits to a *"satanisch"* strain (in a letter of 1929),[30] he equates Satan with Mammon, condemning him in rousing terms in "The Risen Lord": "This time, if Satan attempted temptation in the wilderness, the Risen Lord would answer: Satan, your silly temptations no longer tempt me. . . . You are the selfish hog that's got hold of all the world, aren't you? . . . Whom do you think the earth belongs to, you stale old rat? The earth is the Lord's and is given to men who have died and had the power to rise again" (*PII* 575-76).

In *The Ladybird,* as in this essay and in *The Man Who Died,* his interest continues to be the theme of resurrection. If the story of the "man who died" runs counter to biblical typology's transcendent "main thrust," as Frye says, the tales of the "dark" characters like Psanek take the main line, turning intensely to the millennial future and the next world. It is noteworthy that these power figures, often harking back to primitive patriarchs and heroes like Adam and Samson, are the truer heirs of Lawrence's peculiar typological pattern than are the "light" figures; at the same time that they represent tribal or ancient aristocratic values, they borrow one feature from the antitype—the pattern of resurrection. They are men in extremis, vaunting their ability to descend into the underworld and rise again, in terms suggesting the Bible as often as Frazer.

Lawrence's concern with the underworld is like his interest in the dead men I have considered earlier. It reminds him of the potential for rebirth, both metaphorical and literal. "Every new conquest of life means a 'harrowing of hell,' " he states (*A* 109). In describing the initiations of the ancient world, he cares most urgently about how the soul retains its life at the lowest ebb, "in Hades," and, "at the very instant of extinction," emerges as "a new whole cloven flame" (*A* 105). In a 1926 letter, he suggests to Rolf Gardiner, "We'll have to establish some spot on earth, that will be *the fissure into the under world,* like the oracle at Delphos" (*Letters*

28. The term is that of Tannenbaum on Blake, in *Biblical Tradition,* 112.
29. See especially Widmer, *The Art of Perversity.*
30. See Frieda Lawrence, *Not I, But the Wind. . .,* 286. L. D. Clark also quotes the letter of June 1929, including this statement (*PS* xlvii).

5:591; emphasis mine); two years later, to the same correspondent, he repeats his vision of "a holy centre: whole, heal, hale" (6:258). It is, of course, no news that Lawrence desired a utopian "center," but its association with "the underworld" is instructive, for this is evidently the place to gain truth and achieve healing. Never has the underworld appeared in less sinister guise. It is easy to see in the letter-writer the creator of the beckoning underground in *Etruscan Places* and some of the *Last Poems*.

Now it is possible to notice that some of Lawrence's most striking depictions of this underground, or afterlife, are related to the iconography of death and resurrection considered earlier in this chapter. In "Bavarian Gentians" it is Dis, the place where "black lamps" lead the dead man to a wedding (*CP* 697). Keith Sagar links this afterlife to the account in *Apocalypse* of the rekindling of life "in Hades."[31] The earliest draft of what became "Bavarian Gentians" had the significant title "State of Grace."[32] Even a rather puzzling Lawrence painting of 1928, *Accident in a Mine* (Fig. 18), may depict features of the underworld. Since early *Pietà* scenes in "Odour of Chrysanthemums" and *The Widowing of Mrs. Holroyd* both cast miners as "Christ figures," the painting's unpromising title need not preclude its more symbolic content. It reveals unexpected aspects of sacred art, including the lighted Gothic arch behind the central figure. Of course, the fallen man is not Christ, but he has affinities with the earlier dead miners; the painting is not a *Lamentation,* but it has features in common with one.[33] Although neither the Virgin Mary nor Mary Magdalene (nor St. John) supports the prone man in the painting, the central figure bends over him solicitously; it is hard to say definitively if it is a man or a woman, and, in the unusual lighting from the ecclesiastical arch, it seems almost haloed. The chapel-like cavern, the elemental nakedness of the "miners," their stylized postures: all show that the situation is no ordinary mining accident. Rather, an archetypal ritual is enacted just at the borderline of death, the mother's arms of a *Lamentation* replaced by the earth itself and by the stooping attendants. The light, along with the illuminated

31. Sagar, *D. H. Lawrence: Life into Art,* 351.

32. In this early version, transcribed by Mandell in *The Phoenix Paradox,* 228, the dark flowers provide a "baptism."

33. It may have distant affinities, too, with another iconographic pose sometimes related to the *Lamentation,* the *Not Gottes,* in which God the Father supports Christ as the Man of Sorrows in a cosmic setting expanding beyond Calvary (Schiller 2:219–20).

central figure fronting the Gothic arch, gives the only hint in the dark painting that aid or rebirth may be near. I include this example to show that, even in some of the least likely contexts, Lawrence reproduces elements of ecclesiastical art.

This painting might almost illustrate a passage in one of the "written hymns" of *The Plumed Serpent,* in which Quetzalcoatl describes the afterlife:

> "And at the heart of all the worlds those were waiting whose faces I could not see. . . .
>
> "Then with hands I could see, they took my hands, and in their arms that I could not see, at last I died.
>
> ....
>
> *"He is dead,* they said, *but unrelinquished.*
>
> "So they took the oil of the darkness, and laid it on my brow and my eyes . . . in my ears and nostrils and my mouth . . . on the two-fold silence of my breasts, and on my sunken navel, and on my secret places . . . and in the palms of my hands, and on the mounds of my knees, and under the tread of my feet.
>
> "Lastly, they anointed all my head with the oil that comes out of the darkness. Then they said: He is sealed up. Lay him away.
>
> So they laid me in the fountain that bubbles darkly at the heart of all the worlds, far, far behind the sun, and there lay I . . . in warm oblivion." (225-26)

This is certainly not the Christian heaven of Fra Angelico's *Last Judgment* that still interests several characters in *The Rainbow.* Rather, it celebrates immortality in more elemental, more archetypal terms. Significantly, however, it is evidently the "place" where Christ is imagined as going in his turn in the mythology of *The Plumed Serpent* — to "the bath of forgetting and peace and renewal" (125). The sealing of the dead man's body recalls the system of *chakras* by which Lawrence characters elsewhere gain cosmic awareness, the same system that is adjusted to the Christ figure's wounds, which are similarly anointed with oil in *The Man Who Died.* Ministering now to the dead, this regimen preserves the bodily senses for rebirth. The cosmology in the *Plumed Serpent*

Fig. 18. *Accident in a Mine,* oil painting by D. H. Lawrence (1928), whereabouts unknown.

passage is related in some respects to the worldview examined in chapter 5 above; existing in a system of correspondences, it is set in the otherworldly counterpart of a terrestrial realm, in which initiation echoes the greater mysteries beyond life.[34] The way the earth itself enfolds the dead man in the underworld somewhat suggests imagery in some of Lawrence's late poems, like "Abysmal Immortality," focusing on "the hands of the living God" that "are so large" and "cradle so much of a man" (*CP* 700). Seemingly, they are the "hands" of the cosmos or the life force, from which one can become separated by asserting the division. Whether these "hands" would be male or female in a mythic sense is a great question, for I have shown that the matriarchal and patriarchal visions contend with each other in many Lawrence works. The scheme suggested by biblical typology is patriarchal, as are the "dark gods," whose mastery is well illustrated in Daphne's washing Psanek's feet with her tears in *The Ladybird*. Significantly, the like submission is repudiated in *The Man Who Died*, pointing to Lawrence's 1928 disavowal, or at least moderation, of the "leadership" doctrine and his assertion of new relationships of "tenderness" between the sexes and among men (*Letters* 6:321). Although the "man who died" must learn, in contrast to his democratic leanings,[35] "the irrevocable *noli me tangere* which separates the re-born from the vulgar" (68), he no longer tries to lead others and is clearly in no dominant position over the priestess. On the contrary, he contrasts his destiny of death with hers of life, glorifying the goddess: "Great is Isis!" he says. "In her search she is greater than death" (70).

Sandra M. Gilbert finds even *The Ladybird* ultimately "a tale of female power," for Daphne, likened passingly to Isis, is the force that keeps both of her men going after their wartime experiences.[36] Because of the war, Lawrence states, the image of the merciful Madonna "broke" in men, leaving that of crucified man in its

34. In keeping with these correspondences, the people in *The Plumed Serpent* are adjured to apply the myth of death and rebirth in their own lives as sacramental initiation rituals: "put oil on your hands and your feet, on your mouth and eyes and ears and nostrils, on your breast and navel and on the secret places of your body, that nothing of the dead days . . . may pass into you," for each must "have a new body" (*PS* 200).

35. Aspects of democracy and aristocracy are somewhat mixed in this tale. Although I have argued that no new epoch arrives in *The Man Who Died*, the man himself enters an aristocratic world unlike the democratic one that Lawrence ascribes to Christendom. As a natural aristocrat, he has, however, less of a public role than when he was the leader of masses.

36. Gilbert, "Potent Griselda," 145.

place—and "Christ Crucified is essentially womanless," although
women strive still to preserve the madonna image as a sign of
their power (*PII* 572). The statement seems amazing in the light
of the steadfastness of Christ's women followers before, during,
and after the Crucifixion, but Lawrence ignores them only at
some times and not others. His statement helps to explain some of
his bitterest uses of the *Pietà* situation, merged with that of
Madonna and Child. Sometimes the "dead" man's dependence on
the woman who props him up, like Clifford's on Mrs. Bolton in
Lady Chatterley's Lover, yields only a false and parodic resurrection.[37] But the "womanless" stage is fleeting in Lawrence's
works, and sometimes the woman supporting the man is the
dispenser of the life force, as in *The Man Who Died* and the poem
"Invocation to the Moon." Much earlier, the women and the dead
miners, being partly modeled on Mary and Christ, may suggest
rival deities, matriarchy and patriarchy side by side; for, if the
women are the strong survivors, yet they recognize something
lordly in the men in their deaths. Most characters in the "leadership"
period, with Aaron Sisson as a noteworthy exception, do not try to
free themselves altogether from woman. In *The Plumed Serpent*,
for example, Ramón "doesn't believe in womanless gods" (234), a
fact in keeping with a statement in Lawrence's later nonfiction
that religions of power, unlike those of renunciation, "must have a
queen" (*A* 120). It is perhaps only partly in this spirit that the man
and the priestess meet as two "gods" in *The Man Who Died*, for
theirs is a very modest aristocratic enclave in a limited location
and not in a power epoch, and, unlike Kate and Cipriano, they
avoid the issue of dominance between them.

   While a number of Lawrence heroines have male "saviors"
—including Ursula, Kate, and Connie—they are mutual saviors to
their men. Although most criticism of *Lady Chatterley's Lover*
focuses, for example, on Connie's revitalization, Mellors (who has
gone through the war) is reborn as well. Like the "man who died,"
he has dropped out of human contact before Connie has "connected
him up again" (*LCL* 132). Although this connection does not
make him a herald of a new age, he proclaims a significant
prophecy from Psalms: "Lift up your heads o' ye gates, that the
king of glory may come in" (237).[38] Psalm 24:7, sometimes seen

   37. Teunissen and Hinz, "The Attack on the *Pietà,*" 49. See also Harris,
"The Many Faces of Lazarus," 303.
   38. See Sheerin, "John Thomas," 297-300.

as foretelling the coming of the antitype, Christ, is adapted to form a phallic joke with a serious meaning: through sexual desire, a new world dawns for the individual couple, replacing the modern consciousness and the deadly mechanisms of wartime with the sensuous life-style of the types, like Adam and Eve.

Throughout his works, Lawrence attempts to reveal in his characters the need for this rejuvenation. Transformation is often seen in terms of two major image patterns, the return to Eden and the reversal of crucifixion, and the two are inextricably linked through biblical typology. The return to Eden appears in very early work, like the poem "Paradise Re-entered"; in "middle" work, like *Quetzalcoatl* and *The Plumed Serpent;* and in late work, like "A Propos of *Lady Chatterley's Lover,*" with its aim of regaining "the Park of Eden" (*PII* 506). The reversal of crucifixion, too, appears early, as in "The Thorn in the Flesh"; centrally, as in "Almond Blossom"; and late, as in *The Man Who Died.* To reverse crucifixion by resurrection *is* to regain Eden—or at least the primal consciousness that Lawrence associates with it—and this is largely in accord with the scheme of redemption and rebirth in biblical typology despite his revaluation of physical and spiritual. Lawrence's urgency to present and reiterate this model arises from his belief that modern people, especially during and after the war, are "dead" in essential ways. In 1915, writing to Lady Cynthia Asquith, he deplores "all these Gethsemane Calvary and Sepulchre stages" and calls for "a resurrection with sound hands and feet and a whole body and a new soul" (*Letters* 2:454). In a letter to Trigant Burrow in 1927, the situation has not changed: "Now is the time between Good Friday and Easter. We're absolutely in the tomb. If only one saw a chink of light in the tomb door" (*Letters* 6:113). And in "The Risen Lord," two years later, it is still the same: people must rouse from "those grey empty days between Good Friday and Easter" (*PII* 573). In view of this overwhelming sense of the general need to emerge from deathliness, it is no wonder that Lawrence was attracted to a typology of resurrection.

Bibliography

Works by D. H. Lawrence

Cambridge Edition

Cambridge Edition of the Letters and Works of D. H. Lawrence, gen. eds. James T. Boulton and Warren Roberts (Cambridge: Cambridge University Press):

   Aaron's Rod. Ed. Mara Kalnins. 1988.

   Apocalypse and the Writings on Revelation. Ed. Mara Kalnins. 1983.

   The Boy in the Bush. And M. L. Skinner. Ed. Paul Eggert. 1990.

   England, My England and Other Stores. Ed. Bruce Steele. 1990.

   The Letters of D. H. Lawrence. 6 vols. to date.

      Letters 1 (1901-13). Ed. James T. Boulton. 1979.

      Letters 2 (1913-16). Ed. George J. Zytaruk and James T. Boulton. 1981.

      Letters 3 (1916-21). Ed. James T. Boulton and Andrew Robertson. 1984.

      Letters 4 (1921-24). Ed. James T. Boulton, Elizabeth Mansfield, and Warren Roberts. 1987.

      Letters 5 (1924-27). Ed. James T. Boulton, Lindeth Vasey, and John Worthen. 1989.

      Letters 6 (1927-28). Ed. James T. Boulton and Margaret H. Boulton, with Gerald M. Lacy. 1991.

   The Lost Girl. Ed. John Worthen. 1981.

Movements in European History. Ed. Philip Crumpton. 1989.
The Plumed Serpent. Ed. L. D. Clark. 1987.
The Prussian Officer and Other Stories. Ed. John Worthen. 1983.
The Rainbow. Ed. Mark Kinkead-Weekes. 1989.
Reflections on the Death of a Porcupine. Ed. Michael Herbert. 1988.
St. Mawr and Other Stories. Ed. Brian Finney. 1983.
Study of Thomas Hardy and Other Essays. Ed. Bruce Steele. 1985.
Women in Love. Ed. David Farmer, Lindeth Vasey, and John Worthen.
    1987.

Other Editions and Materials

"A Propos of Lady Chatterley's Lover." Holograph manuscript ["Continuation
    of Jolly Roger article"] at the Harry Ransom Humanities Research Center,
    the University of Texas at Austin.
"The Blind" [later "Elysium"]. Holograph manuscript at the Harry Ransom
    Humanities Research Center, the University of Texas at Austin.
"The Border Line." Holograph manuscript in the collection of Mr. George
    Lazarus.
"The Border Line." *Smart Set* (September 1924), 11–25.
The Complete Plays of D. H. Lawrence. New York: Viking, 1965.
The Complete Poems of D. H. Lawrence. Ed. Vivian de Sola Pinto and Warren
    Roberts. New York: Viking, 1971.
The Complete Short Novels of D. H. Lawrence. Ed. Keith Sagar and Melissa
    Partridge. Harmondsworth: Penguin, 1982.
The Complete Short Stories of D. H. Lawrence. 3 vols. New York: Viking,
    1972.
"England, My England." *English Review* 21 (October 1915), 238–52.
The Escaped Cock. Ed. Gerald M. Lacy. Los Angeles: Black Sparrow, 1973.
Etruscan Places, in *D. H. Lawrence and Italy.* New York: Viking, 1972.
Fantasia of the Unconscious, in *Psychoanalysis and the Unconscious* and
    Fantasia of the Unconscious. Introduction by Philip Rieff. New York:
    Viking, 1960.
"Honor and Arms." *English Review* 18 (August 1914): 24–43.
Kangaroo. Introduction by Richard Aldington. New York: Viking, 1960.
Lady Chatterley's Lover. Preface by Archibald MacLeish. Introduction by
    Mark Schorer. New York: Modern Library, 1983.
Letter to Frederick Carter (1929). Holograph manuscript at the Harry Ran-
    som Humanities Research Center, the University of Texas at Austin.
The Man Who Died. London: Martin Secker, 1931.
Memoir of Maurice Magnus. Ed. Keith Cushman. Santa Rosa, Calif.: Black
    Sparrow Press, 1987.
Mornings in Mexico and *Etruscan Places.* Introduction by Richard Aldington.
    London: Heinemann, 1956.
"Passages from *Ecce Homo*" [later "Eloi, Eloi, Lama Sabachthani?"]. Holo-
    graph manuscript [in Harriet Monroe's hand?] at the Regenstein Library,
    the University of Chicago. In Alvin Sullivan, "D. H. Lawrence and *Poetry,*"
    D. H. Lawrence Review 9 (1976), 269–71.

Phoenix: The Posthumous Papers of D. H. Lawrence. Ed. Edward D. McDonald. New York: Viking, 1936.

Phoenix II: Uncollected, Unpublished, and Other Prose Works by D. H. Lawrence. Ed. Warren Roberts and Harry T. Moore. New York: Viking, 1968.

"The Prodigal Husband" [later "Samson and Delilah"]. Holograph manuscript at the Harry Ransom Humanities Research Center, the University of Texas at Austin.

Psychoanalysis and the Unconscious, in *Psychoanalysis and the Unconscious* and *Fantasia of the Unconscious.* Introduction by Philip Rieff. New York: Viking, 1960.

Quetzalcoatl [early version of *The Plumed Serpent*]. Typescript at the Houghton Library, Harvard University; holograph manuscript at the Harry Ransom Humanities Research Center, the University of Texas at Austin. (Publication forthcoming, edited with an introduction by Louis Martz: Redding Ridge, Conn.: Black Swan Books.)

"Samson and Delilah." *English Review* 24 (March 1917), 209–24.

Sea and Sardinia, in *D. H. Lawrence and Italy.* New York: Viking, 1972.

Sons and Lovers: A Facsimile of the Manuscript. Ed. Mark Schorer. Berkeley, Los Angeles, and London: University of California Press, 1977.

Studies in Classic American Literature. New York: Viking, 1961.

Sun. Paris: Black Sun, 1928.

The Symbolic Meaning: Uncollected Versions of Studies in Classic American Literature. Ed. Armin Arnold. Fontwell: Centaur, 1962.

Twilight in Italy, in *D. H. Lawrence and Italy.* New York: Viking, 1972.

"Vin Ordinaire." *English Review* 17 (June 1914), 298–315.

The Wedding Ring [later *The Rainbow*]. Holograph and typescript at the Harry Ransom Humanities Research Center, the University of Texas at Austin.

Works about D. H. Lawrence

Alexander, Edward. "Thomas Carlyle and D. H. Lawrence: A Parallel." *University of Toronto Quarterly* 37 (1968), 248–67.

Alldritt, Keith. *The Visual Imagination of D. H. Lawrence.* London: Edward Arnold, 1971.

Anderson, Walter E. "'The Prussian Officer': Lawrence's Version of the Fall of Man Legend." *Essays in Literature* (Macomb, Illinois) 12 (1985), 215–23.

Baker, Paul G. "Profile of an Anti-Hero: Aaron Sisson Reconsidered." *D. H. Lawrence Review* 10 (1977), 182–92.

———. *A Reassessment of D. H. Lawrence's* Aaron's Rod. Studies in Modern Literature. Ann Arbor, Mich.: UMI Research Press, 1983.

Balbert, Peter. *D. H. Lawrence and the Phallic Imagination: Essays on Sexual Identity and Feminist Misreading.* New York: St. Martin's Press, 1989.

Ballin, Michael G. "D. H. Lawrence's Esotericism: D. H. Lawrence and William Blake in *Women in Love.*" In *D. H. Lawrence's* Women in Love: *Contexts and Criticism.* Ed. Michael G. Ballin. Waterloo, Ont.: Wilfrid Laurier University Press, n.d., 70–87.

———. "Lewis Spence and the Myth of Quetzalcoatl in D. H. Lawrence's *The Plumed Serpent.*" *D. H. Lawrence Review* 13 (1980), 63–78.

Barr, William R. "*Aaron's Rod* as D. H. Lawrence's Picaresque Novel." *D. H. Lawrence Review* 9 (1976), 213–25.

Beards, Richard D. "D. H. Lawrence and the *Study of Thomas Hardy,* His Victorian Predecessor." *D. H. Lawrence Review* 2 (1969), 210–29.

Black, Michael. *D. H. Lawrence: The Early Fiction: A Commentary.* Macmillan Studies in Twentieth-Century Literature. Houndmills and London: Macmillan, 1986.

Blanchard, Lydia. "Lawrence, Foucault, and the Language of Sexuality." In *D. H. Lawrence's 'Lady': A New Look at* Lady Chatterley's Lover. Ed. Michael Squires and Dennis Jackson. Athens: University of Georgia Press, 1985.

Bonds, Diane S. *Language and the Self in D. H. Lawrence.* Studies in Modern Literature. Ann Arbor, Mich.: UMI Research Press, 1987.

Burwell, Rose Marie. "A Checklist of Lawrence's Reading." In *A D. H. Lawrence Handbook.* Ed. Keith Sagar. Manchester: Manchester University Press; New York: Barnes and Noble, 1982. 59–125.

Butler, Gerald J. *This Is Carbon: A Defense of D. H. Lawrence's 'The Rainbow' Against His Admirers.* Seattle, Wash.: Genitron Press, 1986.

Carter, Frederick. *D. H. Lawrence and the Body Mystical.* London: Denis Archer, 1932.

Chambers, Jessie. (E.T.) *D. H. Lawrence: A Personal Record* (1935). 2d ed., with new material. New York: Barnes and Noble, 1965.

Clark, L. D. "The Apocalypse of Lorenzo." *D. H. Lawrence Review* 3 (1970), 141–59.

———. *Dark Night of the Body: D. H. Lawrence's* The Plumed Serpent. Austin: University of Texas Press, 1964.

———. "Immediacy and Recollection: The Rhythm of the Visual in D. H. Lawrence." In *D. H. Lawrence: The Man Who Lived.* Ed. Robert B. Partlow, Jr., and Harry T. Moore. Carbondale and Edwardsville: Southern Illinois University Press, 1980. 121–35.

———. *The Minoan Distance: The Symbolism of Travel in D. H. Lawrence.* Tucson: University of Arizona Press, 1980.

Clarke, Bruce. "The Eye and the Soul: A Moment of Clairvoyance in *The Plumed Serpent.*" *Southern Review* n.s. 19 (1983), 289–301.

Clarke, Colin. *River of Dissolution: D. H. Lawrence and English Romanticism.* New York: Barnes and Noble; London: Routledge and Kegan Paul, 1969.

Colmer, John. "Lawrence and Blake." In *D. H. Lawrence and Tradition.* Ed. Jeffrey Meyers. Amherst: University of Massachusetts Press, 1985. 9–20.

Cowan, James C. "Allusions and Symbols in D. H. Lawrence's *The Escaped Cock.*" In *Critical Essays on D. H. Lawrence.* Ed. Dennis Jackson and Fleda Brown Jackson. Boston: G.K. Hall, 1988. 174–88.

———. "D. H. Lawrence and the Resurrection of the Body." In *D. H. Lawrence: The Man Who Lived.* Ed. Robert B. Partlow, Jr., and Harry T. Moore. Carbondale and Edwardsville: Southern Illinois University Press, 1980, 94–104.

———. *D. H. Lawrence and the Trembling Balance.* University Park: Pennsylvania State University Press, 1990.

————. *D. H. Lawrence's American Journey: A Study of Literature and Myth.* Cleveland, Ohio: Case Western Reserve University Press, 1970.

Cushman, Keith. "The Achievement of *England, My England and Other Stories.*" In *D. H. Lawrence: The Man Who Lived.* Ed. Robert B. Partlow, Jr., and Harry T. Moore. Carbondale and Edwardsville: Southern Illinois University Press, 1980. 27–38.

————. *D. H. Lawrence at Work: The Emergence of the* Prussian Officer *Stories.* Charlottesville: University Press of Virginia, 1978.

————. " 'I Am Going through a Transition Stage': *The Prussian Officer* and *The Rainbow.*" *D. H. Lawrence Review* 8 (1975): 176–97.

Daalder, Joost. "Background and Significance of D. H. Lawrence's 'The Ladybird.' " *D. H. Lawrence Review* 15 (1982): 107–28.

Daleski, H. M. *The Forked Flame: A Study of D. H. Lawrence.* London: Faber, 1965.

Delany, Paul. *D. H. Lawrence's Nightmare: The Writer and His Circle in the Years of the Great War.* New York: Basic Books, 1978.

————. "Lawrence and Carlyle." In *D. H. Lawrence and Tradition.* Ed. Jeffrey Meyers. Amherst: University of Massachusetts Press, 1985. 21–34.

Delavenay, Emile. "Lawrence and the Futurists." In *The Modernists: Studies in a Literary Phenomenon: Essays in Honor of Harry T. Moore.* Ed. Lawrence B. Gamache and Ian S. MacNiven. London and Toronto: Associated University Presses; Rutherford, Madison, and Teaneck, N.J.: Fairleigh Dickinson University Press, 1987. 140–62.

DiBattista, Maria. "*Women in Love:* D. H. Lawrence's Judgment Book." In *D. H. Lawrence: A Centenary Consideration.* Ed. Peter Balbert and Phillip L. Marcus. Ithaca, N.Y., and London: Cornell University Press, 1985. 67–90.

Dix, Carol. *D. H. Lawrence and Women.* Totowa, N.J.: Rowman and Littlefield, 1980.

Doherty, Gerald. "Connie and the Chakras: Yogic Patterns in D. H. Lawrence's *Lady Chatterley's Lover.*" *D. H. Lawrence Review* 13 (1980), 79–92.

————. "The Salvator Mundi Touch: Messianic Typology in *Women in Love.*" *Ariel* 13.3 (1982), 53–71.

————. "The Third Encounter: Paradigms of Courtship in D. H. Lawrence's Shorter Fiction." *D. H. Lawrence Review* 17 (1984), 135–51.

————. "White Mythologies: D. H. Lawrence and the Deconstructive Turn." *Criticism* 29 (1987), 477–96.

Eggert, Paul. "D. H. Lawrence and the Crucifixes." *Bulletin of Research in the Humanities* 86 (1983), 67–85.

Eliot, T. S. *After Strange Gods: A Primer of Modern Heresy.* London: Faber, 1934.

Fiderer, Gerald. "D. H. Lawrence's *The Man Who Died:* The Phallic Christ." *American Imago* 25 (1968), 91–96.

Ford, George. *Double Measure: A Study of the Novels and Stories of D. H. Lawrence.* New York: Norton, 1966.

————. "The Eternal Moment: D. H. Lawrence's *The Rainbow* and *Women in Love.*" In *The Study of Time III: Proceedings of the Third Conference of the International Society for the Study of Time.* Ed. J. T. Fraser, N. Lawrence, and D. Park. Alpbach, Heidelberg, and Berlin: Springer, 1978. 512–36.

Freeman, Mary. *D. H. Lawrence: A Basic Study of His Ideas*. Gainesville: University of Florida Press, 1955.

Gamache, Lawrence B. "Lawrence's *David*: Its Religious Impulse and Its Theatricality." *D. H. Lawrence Review* 15 (1982), 235–48.

Gilbert, Sandra M. "D. H. Lawrence's Uncommon Prayers." In *D. H. Lawrence: The Man Who Lived*. Ed. Robert B. Partlow, Jr., and Harry T. Moore. Carbondale and Edwardsville: Southern Illinois University Press, 1980. 73–93.

———. "Potent Griselda: 'The Ladybird' and the Great Mother." In *D. H. Lawrence: A Centenary Consideration*. Ed. Peter Balbert and Phillip L. Marcus. Ithaca, N.Y., and London: Cornell University Press, 1985. 130–61.

Glazer, Myra. "Why the Sons of God Want the Daughters of Men: On William Blake and D. H. Lawrence." In *William Blake and the Moderns*. Ed. Robert J. Bertholf and Annette S. Levitt. Albany: State University of New York Press, 1982. 164–85.

Goodheart, Eugene. *The Utopian Vision of D. H. Lawrence*. Chicago: University of Chicago Press, 1963.

Hagen, Patricia L. "Astrology, Schema Theory, and Lawrence's Poetic Method." *D. H. Lawrence Review* 22 (1990), 23–37.

Harris, Janice Hubbard. "The Many Faces of Lazarus: *The Man Who Died* and Its Context." *D. H. Lawrence Review* 16 (1983), 291–311.

———. *The Short Fiction of D. H. Lawrence*. New Brunswick, N.J.: Rutgers University Press, 1984.

Heywood, Annemarie. "Reverberations: 'Snapdragon.'" In *D. H. Lawrence: New Studies*. Ed. Christopher Heywood. Macmillan Studies in Twentieth-Century Literature. Houndmills and London: Macmillan, 1987. 158–81.

Heywood, Christopher. "*Birds, Beasts and Flowers*: The Evolutionary Context and Lawrence's African Source." *D. H. Lawrence Review* 15 (1982), 87–105.

Hill, Ordelle G., and Peter Woodberry. "Ursula Brangwen of *The Rainbow*: Christian Saint or Pagan Goddess?" *D. H. Lawrence Review* 4 (1971), 274–79.

Hinz, Evelyn J. "*Ancient Art and Ritual* and *The Rainbow*." *Dalhousie Review* 58 (1979), 617–37.

———. "*The Rainbow*: Ursula's Liberation." *Contemporary Literature* 17 (1976), 24–43.

———. "*Sons and Lovers*: The Archetypal Dimensions of Lawrence's Oedipal Tragedy." *D. H. Lawrence Review* 5 (1972), 26–53.

Hinz, Evelyn J., and John Teunissen. "Savior and Cock: Allusion and Icon in Lawrence's *The Man Who Died*." *Journal of Modern Literature* 5 (1976), 279–96.

———. "War, Love, and Industrialism: The Ares/Aphrodite/Hephaestus Complex in *Lady Chatterley's Lover*." In *D. H. Lawrence's 'Lady': A New Look at* Lady Chatterley's Lover. Ed. Michael Squires and Dennis Jackson. Athens: University of Georgia Press, 1985. 197–221.

Hough, Graham. *The Dark Sun: A Study of D. H. Lawrence*. New York: Macmillan, 1957.

Howe, Marguerite Beede. *The Art of the Self in D. H. Lawrence*. Athens: Ohio University Press, 1977.

Hudspeth, Robert N. "Duality as Theme and Technique in D. H. Lawrence's 'The Border Line.'" *Studies in Short Fiction* 4 (1966), 51–56.

Humma, John B. "The Imagery of *The Plumed Serpent:* The Going-Under of Organicism." *D. H. Lawrence Review* 15 (1982), 197–217.

———. "Lawrence's 'The Ladybird' and the Enabling Image." *D. H. Lawrence Review* 17 (1984), 219–32.

———. "Melville's *Billy Budd* and Lawrence's 'The Prussian Officer': Old Adams and New." *Essays in Literature* (Macomb, Ill.) 1 (1974), 83–88.

———. *Metaphor and Meaning in D. H. Lawrence's Later Novels.* Columbia: University of Missouri Press, 1990.

Hyde, Virginia. "*Aaron's Rod:* D. H. Lawrence's Revisionist Typology," *Mosaic* 20.2 (1987), 111–26.

———. "Architectural Monuments: Centers of Worship in *Women in Love.*" *Mosaic* 17.4 (1984), 73–92.

———. "Will Brangwen and Paradisal Vision in *The Rainbow* and *Women in Love.*" *D. H. Lawrence Review* 8 (1975), 346–57.

Iida, Takeo. "On a Topos Called the Sun Shining at Midnight in D. H. Lawrence's Poetry." *D. H. Lawrence Review* 15 (1982), 271–90.

Jarrett-Kerr, Martin. [Father William Tiverton.] *D. H. Lawrence and Human Existence.* Rev. ed. London: Rockliff, 1961.

Kalnins, Mara. "D. H. Lawrence's 'Odour of Chrysanthemums': The Three Endings." In *Critical Essays on D. H. Lawrence.* Ed. Dennis Jackson and Fleda Brown Jackson. Boston: G.K. Hall, 1988. 145–53.

———. "Symbolic Seeing: Lawrence and Heraclitus." In *D. H. Lawrence: Centenary Essays.* Ed. Mara Kalnins. Bristol: Bristol Classical Press, 1986. 173–90.

Kermode, Frank. *D. H. Lawrence.* Modern Masters Series. New York: Viking, 1973.

———. "Lawrence and the Apocalyptic Types." *Critical Quarterly* 10 (1968), 14–38.

Kessler, Jascha. "Descent into Darkness: The Myth of *The Plumed Serpent.*" In *A D. H. Lawrence Miscellany.* Ed. Harry T. Moore. Carbondale: Southern Illinois University Press, 1959. 239–61.

Kinkead-Weekes, Mark. "The Marble and the Statue: The Exploratory Imagination of D. H. Lawrence." In *Imagined Worlds: Essays in Honor of John Butt.* Ed. Maynard Mack and Ian Gregor. London: Methuen, 1968. 371–418.

———. "The Marriage of Opposites in *The Rainbow.*" In *D. H. Lawrence: Centenary Essays.* Ed. Mara Kalnins. Bristol: Bristol Classical Press, 1986. 21–39.

Knight, G. Wilson. "Lawrence, Joyce and Powys." *Essays in Criticism* 11 (1961), 403–17.

Laird, Holly A. *Self and Sequence: The Poetry of D. H. Lawrence.* Charlottesville: University Press of Virginia, 1988.

Landow, George P. "Lawrence and Ruskin: The Sage as Word-Painter." In *D. H. Lawrence and Tradition.* Ed. Jeffrey Meyers. Amherst: University of Massachusetts Press, 1985.

Langbaum, Robert. "Hardy and Lawrence." *Thomas Hardy Annual* 3 (1985), 15–38.

Lawrence, Frieda. *Not I, But the Wind. . . .* London: Heinemann, 1935.

LeDoux, Larry V. "Christ and Isis: The Function of the Dying and Reviving God in *The Man Who Died.*" *D. H. Lawrence Review* 5 (1972), 132–48.

Levy, Mervyn, ed. *The Paintings of D. H. Lawrence.* New York: Viking, 1964.

Lindsay, Jack. "The Impact of Modernism on Lawrence." In *The Paintings of D. H. Lawrence.* Ed. Mervyn Levy. New York: Viking, 1964. 35–53.

Luhan, Mabel Dodge. *Lorenzo in Taos.* New York: Alfred A. Knopf, 1932.

Mandell, Gail Porter. *The Phoenix Paradox: A Study of Renewal Through Change in the* Collected Poems *and* Last Poems *of D. H. Lawrence.* Carbondale and Edwardsville: Southern Illinois University Press, 1984.

Manicom, David. "An Approach to the Imagery: A Study of Selected Biblical Analogues in D. H. Lawrence's *The Rainbow.*" *English Studies in Canada* 11 (1985), 474–83.

Marcus, Phillip L. "Lawrence, Yeats, and 'the Resurrection of the Body.'" In *D. H. Lawrence: A Centenary Consideration.* Ed. Peter Balbert and Phillip L. Marcus. Ithaca, N.Y., and New York: Cornell University Press, 1985. 210–36.

Marshall, Tom. *The Psychic Mariner: A Reading of the Poems of D. H. Lawrence.* New York: Viking, 1970.

Martz, Louis. "Introduction." In *Quetzalcoatl.* By D. H. Lawrence. Redding Ridge, Conn.: Black Swan Books, forthcoming.

———. "Portrait of Miriam." In *D. H. Lawrence.* Ed. Harold Bloom. New York, New Haven, Conn., and Philadelphia: Chelsea House, 1986. 73–91.

Merivale, Patricia. *Pan the Goat-God: His Myth in Modern Times.* Cambridge, Mass.: Harvard University Press, 1969. 194–219.

Meyers, Jeffrey. *D. H. Lawrence: A Biography.* New York: Alfred A. Knopf, 1990.

———. *Painting and the Novel.* Manchester: Manchester University Press; New York: Barnes and Noble, 1975. 53–64.

Michaels-Tonks, Jennifer. *D. H. Lawrence: The Polarity of North and South — Germany and Italy in His Prose Works.* Studien zur Germanistik, Anglistik, und Komparatistik. Ed. Armin Arnold and Alois M. Haas. Bonn: Bouvier Verlag, Herbert Gründmann, 1976.

Miles, Thomas H. "Birkin's Electro-Mystical Body of Reality: D. H. Lawrence's Use of Kundalini." *D. H. Lawrence Review* 9 (1976), 194–212.

Miliaras, Barbara A. *Pillar of Flame: Foundations of D. H. Lawrence's Sexual Philosophy.* American University Studies. New York, Frankfurt am Main, and Paris: Peter Lang, 1987.

Millett, Robert W. *The Vultures and the Phoenix: A Study of the Mandrake Press Edition of the Paintings of D. H. Lawrence.* Philadelphia: Art Alliance Press; London: Associated University Presses, 1983.

Milton, Colin. *Lawrence and Nietzsche: A Study in Influence.* Aberdeen: Aberdeen University Press, 1987.

Moore, Harry T. "D. H. Lawrence and His Paintings." In *The Paintings of D. H. Lawrence.* Ed. Mervyn Levy. New York: Viking, 1964. 17–34.

———. *The Priest of Love: A Life of D. H. Lawrence.* Rev. ed. New York: Farrar, Straus and Giroux, 1974.

Moynahan, Julian. *The Deed of Life: The Novels and Tales of D. H. Lawrence.* Princeton, N.J.: Princeton University Press, 1963.

Nehls, Edward, ed. *D. H. Lawrence: A Composite Biography.* 3 vols. Madison: University of Wisconsin Press, 1957–1959.

Nixon, Cornelia. *Lawrence's Leadership Politics and the Turn Against Women.* Berkeley, Los Angeles, and London: University of California Press, 1986.

Panichas, George A. *Adventures in Consciousness: The Meaning of D. H. Lawrence's Religious Quest.* The Hague: Mouton, 1964.

Paulin, Tom. " 'Hibiscus and Salvia Flowers': The Puritan Imagination." In *D. H. Lawrence in the Modern World.* Ed. Peter Preston and Peter Hoare. Cambridge: Cambridge University Press, 1989. 180–92.

Pinkney, Tony. *D. H. Lawrence and Modernism.* Iowa City: University of Iowa Press. 1990.

Pinto, Vivian de Sola. "The Burning Bush: D. H. Lawrence as Religious Poet." In *Mansions of the Spirit: Essays in Literature and Religion.* Ed. George A. Panichas. New York: Hawthorn, 1967. 213–38.

———. "Lawrence and the Nonconformist Hymns." In *A D. H. Lawrence Miscellany.* Ed. Harry T. Moore. Carbondale: Southern Illinois University Press, 1959. 103–13.

———. "William Blake and D. H. Lawrence." In *William Blake: Essays for S. Foster Damon.* Ed. Alvin Rosenfeld. Providence, R.I.: Brown University Press, 1969. 84–106.

Pollnitz, Christopher. " 'I Didn't Know His God': The Epistemology of 'Fish.' " *D. H. Lawrence Review* 13 (1982), 1–50.

———. " 'Raptus Virginis': The Dark God in the Poetry of D. H. Lawrence." In *D. H. Lawrence: Centenary Essays.* Ed. Mara Kalnins. Bristol: Bristol Classical Press, 1986. 111–38.

Poston, Murray. *Biblical Drama in England: From the Middle Ages to the Present Day.* Evanston, Ill.: Northwestern University Press, 1968. 264–79.

Read, Herbert. "Lawrence as a Painter." In *The Paintings of D. H. Lawrence.* Ed. Mervyn Levy. New York: Viking, 1964. 55–64.

Remsbury, John. " 'Real Thinking': Lawrence and Cézanne," *Cambridge Quarterly* 2 (1967), 117–47.

Rieff, Philip. "Introduction." In *Psychoanalysis of the Unconscious* and *Fantasia of the Unconscious.* By D. H. Lawrence. New York: Viking, 1960.

Roberts, Warren. *A Bibliography of D. H. Lawrence.* 2d ed. Cambridge: Cambridge University Press, 1982.

Rosenzweig, Paul. "A Defense of the Second Half of *The Rainbow:* Its Structure and Characterization." *D. H. Lawrence Review* 13 (1980), 150–60.

Ross, Charles L. *The Composition of* The Rainbow *and* Women in Love: *A History.* Charlottesville: University Press of Virginia, 1980.

———. "The Revisions of the Second Generation in *The Rainbow.*" *Review of English Studies* 27 (1976), 277–95.

Ross, Michael. " 'More or Less a Sequel': Continuity and Discontinuity in Lawrence's Brangwensaga." *D. H. Lawrence Review* 14 (1981), 263–88.

Rossman, Charles. "*The Boy in the Bush* in the Lawrence Canon." In *D. H. Lawrence: The Man Who Lived.* Ed. Robert B. Partlow, Jr., and Harry T. Moore. Carbondale and Edwardsville: Southern Illinois University Press, 1979. 185–94.

———. "D. H. Lawrence and Mexico." In *D. H. Lawrence: A Centenary Consideration.* Ed. Peter Balbert and Phillip L. Marcus. Ithaca, N.Y., and London: Cornell University Press, 1985. 180–209.

Ruderman, Judith. *D. H. Lawrence and the Devouring Mother: The Search for a Patriarchal Ideal of Leadership.* Durham, N.C.: Duke University Press, 1984.

———. "The New Adam and Eve in Lawrence's *The Fox* and Other Works." *Southern Humanities Review* 17 (1983), 225–36.

Sagar, Keith. *The Art of D. H. Lawrence.* Cambridge: Cambridge University Press, 1966.

───── . *D. H. Lawrence: A Calendar of His Major Works.* With *A Checklist of the Manuscripts of D. H. Lawrence* by Lindeth Vasey. Manchester: Manchester University Press, 1979.

───── , ed. *A D. H. Lawrence Handbook.* Manchester: Manchester University Press; New York: Barnes and Noble, 1982.

───── . *D. H. Lawrence: Life into Art.* New York: Viking, 1985.

Sanders, Scott. "D. H. Lawrence and the Resacralization of Nature." In *D. H. Lawrence: The Man Who Lived,* ed. Robert B. Partlow, Jr., and Harry T. Moore. Carbondale and Edwardsville: Southern Illinois University Press, 1980. 159-67.

Schneider, Daniel J. "Alternatives to Logocentrism in D. H. Lawrence." *South Atlantic Review* 51.2 (1986), 35-47.

───── . *The Consciousness of D. H. Lawrence: An Intellectual Biography.* Lawrence: University of Kansas Press, 1986.

───── . "D. H. Lawrence and the Early Greek Philosophers." *D. H. Lawrence Review* 17 (1984), 97-109.

───── . " 'Strange Wisdom': Leo Frobenius and D. H. Lawrence." *D. H. Lawrence Review* 16 (1983), 183-93.

Schnitzer, Deborah. *The Pictorial in Modernist Fiction from Stephen Crane to Ernest Hemingway.* Studies in Modern Literature. Ann Arbor, Mich.: UMI Research Press, 1988. 138-58.

Schvey, Henry. "Lawrence and Expressionism." In *D. H. Lawrence: New Studies.* Ed. Christopher Heywood. Houndmills and London: Macmillan, 1987. 124-36.

Scott, James F. "D. H. Lawrence's *Germania:* Ethnic Psychology and Cultural Crisis in the Shorter Fiction." *D. H. Lawrence Review* 10 (1977), 142-64.

───── . "Thimble into *Ladybird:* Nietzsche, Frobenius, and Bachofen in the Later Works of D. H. Lawrence." *Arcadia* 13 (1978), 161-76.

Sheerin, Daniel J. "John Thomas and the King of Glory: Two Analogues to D. H. Lawrence's Use of Psalm 24:7 in Chapter XIV of *Lady Chatterley's Lover.*" *D. H. Lawrence Review* 11 (1978), 297-300.

Siegel, Carol. *Lawrence among the Women: Wavering Boundaries in Women's Literary Traditions.* Charlottesville: University Press of Virginia, 1991.

Simpson, Hilary. *D. H. Lawrence and Feminism.* De Kalb: Northern Illinois University Press, 1982.

Spilka, Mark. *The Love Ethic of D. H. Lawrence.* Bloomington: Indiana University Press, 1955.

Squires, Michael. "Scenic Construction and Rhetorical Signals in Hardy and Lawrence." *D. H. Lawrence Review* 8 (1975), 125-45.

Stewart, Jack F. "Expressionism in *The Rainbow.*" In *Critical Essays on D. H. Lawrence.* Ed. Dennis Jackson and Fleda Brown Jackson. Boston: G.K. Hall, 1988. 72-92.

───── . "Lawrence and Gauguin." *Twentieth Century Literature* 26 (1980), 385-401.

───── . "Lawrence on Van Gogh." *D. H. Lawrence Review* 16 (1983), 1-24.

───── . "Primitivism in *Women in Love.*" *D. H. Lawrence Review* 13 (1980), 45-62.

———. "The Vital Art of Lawrence and Van Gogh." *D. H. Lawrence Review* 19 (1987), 123–48.

Storch, Margaret. *Sons and Adversaries: Women in William Blake and D. H. Lawrence.* Knoxville: University of Tennessee Press, 1990.

Stroupe, John H. "Ruskin, Lawrence, and Gothic Naturalism." *Ball State Forum* 11 (1970), 3–9.

Sullivan, Alvin. "D. H. Lawrence and *Poetry.*" *D. H. Lawrence Review* 9 (1976), 266–77.

Swigg, Richard. *Lawrence, Hardy, and American Literature.* London: Oxford University Press, 1972.

Teunissen, John, and Evelyn Hinz. "The Attack on the *Pietà:* An Archetypal Analysis." *Journal of Aesthetics and Art Criticism* 33 (Fall 1974), 43–50.

Thomas, Marlin. "Somewhere Under *The Rainbow:* D. H. Lawrence and the Typology of Hermeneutics." *Mid-Hudson Language Studies* 6 (1983), 57–65.

Tindall, William York. *D. H. Lawrence and Susan His Cow.* New York: Columbia University Press, 1939.

———. "Introduction." In *The Plumed Serpent.* By D. H. Lawrence. New York: Knopf, 1952.

Torgovnick, Marianna. *The Visual Arts, Pictorialism, and the Novel: James, Lawrence, and Woolf.* Princeton, N.J.: Princeton University Press, 1985. 37–69, 124–56.

Tracy, Billy T., Jr. *D. H. Lawrence and the Literature of Travel.* Studies in Modern Literature. Ann Arbor, Mich.: UMI Research Press, 1983.

Trail, George Y. "West by East: The Psycho-Geography of *Birds, Beasts and Flowers.*" *D. H. Lawrence Review* 11 (1979), 241–55.

Urang, Sarah. *Kindled in the Flame: The Apocalyptic Scene in D. H. Lawrence.* Studies in Modern Literature. Ann Arbor, Mich.: UMI Research Press, 1983.

Vasey, Lindeth. "A Checklist of the Manuscripts of D. H. Lawrence." In *D. H. Lawrence: A Calendar of His Works.* By Keith Sagar. Manchester: Manchester University Press, 1979. 191–266.

Verduin, Kathleen. "Lawrence and the Middle Ages." *D. H. Lawrence Review* 18 (1985–86), 169–81.

Vickery, John B. "D. H. Lawrence and the Fantasias of Consciousness." In *The Spirit of D. H. Lawrence: Centenary Studies.* Ed. Gāmini Salgādo and G. K. Das. Totowa, N.J.: Barnes and Noble, 1988. 163–80.

———. *The Literary Impact of* The Golden Bough. Princeton, N.J.: Princeton University Press, 1973. 294–325.

———. "*The Plumed Serpent* and the Renewing God." *Journal of Modern Literature* 2 (1971–72), 503–32.

Vivas, Eliseo. *D. H. Lawrence: The Failure and the Triumph of Art.* Evanston, Ill.: Northwestern University Press, 1960.

Whelan, P. T. *D. H. Lawrence: Myth and Metaphysic in* The Rainbow *and* Women in Love. Studies in Modern Literature. Ann Arbor, Mich.: UMI Research Press, 1988.

Widmer, Kingsley. *The Art of Perversity: D. H. Lawrence's Shorter Fictions.* Seattle: University of Washington Press, 1962.

———. "Lawrence and the Nietzschean Matrix." In *D. H. Lawrence and Tradition.* Ed. Jeffrey Meyers. Amherst: University of Massachusetts Press, 1985. 115–31.

Wilt, Judith. *Ghosts of the Gothic: Austen, Eliot, and Lawrence.* Princeton, N.J.: Princeton University Press, 1980. 231-303.

Woodman, Leonora. "'The Big Old Pagan Vision': The Letters of D. H. Lawrence to Frederick Carter." *Library Chronicle of the University of Texas* n.s. no. 34 (1986), 39-51.

———. "D. H. Lawrence and the Hermetic Tradition." *Cauda Pavonis* n.s. 8.2 (1989), 1-6.

Worthen, John. *D. H. Lawrence and the Idea of the Novel.* Totowa, N.J.: Rowman and Littlefield, 1979.

Young, Richard O. "'Where Even the Trees Come and Go': D. H. Lawrence and the Fourth Dimension." *D. H. Lawrence Review* 13 (1980), 30-44.

Other Works

Abrams, M. H. *Natural Supernaturalism: Tradition and Revolution in Romantic Literature.* New York: Norton, 1971.

Allen, Don Cameron. *Mysteriously Meant: The Rediscovery of Pagan Symbolism and Allegorical Interpretation in the Renaissance.* Baltimore, Md., and London: Johns Hopkins University Press, 1970.

Anderson, William, and Clive Hicks. *Cathedrals in Britain and Ireland from Early Times to the Reign of Henry VIII.* New York: Scribner, 1978.

Appleton, LeRoy H., and Stephen Bridges. Introduction by Maurice Lavanoux. *Symbolism in Liturgical Art.* New York: Scribner's, 1959.

Bercovitch, Sacvan. *The American Jeremiad.* Madison: University of Wisconsin Press, 1978.

Besant, Annie. *Mysticism.* London: Theosophical Publishing Society, 1914.

Blavatsky, Madame Helena. *Isis Unveiled: A Master Key to the Mysteries of Ancient and Modern Science and Theology.* 2 vols. in one. London, 1901.

———. *The Secret Doctrine: A Facsimile of the Original Edition of 1888.* 2 vols. in one. Los Angeles: Theosophy, 1925.

Bloom, Harold. *Kabbalah and Criticism.* A Continuum Book. New York: Seabury Press, 1975.

Brumm, Ursula. *American Thought and Religious Typology.* Trans. John Hoaglund. New Brunswick, N.J.: Rutgers University Press, 1970.

Burnet, John. *Early Greek Philosophy.* London: Adam and Charles Black, 1908.

Carr, Stephen Leo. "Illuminated Printing: Toward a Logic of Difference." In *Unnam'd Forms: Blake and Textuality.* Ed. Nelson Hilton and Thomas A. Vogler. Berkeley, Los Angeles, and London: University of California Press, 1986. 177-96.

Carter, Frederick. "The Ancient Science of Astrology." *Adelphi* 2 (1924), 1001.

———. *The Dragon of the Alchemists.* London: Elkin Mathews, 1926.

———. *Symbols of Revelation.* London: Adam Fitzadam, [1934]. [Formerly *The Dragon of Revelation.* London: Desmond Harmsworth, 1931.]

Cavendish, Richard. *King Arthur and the Grail: The Arthurian Legends and Their Meaning.* New York: Taplinger, 1985.

Clark, Kenneth. *Piero della Francesca.* 2d ed., rev. London and New York: Phaidon, 1969.

Clifton-Taylor, Alec. *The Cathedrals of England.* New York: Association Press, 1970.

Cohn, Norman. *The Pursuit of the Millennium: Revolutionary Messianism in Medieval and Reformation Europe and Its Bearing on Modern Totalitarian Movements.* New York: Harper and Row, 1961.

Cook, G. H. *The English Cathedral through the Centuries.* London: Phoenix House, 1969.

Coulton, G. G. *From St. Francis to Dante: A Translation of All That Is of Primary Interest in the Chronicle of the Franciscan Salimbenei (1221-1228) Together with Notes and Illustrations from Other Medieval Sources.* London: Duckworth, 1908.

Eliade, Mircea. *Patterns in Comparative Religion.* Trans. Rosemary Sheed. New York: New American Library, 1963.

———. *The Sacred and the Profane: The Nature of Religion.* Trans. Willard R. Trask. New York and London: Harcourt Brace Jovanovich, 1957.

Eliot, T. S. *Complete Poems and Plays, 1909-1950.* New York: Harcourt, Brace, and World, 1971.

Essick, Robert N. "How Blake's Body Means." In *Unnam'd Forms: Blake and Textuality.* Ed. Nelson Hilton and Thomas A. Vogler. Berkeley, Los Angeles, and London: University of California Press, 1986. 197-217.

Evans, E. P. *Animal Symbolism in Ecclesiastical Architecture.* London: Heinemann, 1896.

Frazer, James G. *Folk-Lore in the Old Testament: Studies in Comparative Religion, Legend and Law.* 3 vols. London: Macmillan, 1919.

———. *The Golden Bough: A Study in Magic and Religion.* 3d ed. 12 vols. London: Macmillan, 1907-15. Individual volumes cited—2: *The Magic Art and the Evolution of Kings* (1911); 5: *Adonis, Attis, Osiris: Studies in the History of Oriental Religion* (1907); 7: *Spirits of the Corn and of the Wild* (1912).

Frye, Northrop. "Agon and Logos: Revolution and Revelation." In *The Prison and the Pinnacle: Papers to Commemorate the Tercentenary of 'Paradise Regained' and 'Samson Agonistes,' 1671-1971.* Ed. Balachandra Rajan. Toronto: University of Toronto Press, 1973.

———. *The Great Code: The Bible and Literature.* New York and London: Harcourt Brace Jovanovich, 1982.

Galdon, Joseph A., S.J. *Typology in Seventeenth-Century Literature.* The Hague: Mouton, 1975.

Gamache, Lawrence B. "Toward a Definition of 'Modernism.'" In *The Modernists: Studies in a Literary Phenomenon: Essays in Honor of Harry T. Moore.* Ed. Lawrence B. Gamache. London and Toronto: Associated University Presses; Rutherford, Madison, and Teaneck, N.J.: Fairleigh Dickinson University Press, 1987. 32-45.

Gettings, Fred. *The Occult in Art.* A Studio Vista Book. New York: Rizzoli, 1978.

Gombrich, E. H. *The Image and the Eye: Further Studies in the Psychology of Pictorial Representation.* Ithaca, N.Y.: Cornell University Press/Phaidon, 1982.

Harrison, Jane. *Ancient Art and Ritual.* London: Williams and Norgate, 1913.

Halevi, Z'ev ben Shimon. *Tree of Life: An Introduction to the Cabala.* London: Rider, 1972.

Heilbrun, Carolyn. *Towards a Recognition of Androgyny.* New York: Harper and Row, 1974. 102-10.

Hilton, Nelson, and Thomas A. Vogler, eds. *Unnam'd Forms: Blake and Textuality.* Berkeley and Los Angeles: University of California Press, 1986.

Hinz, Evelyn J. "Hierogamy versus Wedlock: Types of Marriage Plots and Their Relationship to Genres of Prose Fiction." *PMLA* 91 (1976), 900-913.

Hoefer, Hartmut. *Typologie im Mittelalter: zur Übertragbarkeit typologischer Interpretation auf weltliche Dichtung.* Göppingen Arbeiten zur Germanistik. Ed. Ulrich Müller, Franz Hundsnurscher, and Cornelius Sommer. Göppingen: Alfred Kümmerle, 1971.

Jeffares, A. Norman. *A New Commentary on the Poems of W. B. Yeats.* London: Macmillan, 1984.

Jenner, Mrs. Henry [Katherine L.]. *Christian Symbolism.* Little Books on Art. Gen. ed. Cyril Davenport. London: Methuen, 1910.

Jung, C. G. *The Collected Works.* Trans. R.F.C. Hull. Bollingen Series 20. Ed. Herbert Read, Michael Fordham, and Gerhard Adler. 21 vols. New York: Pantheon Books, 1953-79. Individual volumes cited—9: *The Archetypes and the Collective Unconscious* (1959); 11: *Psychology and Religion: West and East* (1958); 12: *Psychology and Alchemy* (1953, 1968); 14: *Mysterium Coniunctionis: An Inquiry into the Separation and Synthesis of Psychic Opposites in Alchemy* (1963).

Kaufmann, Lynn Frier. *The Noble Savage: Satyrs and Satyr Families in Renaissance Art.* Studies in Renaissance Art History. Ann Arbor, Mich.: UMI Research Press, 1984.

Kermode, Frank. *The Sense of an Ending: Studies in the Theory of Fiction.* London: Oxford University Press, 1967.

Kestner, Joseph A. *Mythology and Misogyny: The Social Discourse of Nineteenth-Century British Classical-Subject Painting.* Madison: University of Wisconsin Press, 1989.

Knapp, Bettina L. *Archetype, Architecture, and the Writer.* Bloomington: Indiana University Press, 1986.

Korshin, Paul J. "The Development of Abstracted Typology in England, 1650-1820." In *Literary Uses of Typology from the Late Middle Ages to the Present.* Ed. Earl Miner. Princeton, N.J.: Princeton University Press, 1977. 147-203.

———. *Typologies in England, 1650-1820.* Princeton, N.J.: Princeton University Press, 1982.

Krouse, F. Michael. *Milton's Samson and the Christian Tradition.* New York: Princeton, N.J.: Princeton University Press, 1949.

Landow, George P. *The Aesthetic and Critical Theories of John Ruskin.* Princeton, N.J.: Princeton University Press, 1971.

———. "Bruising the Serpent's Head: Typological Symbolism in Victorian Poetry." *Victorian Newsletter* 55 (Spring 1979), 11-14.

———. *Images of Crisis: Literary Iconology, 1750 to the Present.* Boston: Routledge and Kegan Paul, 1982.

———. "Moses Striking the Rock: Typological Symbolism in Victorian Poetry."

In *Literary Uses of Typology from the Late Middle Ages to the Present.* Ed. Earl Miner. Princeton, N.J.: Princeton University Press, 1977. 315–44.

———. "The Rainbow: A Problematic Image." In *Nature and the Victorian Imagination.* Ed. U.C. Knoepflmacher and G. B. Tennyson. Berkeley and Los Angeles: University of California Press, 1977. 341–69.

———. *Victorian Types, Victorian Shadows: Biblical Typology in Victorian Literature, Art, and Thought.* Boston: Routledge and Kegan Paul, 1980.

———. *William Holman Hunt and Typological Symbolism.* Princeton, N.J.: Princeton University Press, 1979.

———. "William Holman Hunt's 'The Shadow of Death.'" *Bulletin of the John Rylands University Library of Manchester* 55 (1972), 212–15.

Lowance, Mason I., Jr. "Typology and Millennial Eschatology in Early New England." In *Literary Uses of Typology from the Late Middle Ages to the Present.* Ed. Earl Miner. Princeton, N.J.: Princeton University Press, 1977. 228–73.

Mattes, Eleanor Bustin. *'In Memoriam': The Way of a Soul. A Study of Some Influences That Shaped Tennyson's Poem.* New York: Exposition Press, 1951.

Milton, John. *Complete Poems and Major Prose.* Ed. Merritt Y. Hughes. New York: Odyssey, 1957.

Miner, Earl. "Afterword." In *Literary Uses of Typology from the Late Middle Ages to the Present.* Ed. Earl Miner. Princeton, N.J.: Princeton University Press, 1977. 370–94.

Miner, Paul. "William Blake's 'Divine Analogy.'" *Criticism* 3 (1961), 46–61.

Montgomery, Lyna Lee. "The Phoenix: Its Use as a Literary Device in English from the Seventeenth Century to the Twentieth Century." *D. H. Lawrence Review* 5 (1972), 268–323.

Murray, Gilbert. *Four Stages of Greek Religion.* New York: Columbia University Press, 1912.

Pryse, James M. *The Apocalypse Unsealed: Being an Esoteric Interpretation of the Initiation of Ioannes, Commonly Called the Revelation of* [St.] *John.* 2d ed. New York: John M. Pryse, 1910.

Raine, Kathleen. *Yeats, the Tarot and the Golden Dawn.* Dublin: Dolmen Press, 1972.

Reeves, Marjorie, and Warwick Gould. *Joachim of Fiore and the Myth of the Eternal Evangel in the Nineteenth Century.* Oxford: Clarendon, 1987.

Reeves, Marjorie, and Beatrice Hirsch-Reich. *The Figurae of Joachim of Fiore.* Oxford: Clarendon, 1972.

Rosenau, Helen. *Vision of the Temple: The Image of the Temple of Jerusalem in Judaism and Christianity.* London: Oresko, 1979.

Rothenberg, Molly. "The Provisional Vision of Blake's *Jerusalem.*" *Word and Image* 3 (1987), 305–11.

Ruskin, John. *The Works of John Ruskin.* Library Edition. Ed. E. T. Cook and Alexander Wedderburn. 39 vols. London: George Allen, 1903–12.

Schiller, Gertrud. *Ikonographie der christlichen Kunst.* 5 vols. Gütersloh: Gütersloher Verlagshaus Gerd Mohn, 1966–83. [The early volumes are also in translation: *Iconography of Christian Art.* Trans. Janet Seligman. 2 vols. Greenwich, Conn.: New York Graphic Society, 1972.]

Scholem, Gershom. *Kabbalah.* New York and Scarborough, N.Y.: New American Library, 1974.

Skinner, Mollie. *The Fifth Sparrow: An Autobiography.* Sydney: Sydney University Press, 1972.

Sussman, Herbert. *Fact into Figure: Typology in Carlyle, Ruskin, and the Pre-Raphaelite Brotherhood.* Columbus: Ohio State University Press, 1979.

Tannenbaum, Leslie. *Biblical Tradition in Blake's Early Prophecies: The Great Code of Art.* Princeton, N.J.: Princeton University Press, 1982.

Taylor, Thomas. *Christ revealed: or The Old Testament explained.* London, 1635.

Tennyson, Alfred Lord. *The Poems of Tennyson.* Ed. Christopher Ricks. 2d ed. 3 vols. Longman Annotated English Poets. Gen. eds. F. W. Bateson and John Barnard. Harlow: Longman, 1987.

Von Simson, Otto. *The Gothic Cathedral: Origins of Gothic Architecture and the Medieval Concept of Order.* 2d ed. Bollingen Series 48. Princeton, N.J.: Princeton University Press, 1988.

Waite, Arthur Edward. *The Pictorial Key to the Tarot.* New York: U.S. Games Systems, 1983. [First published in 1910.]

Werner, Martin. "On the Origin of Zoanthropomorphic Symbols: The Early Christian Background." *Studies in Iconography* 10 (1984–86), 1–35.

West, Delno C., and Sandra Zimders-Swartz. *Joachim of Fiore: A Study in Spiritual Perception and History.* Bloomington: Indiana University Press, 1983.

Whitman, Jon. *Allegory: The Dynamics of an Ancient and Medieval Technique.* Oxford: Clarendon, 1987.

Wilson, F.A.C. *Yeats's Iconography.* London: Victor Gollancz, 1969.

Yarden, L. *The Tree of Light: A Study of the Menorah the Seven-Branched Lampstand.* Ithaca, N.Y.: Cornell University Press, 1971.

Yeats, W. B. *Autobiographies.* London: Macmillan, 1955.

———. *Essays and Introductions.* London and New York: Macmillan, 1961.

———. *The Variorum Edition of the Poems.* Ed. Peter Allt and Russell K. Alspach. New York: Macmillan, 1968.

Ziolkowski, Theodore. *Fictional Transfigurations of Jesus.* Princeton, N.J.: Princeton University Press, 1972.

———. "Some Features of Religious Figuralism in Twentieth-Century Literature." In *Literary Uses of Typology from the Late Middle Ages to the Present.* Ed. Earl Miner. Princeton, N.J.: Princeton University Press, 1977. 345–69.

Index